The People's Writer

Erskine Caldwell and the South

Minds of the New South

ROBERT F. MARTIN
Howard Kester and the Struggle for Social
Justice in the South, 1904–77

JANIS P. STOUT
Katherine Anne Porter: A Sense of the Times

WAYNE MIXON
The People's Writer: Erskine Caldwell and the South

The People's Writer

Erskine Caldwell
and the South

Wayne Mixon

University Press of Virginia

Charlottesville & London

THE UNIVERSITY PRESS OF VIRGINIA
Copyright © 1995 by the Rector and Visitors
of the University of Virginia

First published 1995

Library of Congress Cataloging-in-Publication Data
Mixon, Wayne.
  The people's writer: Erskine Caldwell and the South / Wayne
Mixon.
      p. cm. — (Minds of the new South)
    Includes bibliographical references and index.
    ISBN 0-8139-1627-5 (cloth: alk. paper)
      1. Caldwell, Erskine, 1903–   —Knowledge—Southern States.
    2. Literature and society—Southern States—History—20th century.
    3. Popular literature—Southern States—History and criticism.
    4. Southern States—In literature. 5. Social problems in
    literature. I. Title. II. Series.
    PS3505.A322Z75   1995
    813'.52—dc20   95–8291
                                                                    CIP

Printed in the United States of America

For Eleanor and Phillip
and, again, for Fran

CONTENTS

Preface   ix

Acknowledgments   xiii

Introduction: The Character of Erskine Caldwell   1

ONE   The Maverick Preacher's Wayward Son   5

TWO   The Making of a Writer   23

THREE   The Godforsaken South: The Fiction of the Thirties   37

FOUR   Radical Activism: The Nonfiction of the Thirties   93

FIVE   Changing South, Unchanging Writer: Caldwell in Decline—and in Resurgence   118

SIX   Caldwell's Achievement   155

Notes   169

Select Bibliography   198

Index   209

PREFACE

My intention in the pages that follow is to present an intellectual biography of the writer Erskine Caldwell. I hope to reveal the sources and to trace the development of the ideas and attitudes that informed his writing. The circumstances of his life that figured large in the making of his work receive full play. The experiences that had little bearing on the substance of his work are treated summarily if at all.

Just as this book is not intended to be a comprehensive account of Caldwell's life, neither does it include commentary on everything that he wrote. Although he produced fiction and nonfiction with settings from Mexico to Moscow—some of that work, such as the documentary *North of the Danube* and the Maine story "Country Full of Swedes," being excellent—my purpose is to examine his portrayal of the American South, his native ground. Moreover, my emphasis is on his early southern work, the writing of the 1930s and early 1940s, for therein lies his significance. Furthermore, my focus is directed toward those examples of the early southern writing that depict social injustice, for therein lies his greatness.

Throughout his career, Caldwell considered himself to be the people's writer. By and large, he intended to portray what he perceived as the reality of the lives of men and women existing on the margins of society. In the South, such people were blacks and poor whites. In his prime, during the era of the Great Depression, Caldwell brought great art to his deep concern for down-and-out southerners. Later, as his creative powers waned, the art suffered; the anger at social injustice, however, lost none of its fervor.

Because Caldwell considered himself a champion of the South's downtrodden and a critic of the South's elite, I attempt to assay the responses of southerners to his work. Fittingly, what the people thought of his writing was a matter of much interest to the people's writer. In my research, I found that many southerners vehemently rejected his rendition of the South, but I also learned that many other southerners warmly applauded it. Because, like countless others of my generation, I became acquainted with Caldwell's books by way of their alluring covers that beckoned from drugstore racks, I expected the denunciation. The approbation caught me by surprise.

I also was surprised by the great neglect that Caldwell had suffered from scholars. Although it is not within the scope of this book to treat at length his critical reputation, a few observations at the outset may be in order. The man that William Faulkner once ranked among the five best writers in America has received relatively little attention from scholars. The reasons are puzzling. It cannot be that his best work is unworthy of scholarly notice. Perhaps the neglect by experts results from Caldwell's oft-expressed disdain for them, from his plain style of writing in which form is secondary to content, from his prolificacy, from a conflation by critics of his worst work with his best, and from the immense popularity—albeit brief in his own country—of paperback editions of his books. Whatever the reasons for scholarly neglect, probably no other American writer of comparable talent has been so ignored by academicians.

It is true that, from the 1930s on, there has been a trickle of scholarly commentary on Caldwell's work, some of which is thoughtful and perceptive. Yet it was not until 1981, when Caldwell was almost eighty years old, that the first collection of criticism appeared. Scott MacDonald's *Critical Essays on Erskine Caldwell* helped to usher in a scholarly reevaluation of his work. Three years later, Twayne Publishers inducted Caldwell into its United States Authors Series, which already included a legion of writers less worthy than he. Unfortunately for anyone desiring a greater understanding of Caldwell, the Twayne volume suffers from the space limitations imposed by the publisher and from the author's lack of familiarity with the South. Not until 1991 did there appear a full-length critical study of Caldwell's work written by a single hand. *Erskine Caldwell and the Fiction of Poverty*, by Sylvia Jenkins Cook, a scholar long interested in his work, adds much to our understanding of Caldwell the writer. Not until 1993, ninety years after Caldwell's birth, was a biography published. *Erskine Caldwell*, by Harvey L. Klevar, a scholar long interested in his life, adds much to our understanding of Caldwell the man. So, too, does Dan B. Miller's recent biography, *Erskine Caldwell*.[1] There is now under way a long-overdue Caldwell revival. I am grateful for the opportunity to contribute my mite to that worthy cause.

Throughout this book, I try to see as Caldwell saw, as I attempt to portray his relationship to the region of his birth and upbringing. I hope that my effort contributes to a fuller understanding of a complex man and a complex land.

Although Caldwell was a first-class writer, he never won any spelling bees. Moreover, he usually typed his personal correspondence and did not proofread it. To avoid strewing *sic* throughout the text, wherever typewritten correspondence is quoted, I have corrected errors.

ACKNOWLEDGMENTS

I could not have written this book without the help of nearly a hundred people. Librarians, archivists, and other officials at fifty-odd institutions from Maine to California that house material relating to Erskine Caldwell answered my queries and supplied information quickly and competently. To name all of the people and to identify their institutions would produce acknowledgments of undue length. I am obliged, however, to mention specifically the librarians and archivists who suffered my presence: Linda Matthews and her staff at Emory University; Thomas Camden and his staff at the University of Georgia; Edmund Berkeley Jr. and his staff at the University of Virginia; and Philip N. Cronenwett and his staff at Dartmouth College.

I am especially indebted to Mr. Cronenwett and his staff. For four weeks in the summer of 1990, they labored diligently to supply me with material from Dartmouth's enormous Caldwell Collection. Since then, they have furnished supplemental material graciously and expeditiously. Mr. Cronenwett's knowledge of Caldwelliana has been particularly helpful.

At Mercer University, Virginia Cairns processed scores of interlibrary loan requests capably and cheerfully. I am grateful for her assistance. I am also thankful for a grant from Mercer that helped to defray the costs of research.

In addition to manuscript sources, interviews with people who knew Caldwell or his parents well provided indispensable information. For willingly and candidly sharing their recollections and for allowing me to use them, I am deeply indebted to Henrietta Boyce, Erskine Caldwell Jr., Virginia Caldwell Hibbs, Annette Johnson, Leroy Lewis, Mary M. Maner, Lucille M. Parrish, Ralph Stephens, Helen Williams, and Harry P. Wren. Not long before I completed my work on this book, Ralph Stephens passed away. I was deeply saddened to learn of the death of a man who, as director of the University of Georgia Press for many years, contributed much to our understanding of the South and who, on his sickbed, contributed much to my understanding of Erskine Caldwell.

My gratitude to Mary Maner is immense. Not only did Miss Maner, Caldwell's first cousin, grant me numerous interviews, she also arranged for me to interview other people, allowed me to examine material in her possession relating to Caldwell's family, conducted research, and read portions of my manuscript. Among the greatest pleasures of engaging in this project was the renewal of acquaintance with Miss Maner, my highschool biology teacher.

My gratitude to Virginia Caldwell Hibbs is equally great. Mrs. Hibbs gave me permission to examine her late husband's correspondence, granted me interviews despite the emotional difficulty involved, allowed me to use photographs, and read my manuscript. Throughout this endeavor, she has been unfailingly gracious, cooperative, and encouraging.

Other people who contributed directly to my research also have my thanks. They are as follows: George and Lucia Caldwell, Stetson Kennedy, James E. Kibler Jr., John Densmore Smith, and John O. West. For helping me in other ways, I am grateful to Florence Eichin and Jonathan B. White.

William A. Sutton's contribution to my work was indirect but nonetheless significant. His unpublished biography of Caldwell, written in the 1970s and based in part on interviews with people no longer living, provides a wealth of information.

Other Caldwell scholars—Erik Bledsoe, Harvey L. Klevar, and Dan B. Miller—also helped me in important ways. Each of them read my manuscript and made useful suggestions. Professor Klevar and Dr. Miller allowed me to read in manuscript their biographies of Caldwell. My work has benefited from their generosity, and I am grateful to all of them.

Shortly after this project was begun, members of the advisory board of the series in which this volume appears made suggestions regarding how I should proceed. Shortly before this project was finished, readers who examined the completed manuscript for the publisher made suggestions regarding how I could improve it. I am grateful to all of those scholars who helped me—from beginning to end.

Other scholars of the history and literature of the American South read my work in draft and offered perceptive criticisms. I am deeply indebted to Michael M. Cass, John Herbert Roper, and Eric J. Sundquist. Professor Sundquist made significant suggestions regarding the manuscript's structure and other matters. Professor Cass read two drafts of the manuscript—the first was so rough that it must have chafed his hands—and he gave pertinent advice. As the editor of the series Minds of the New South, Professor Roper asked me to write this book. Before I completed my work, he relinquished the editorship. Even though he no longer had any obligation to read my manuscript, he read it. And he read it closely, thoroughly, and insightfully. Moreover, he offered encouragement at a time when I needed it very much.

I am also grateful to three other people who read my manuscript. John Gibbs Barnwell, with his fine feel for language, improved my writing. Eugene H. Winick, on behalf of the Caldwell Estate, granted me permission to quote from Caldwell's writings and to reproduce certain photographs. Suzanne Schafer did a superb job of copyediting. None of the readers of the manuscript is responsible for any flaws that may remain, which are my responsibility alone.

It has been a pleasure to work with the staff of the University Press of Virginia. I am especially grateful to acquisitions editor Boyd Zenner, history and social sciences editor Richard Holway, and manuscript editor Gerald Trett for their patience, understanding, and skillful assistance.

My greatest debt is to the people who have had to live with me throughout this project. Over the past seven years, never once did my wife and children complain that I was devoting too much attention to Erskine Caldwell and too little to them. Instead, with unfailing good humor, they encouraged me to do my best. What is more, they helped me directly. My daughter, Eleanor, as she wondered why her father thought that technology was magic, introduced me to the word processor. My son, Phillip, came to the rescue on the countless occasions when I showed that I had not mastered the word processor. My wife, Fran, despite her own busy career, made time to read some of Caldwell's work and portions of my manuscript, and she offered sound counsel. Throughout, Fran, Phil, and Eleanor kept me going. This book is for them.

The People's Writer

Erskine Caldwell and the South

The Character
of Erskine Caldwell

Like most other people, Erskine Caldwell was a welter of contradictions. He was generous and selfish, diffident and egotistical, gentle and cruel. Unlike most other people, he possessed a great gift. His creativity enabled him to fashion some of the finest fiction in American literature. That creativity also presents serious problems to the student of his life.

Lacking independent documentation for some of Caldwell's assertions about himself, I wondered whether always to take him at his word. To do so entails risks. Because his published autobiographies are not always candid, in reconstructing his personal life I have relied primarily on extensive manuscript research and on interviews with people who knew him or his parents well. I have used Caldwell's published comments about his life only when they correlate with the other sources or when, in my judgment, they seem plausible. Sometimes, his accounts appear to be egregiously exaggerated. For example, was he involved in the many sexual incidents that he attributed to his childhood, adolescence, and young manhood? Did he leave home at age fourteen and wander through the Deep South, and Central America to boot? Did he, a decade later, write eight to ten book reviews a week and did he accumulate three thousand review copies of books over a three-year period?[1]

Like many another writer of his generation—I think most readily of F. Scott Fitzgerald, Ernest Hemingway, and William Faulkner—Caldwell created an image of himself that attempted to justify the works he authored. As what the critic Philip Rahv called a "redskin," rather than a "paleface," he valued experience over study, emotion over reason, heart over head.[2] A writer should be a robust man of the world, not a cloistered intellectual. He should know of what he wrote from having encountered it, not from having read about it. He should be a passionate participant in life's struggles, not an aloof commentator on them. That Caldwell was essentially what he depicted himself to be—a writer who had experienced much and who was deeply engaged with the world around him—cannot be denied. Yet I suspect that the hyperbole in the accounts of his life—in publishers' blurbs, in interviews, in autobiographies—reflects an intent to be chief of the redskins.

Just as revealing about Caldwell's character are the omissions from his autobiographies. His tough exterior concealed a fragile psyche. Over the course of his eighty-three years, he made only a few friends. For the first forty years of his life, Caldwell braced himself during most crises on his father. Although the circumstances may be only coincident, the serious decline in his art began as his father's health failed rapidly.

Caldwell's emotional fragility is also evident in his relationships with women, from that with his occasionally overbearing mother to that with the last of his four wives, who, in the course of a thirty-year marriage, came to understand him better than anyone else. He seems to have resented what he feared was his excessive dependence on women. After all, in the culture in which he was reared, women were deemed to be inferior. Their purpose was to serve their men. A man needed a woman in fundamental ways—for sex, for raising children, for performing other domestic duties—but what kind of man needed a woman's approbation to convince him of the worth of his work? Again, the circumstances may be only coincident, but many of Caldwell's best works, early and late, were written during times of domestic tranquillity, sometimes with the help of his wife, and many of the worst ones were written during times of domestic turmoil.[3]

Other omissions from Caldwell's autobiographies further demonstrate their inadequacy for providing a satisfactory understanding of a complex individual. The same man who beat his sons for slight offenses advised them to use great care in unhooking fish so as not to hurt the fish needlessly. The same man who, in hard times, threatened to wring his wife's neck for buying a few items on credit, in flush times provided financial support to a friend for twenty years, loaned money to another writer to enable her to complete a novel, paid for a cousin's vocational training, bought a farm and a town house for his parents, and helped to purchase

four weekly newspapers for his father to edit. The same man who titil-
lated millions of readers with what were considered bawdy tales con-
versed in a manner that reflected his upbringing in parsonages. The same
man who flirted with communism in the 1930s enthusiastically played
the stock market in that decade. The same man who denounced racism
with uncommon fervor remained cordial to a boyhood friend who became one of the South's most vociferous segregationists.[4]

For all the complexity of the private Caldwell, the public Caldwell consistently displayed admirable traits. People who knew him at various
stages of his career commented on the unflagging integrity that informed
his professional dealings, the iron discipline with which he practiced his
craft, and the compassionate forthrightness that characterized his stands
on social issues.[5] Even so, given his tendency to present accounts of his
personal life that were often self-serving and occasionally suspect, could
a scholar, trying his best to be careful, assume that Caldwell's portrayal
of the Depression-era South was reliable?

As a child of a Georgia sharecropper who was forced off the land and
into a Carolina cotton mill by the Great Depression, I heard countless
tales as I was growing up of the desperation that hard times brought to
my family and to people that they knew. Nonetheless, I was not prepared
to believe that conditions were as wretched as Caldwell described. One
of his journalistic accounts seemed incredible. In an east Georgia shack
early in 1935, human babies lay nursing at a dog.[6] I did not believe that
such a thing could have happened. I was convinced that Caldwell had
irresponsibly crossed the line separating fact from fiction. The exaggeration for effect that made much of his fiction so powerful had no place in
a work of reportage.

Early in the afternoon of March 21, 1991, my misgivings about Caldwell's trustworthiness as a social commentator were abruptly dispelled.
Trying to learn more about the personalities of his parents, I was conducting an interview in Wrens, Georgia, with a group of women who had
been their students in high school. Eagerly responding to my questions,
the women emphasized the concern that Caldwell's father displayed for
destitute country people during the Depression. As the interview was
drawing to a close, one of the women, without my solicitation, recounted
an incident that her father had witnessed and had related to her. Along
with Caldwell's father and a Wrens physician, her father had driven into
the country to try to help a sick child. The men found the child lying on

a dirty, ragged cot in a two-room shack whose only other furniture was a wooden box and a bed. On the bed lay a hound and four or five children, including an infant who was no more than nine months old. The baby was nursing at the dog. Unaware that anyone had ever written about the incident, the woman exclaimed excitedly to her companions who expressed disbelief, "It's true; it's absolutely true!"[7] The passing of more than fifty-five years could not dim her recollection.

That an event so inconceivable had actually occurred profoundly affected me. I realized that subjectively to doubt the validity of Caldwell's nonfictional social commentary and, what is more important, simplistically to question the veracity of vision in his best fiction would be to deny the two overarching constants in the life of an otherwise enigmatic man. That Caldwell was unshakably committed to his craft should not be questioned. For sixty years he wrote steadily—all too steadily after his powers waned—producing twelve books of nonfiction, twenty-five novels, and nearly a hundred fifty short stories. That he mounted, throughout his career, an uncompromising assault on social injustice should likewise not be questioned. There was much that was wrong in the world, and Caldwell revealed injustice where, by experience, he knew it best—in the South.

CHAPTER ONE

The Maverick Preacher's
Wayward Son

For a man whose career was stalked by controversy, it is fitting that even the date of Erskine Caldwell's birth be a matter of dispute. Sources agree on the month and day—December 17—but they disagree on the year. Caldwell himself occasionally gave 1902, but usually he cited 1903 because he preferred to have been born in that year. Although the earlier year is listed in the family Bible, his parents attested that the later was correct. The weight of the evidence leans toward December 17, 1903.[1] In light of the achievement of Orville and Wilbur Wright, that date provides an appropriate beginning to the life of a man who from early childhood had much experience with movement and who for all of his days was fascinated by travel, by observing people in places both familiar and unfamiliar.

If there is doubt about the date of Caldwell's birth, the place is certain: White Oak, a small community in Coweta County, Georgia, thirty-five miles southwest of Atlanta. His parents, Caroline Preston Bell and Ira Sylvester Caldwell, neither of whom was Georgian, had established their home there in 1901.[2]

Carrie, as she was known to friends and family, was a proud Virginian whose English ancestors had settled in the Old Dominion by 1670. Among her maternal forebears were English nobility whose descendants held large land grants in eastern Virginia. By the time of the American Revolution, in which both her English and Scots-Irish ancestors fought, many of her family had moved westward, the Cosbys of the paternal line to Louisa County and the Witherses of the maternal side to Fauquier County. All seem to have prospered. During the early nineteenth century,

Carrie's paternal grandfather, Richard Henning Henry, was a physician practicing in Waynesboro, Augusta County, and her maternal grandfather, Jesse Howard Withers Jr., was the master of Oaklawn plantation near Warrenton in Fauquier County. By the time of Carrie's birth in Warrenton in 1872, however, the family had been much reduced by the Civil War. All of her grandparents had died, the oldest at age fifty-eight. Her father, whose name had been changed from Richard Henry to Richard Henry Bell following adoption after his mother's death, earned a living as an accountant and railroad telegrapher.[3]

Carrie was one of eight children of Bell, who, according to a granddaughter, "wasn't very bright in business," and Katherine Elizabeth Withers. She was able to attend Augusta Female Seminary (later Mary Baldwin College) in Staunton, where the family had moved, because she lived at home and because she received a scholarship. Taking courses in mathematics, science, history, Latin, German, and English, Carrie compiled a distinguished record. She won medals for her achievement in German and in English composition. In 1893, after three years at the seminary, she was graduated from the University Course, the equivalent of two years of college work.[4]

Following brief tenures on the faculty of girls' schools in Virginia and Georgia, Carrie accepted an appointment at Due West Female College, an institution located in Abbeville County in the South Carolina upcountry that had been founded in 1860 by members of the Associate Reformed Presbyterian (A.R.P.) church. Like other evangelical denominations in the South, the A.R.P. church was socially and theologically conservative and committed to enforcing strict standards of personal behavior. While Carrie served as teacher of Latin and English at the women's college, she met Ira S. Caldwell, a student at nearby Erskine College, also an A.R.P. school, which had been established in 1839.[5]

Less is known about Ira's forebears than about Carrie's, but family records indicate that the first paternal ancestor to come to America was William Caldwell, a Scots-Irishman who in his early twenties settled in the South Carolina Piedmont shortly before the American Revolution, fought with Patriot forces during the war, moved to Mecklenburg County, North Carolina, married Agnes Henry, of Virginia antecedents, and lived to be almost ninety. William's grandson, John Harvey, married Rose Hunter, who, in December 1870, gave birth to Ira, the oldest of six children in a family of yeoman farmers.[6]

As an adolescent, Ira, when not attending school or working in the fields, sometimes engaged in pranks. His favorite was to lead his schoolmates on nighttime forays that culminated in toppling neighbors' outhouses, on one occasion with an occupant inside. Despite such misadventures, young Ira's nature was fundamentally serious. He joined Back Creek A.R.P. church as a teenager, and he may have been influenced in choosing a vocation by an A.R.P. minister who was also the principal of the high school he attended. Nonetheless, according to one of Ira's brothers, he decided to enter the ministry to satisfy the wishes of his mother, a devout woman who had long worried over the spiritual welfare of her skeptical husband. Even though Ira's speech was marred by an obvious stutter, he set out for Erskine College in 1893 to become a minister of the gospel.[7]

Financing his own education, Ira entered college at an age when other young men were finishing. Even so, he fit well with other students, one of whom remembered him as a man "of an exceptionally strong character" who "was very highly esteemed by his classmates." Ira served as an officer of the Young Men's Christian Association (Y.M.C.A.), played center on the football team, and excelled in the classroom. Pursuing a rigorous curriculum with high standards, he earned A's in humanities courses. In mathematics, chemistry, and astronomy, he usually made B's.[8]

Receiving the A.B. degree in 1897, Ira started the two-year course of study in Erskine Theological Seminary. A transcript of his seminary record, if made, has not survived. In light of his achievement as an undergraduate, one can assume that that record was superior. He would not be able, however, to study systematic theology, church history, homiletics, and other subjects without interruption.[9]

Late in April 1898, six days after the United States declared war against Spain, Ira enlisted in the First North Carolina Infantry, an act that would subsequently provoke criticism from some A.R.P. ministers. His service would not be as an infantryman, however. On June 14, the day the American force steamed out of Tampa Bay for Cuba, he was transferred, probably at his request, to the hospital corps of the regular army, such transfer bringing a reduction in rank and pay. Never one to act in a cowardly manner, he may have wanted to serve his country by helping the wounded rather than by killing the enemy. During his eight months in Cuba, it seems that the only violence Ira committed was directed at other American soldiers. After enduring repeated badgering from two tent mates because of his daily prayers and Bible-reading, he beat the devil out of both of them.[10]

Following his discharge at Havana late in February 1899, three weeks after American ratification of the Treaty of Paris, Ira resumed study at Erskine Seminary. That work completed the next year, he was licensed to preach in the spring of 1900 and ordained to the ministry the following December. Between licensing and ordination, he accepted the pastorate of White Oak A.R.P. Church, a congregation numbering about a hundred. Once established at White Oak, he married Carrie in her hometown of Staunton in October 1901.[11]

In many ways Carrie and Ira were an unlikely couple. She was the proud and proper Virginia lady, meticulous and dainty, blue-eyed, red-haired, and fair-skinned. He was the puckish, disheveled, tobacco-chewing Carolina countryman, big—six-foot-one and nearly two hundred pounds—rough-hewn, dark-skinned, and with a shock of unruly dark hair and a bow tie always askew. The marriage was sometimes rocky, the result primarily of Carrie's inability to express feelings of anger to her husband. Instead, she would retreat into a brooding silence that occasionally lasted for days, a trait that her son, throughout his life, sometimes displayed. Such behavior ceased only after an exasperated Ira, whose patience was eventually exhausted by these episodes, threatened to leave her. Despite such pitfalls, their marriage of nearly forty-five years seems generally to have been felicitous. Their son characterized the relationship as one of "loyalty, congeniality, consideration." Both Ira and Carrie were blessed with a lively sense of humor. A niece who often visited their home recalled that Ira "was very jovial" frequently "making jokes," that Carrie "loved a good laugh," and that "they laughed together a lot." Both were also committed to the cause of social Christianity, although Ira's devotion ran deeper and, as a man in the early-twentieth-century South, he had more opportunities to express that commitment. Throughout their lives both steadfastly supported their controversial son.[12]

Carrie wanted their only child—who with his blue eyes, sandy hair, and fair skin so resembled her—to be "the perfect little gentleman," an expectation doubtlessly encouraged by the matrons of the churches that Ira served. Exceedingly protective, she kept Erskine out of school and taught him at home for much of his early youth. Moreover, she dressed him in Russian blouses and short pants and let his hair grow in long curls to his shoulders. When he was about eight, his father and a visiting aunt spirited him away to a barbershop and a dry goods store to get his hair cut and outfit him in a pair of overalls. Instead of being a little gentleman, Erskine was "a rambunctious boy" whose curiosity often brought him trouble: severe burns from hot grease that left lasting scars, a bee sting to the eye that impaired his vision for the rest of his life, a cut hand from experimenting with his father's razor, and a bout with nausea after drinking kerosene.[13]

During his preadolescent years and especially during the four years that his father served as secretary of the A.R.P. Home Missions Board, an office that required much travel, Erskine made extended visits with his mother to Staunton, where her people lived. As the only grandchild in the family for fifteen years, he was often the center of attention for his grandmother and his unmarried aunts. He developed the habit of getting his way, which, for better and for worse, he would retain for many years to come.[14]

More than anything else, what distinguished Erskine's childhood and adolescence was movement. In 1906, after a little more than five years at White Oak, Ira accepted a call to pastor the seventy-five-member A.R.P. congregation in Prosperity, South Carolina, serving also during his five years there as supply preacher for smaller churches elsewhere in Newberry County. While living in Prosperity, a town whose condition belied its name, the family narrowly escaped death when the firetrap manse burned to the ground.[15]

After the Prosperity pastorate, Ira became secretary of the denomination's Home Missions Board. His principal responsibility was to settle church disputes. There must have been many of them, because during his tenure from 1911 to 1915 he served as supply pastor for churches in Virginia, the Carolinas, Florida, and Tennessee. Carrie and Erskine accompanied him to those stations, although they also frequently visited the Bells in Staunton.[16]

While her husband was refereeing church fights and otherwise attempting to promote goodwill, Carrie was trying to help. For six years, from May 1910 to April 1916, she wrote nearly fifty columns—a few of them poems—for the *Monthly Bulletin* of the denomination's Woman's Presbyterial Missionary Union. Slightly more than half of those columns dealt with matters within the A.R.P. church, but the rest were devoted to spreading the social gospel. Among the many reforms she advocated was the improvement of conditions in prisons, slums, and factories, including higher wages for industrial workers. She also promoted the uplift of blacks. Unlike the virulent racists common to the early-twentieth-century South who believed that blacks had retrogressed since emancipation, Carrie maintained that they had advanced "in intelligence and self-reliance." Even so, she contended maternalistically, "The negro is not yet able to stand alone. He needs support, guidance, instruction." [17]

Although Carrie believed that the American political system benefited from Christian leadership, her columns eschewed partisanship, except on one occasion. During the presidential campaign of 1912, with the solid Presbyterian and Staunton native Woodrow Wilson bearing the Democratic Party's standard, one column, while mentioning no names, gave Wilson a thinly veiled endorsement as it called for the election of "a courageous and uncompromising Christian." Ironically for a woman as intelligent, articulate, and informed as Carrie, the column contained this disclaimer: "Now women are supposed to know nothing of politics and to care less, and indeed, the issues involved in this struggle are too deep and complex for the feminine mind to grapple with." [18]

The welfare of children, of course, was considered the special province of women. Pointing out to her readers that "home conditions can make or mar a life," Carrie observed that "neatness, order, and beauty displayed within four narrow walls tend to give birth to these same qualities in the little lives that unfold within those walls." Reflecting further a deep concern for the well-being of children, Carrie repeatedly called for improvement in public education, beginning with the passage of compulsory school-attendance laws. Thinking particularly of the children of the "less fortunate, or less successful class of tenant farmers," she described them as "absolutely helpless." Their parents, "unable to get an abiding hold upon anything in the way of worldly possessions . . . cease to identify themselves with any interest—community, social, or religious. Often, their children are not in reach of a school. Oftener, they can provide neither clothing nor books for them and though a school be nearby." Such children, she emphasized, "are not far off. They can be found within a few miles of almost any country church. Some of them need medical inspection and attention, many of them, through no fault of their own, are deprived of school advantages, all of them need Christian training." [19]

Carrie's contributions to the *Monthly Bulletin* diminished in frequency in 1915 when Ira relinquished the post of home missions secretary to become pastor of Salem Church near Atoka, Tennessee, thirty miles north of Memphis. With more than three hundred members, the church was by far the largest that he ever served. His experience there highlights his exceptionalism within his denomination.[20]

The Associate Reformed Presbyterians traced their roots to 1730s Scotland, where the Reverend Ebenezer Erskine, for whom the Caldwells named their son, protested the Church of Scotland's practice of forcing congregations to accept pastors. When the governing body of the established church rejected Erskine's protest, he and a group of followers broke away from the Scottish church. Early in the nineteenth century, the descendants of the self-styled Seceders who had emigrated to America formed the A.R.P. church. After 1858, when northern communicants joined the United Presbyterian church, the A.R.P. church became exclusively southern. As of the turn of the twentieth century, it had only ten thousand members, who were concentrated in the upcountry of the Carolinas and in certain other parts of the South, notably in areas of Tennessee and Georgia. The conservative nature of the church was exemplified in the practice of psalmody. Until the middle of the twentieth century, denominational policy prohibited the singing of "uninspired songs" during worship; only versions of the Psalms that had been approved by the denomination's governing body were supposed to be sung.[21]

Carrie's earlier, approving description of the A.R.P. church as "conservative and clannish" proved to be agonizingly apt at Salem. Ira had faced opposition from his co-religionists since the outset of his career. At Erskine Seminary, he was criticized for showing more interest in the welfare of poor people nearby than in the study of church doctrine. A few years later, church members in Prosperity likewise scorned his service to the social gospel, especially his attempts to improve conditions for blacks. Never before, however, had criticism been as virulent as it would become at Salem.[22]

Opposition to Ira developed early, led by a few officers of the church. By late 1917, the discord was so pronounced that some members of the congregation petitioned the Memphis and Louisville Presbytery to oust him. Among the charges brought by the dissidents were that Ira's sermons were not sufficiently biblical, that his attitude toward certain officers of the church "has been very unfriendly," and that he neglected his duties by failing to make pastoral visits to church members, instead spending too much time as master of a Boy Scout troop. The final charge suggests what seems to have been the root of the trouble. Many Salemites opposed what they believed was Ira's excessive attention to people who were not church members. One member who supported him recalled that Ira "was a man ahead of his time . . . [who] was much concerned with social conditions and mixed a good deal with the poorer people of the area." The "conservative, orthodox" church members, however, showed "indifference to, or lack of consciousness of, the needs of share croppers and Negroes."[23]

Ira's commitment to the social gospel led him to establish a mission among the poor, where he preached, conducted Sunday School, and saw to it that the children received gifts at Christmas. On one occasion he carried a four-year-old girl to Memphis at his expense so that she could undergo surgery to correct her harelip. He consistently tried to build the self-esteem of shy children, one of whom suffered a speech defect. Not content to run the mission, Ira regularly brought "outsiders" to Salem services. One member recalled that he "would delight in walking to the back of the church, greeting them, and personally escorting them to the front of the sanctuary."[24]

Although the presbytery rejected the petition for Ira's ouster, opposition to him remained strong and, according to Carrie, was directed also toward the rest of the family. She recalled that his detractors "cursed us loudly and deeply," threatening to prevent Ira from ever holding another pulpit, her from teaching school, and Erskine from making "any progress in education." In the summer of 1919, he and his family having suffered years of criticism that included slurs against his character, Ira resigned the Salem pastorate. The years at Salem figured large in Carrie's recollections of the trials of being a maverick preacher's wife. She had, she said, "suffered, bled, and worse than died backing him while he preached and practiced in his life and works peace on earth, good will to men."[25]

Erskine's recollections of his family's years in Atoka differ dramatically from those of his mother. Near the end of his life, he noted that when he learned that his family was departing the town he, for the first time, "was not eager to leave one place and move to another." Perhaps he did not know that his father's life had been threatened; perhaps his parents explained the shattered window of the family's second-story apartment as an accident. He had to have known, however, that he had himself been beaten unconscious by parties unknown who were rumored to be his father's enemies. No doubt he repressed the memory of that incident because, on balance, residence in Atoka afforded him his first opportunity to enjoy the semblance of a normal life.[26]

Entering adolescence when his father accepted the Salem pastorate, Erskine, although still quiet and reserved, began to emerge from the cocoon that his mother had spun. For the first extended period in his life, he attended public school; he participated in Boy Scouts; he earned money of his own by picking cotton and by plowing for a neighboring farmer; he played baseball; he had a steady girl. He did not excel in school, except at geography, but he read avidly.[27]

Yet Erskine also engaged in activities that were considered hardly proper for a minister's son. Unknown to his parents, he began to smoke, buying Camel cigarettes at a poolroom. Also without his parents' knowledge, he drank moonshine whiskey. To impress his girlfriend, he would occasionally drive his father's car past her house, reclining in the seat and steering with his feet.[28]

Erskine's skill as a driver—with his hands, not with his feet—enabled him to land a job in the summer of 1918 at Millington Field, an army base near Atoka. His duties included chauffering Y.M.C.A. officers stationed there. The destination of a few of those officials was often Memphis's Peabody Hotel, where they had arranged assignations with prostitutes. Moreover, on one occasion, a Y officer directed Erskine to pick up two young mulatto women the officer knew who were waiting outside the fort's gate. Amid "much laughter and giggling" from the man and the women in the back seat, the fifteen-year-old Erskine drove to Memphis. His observation of Memphis and Millington prostitutes may have triggered his lifelong fascination with women, real and imaginary, who were so utterly unlike the ladies in his family.[29]

Upon leaving west Tennessee in July 1919, the Caldwells moved to east Georgia, across the state from Erskine's birthplace. There, in Jefferson County, Ira assumed the pastorate of two churches: one of about a hundred fifty members in the town of Wrens; the other a smaller congregation that worshiped ten miles south of Wrens.[30]

The Caldwells settled in Wrens, a town of roughly a thousand people that had been born of railroad expansion in the 1880s. Situated in the Georgia sandhills, Wrens, like countless other communities in the Deep South, suffered lean times after the cotton economy collapsed in 1920. Ira did not complain when hard times brought a major reduction in his eight-hundred-dollar annual compensation. He and Carrie taught school to supplement his income as a minister, something that they had done previously at other stations. At Wrens Institute, the town's high school, Ira taught literature, history, and sociology. Carrie, from the outset, taught English and Latin. Later, when the principal asked her to add geometry to her offerings, she sought her husband's counsel. Assuaging her fear of teaching a subject outside her expertise, Ira provided assurance: "Sure you can, Carrie; sure you can."[31]

According to many of their students, both Carrie and Ira were inspiring teachers, although their styles differed greatly. Precise, aloof, and firm in discipline, Carrie could be intimidating. Nonetheless, as her students recalled, she was "an excellent teacher," "a wonderful teacher," who "gave the town things it would not otherwise have had—Latin and English literature." More approachable than Carrie, Ira was also considerably more casual in the classroom. Walking about, interpreting a poem, he would duck into the cloakroom from time to time to spit tobacco juice out the window. But his passion for poetry inspired one student to begin memorizing "lots of poems." Because he refused to try to catch students misbehaving, they behaved out of respect for him.[32]

In the pulpit at Wrens, Ira performed just as he had at Salem. Young Baptists and Methodists would often attend Sunday night services at Ira's church because, as one of them later said, "they liked that old man." His sermons were not about "hell-fire"; they dealt with the problems of living. And those sermons, which one listener described as "sociological lectures," were short—twenty minutes—whereas the Baptist and Methodist ministers might preach for an hour.[33]

The litany of Ira's good works in east-central Georgia is virtually endless. Out of his own pocket, he bought equipment for Wrens Institute's athletic teams, which he coached. At least one student, and perhaps others, lived in the Caldwell home so that he could attend school, his poverty and his isolation in the rural part of the county rendering schooling impossible otherwise. With no intention of enriching himself, Ira promoted the Wrens Community Center, a joint-stock enterprise that attempted to create jobs and a measure of prosperity by operating a cottonseed oil mill, a cotton gin, and a chicken hatchery. On Sunday afternoons, he preached to prisoners at the county stockade. Tirelessly, he traveled the back roads of Jefferson County, taking food and clothing to desperately poor tenant farmers.[34]

Somehow, Ira found time to write. In the 1920s and early 1930s, he regularly contributed a column on current issues to the *Chronicle* and the *Herald*, newspapers published in Augusta, thirty miles away. Occasionally, essays that he wrote reached a wider audience, as in the case of a 1928 article published in the *Survey,* a popular magazine of uplift. In "A School That Teaches a Community," he extolled the work of a black school supported in part by the Rosenwald Fund, an agency of northern philanthropy. Located in Keysville, a small, poor settlement in adjacent Burke County, the school had been founded in 1921 by I. E. Bryan, a college-trained black man who served as principal. Over the years, enrollment had increased fivefold, and night classes for adults had been added. The school had a "well-selected library" that included "the best type of monthly magazines and weeklies," a successful canning operation, and an agriculture curriculum that promoted scientific farming. But deficiencies remained. In an indirect appeal for help from a national audience, Ira pointed out that "there is not a desk in any of the school rooms. . . . The school children bring boxes, chairs and benches from their homes." Surely, he implied, such an endeavor as Keysville School merited encouragement. "If there were enough Bryans to man all the schools in Georgia," Ira observed, "the proverbial 'bad Negro' would soon be a thing of the past." [35]

Of all of Ira Caldwell's writings, the one that had the greatest impact on his son was an extended, five-part essay published in the science journal *Eugenics* in 1930. The article hardly seemed appropriate to the journal, which was the organ of the American Eugenics Society (A.E.S.). By 1930, attacks by social scientists, and by some natural scientists as well, had undermined the popularity that eugenics had enjoyed earlier in the century. A movement whose leaders were elitist biologists who wanted to reform human society by biologically "improving" its components had been overwhelmed by other intellectuals. Many of the critics of eugenics were psychologists or sociologists who insisted upon the primacy of environment as a factor in the achievements of human beings. An amateur sociologist of considerable acumen who had taken summer school courses in social science at Columbia University early in the 1920s, Ira Caldwell believed strongly that nurture was more important than nature in an individual's development. Moreover, as a man of God deeply concerned with the welfare of his fellow man, Ira wanted to bridge the gap between religion and science that was to him so agonizingly apparent. Because Caldwell was unknown to the officers of the A.E.S., they were reluctant to accept his manuscript. Yet "because of its interest," which doubtlessly included Ira's cursory endorsement of "negative eugenics"—

controlling the reproduction of "unfit" people—the A.E.S. decided to take a chance on the work.[36]

Entitled "The Bunglers," the article, which was illustrated with photographs taken by Ira, presented the results of his investigation of the history of a family whose type polite society called "poor white trash," a term that Ira disparaged. He had observed and interviewed many members of the family and had traced its genealogy through three generations. Learning that many of the early "Bunglers" had enjoyed "remarkably good health," several living into their nineties without ever having seen a physician, Ira concluded that "this family has had an excellent biological inheritance." An oppressive environment, far more than faulty genes, was the cause of the family's decline.[37]

From a position as landowning farmers seventy-five years before, the Bunglers had fallen into tenancy, almost always on the poorest land. Prisoners of tradition and habit, many refused to give up tilling the soil to seek opportunity elsewhere. Ira emphasized that the family was hard-working, sober, and clean of venereal disease. Even so, the Bunglers suffered physical isolation and social opprobrium. Ravaged by hookworm and poor nutrition, spending as much as a fourth of their meager income on snuff, many of the younger Bunglers suffered "decided physical deterioration." Ignorant of birth control, virtually all of the Bunglers had many more children than they could support. Some of their homes were squalid shacks, "almost wholly devoid of furniture, the beds being piles of rags and straw." One house emitted "a fearful stench." Anticipating the reaction of his audience to his description of such domestic vileness, Ira wrote: "The reader may reason, as some misguided people do, that no matter how poor people are they can keep things clean about the house. The truth is that people can be so poor that they cannot be decent." The source of the Bunglers' misery, the root of their suffering, was poverty "so severe that it grinds vigor out of both body and soul."[38]

"The Bunglers" was much more than a disinterested scientific discourse. It was an impassioned indictment of a callous society, a "bungling civilization" that had missed "a chance to render social justice." "Someone," an enraged Ira wrote, "is responsible for the dwarfed intelligences and lean souls that one sees in these humble people." As Ira's charge suggests, the institutions that had signally failed to fulfill their social obligations were the schools and the churches. Although many school officials were oblivious of the plight of children like those of the Bunglers, even those who sympathized could do little, because "poor white trash" had no political clout. On the few occasions that Bungler children had enrolled in public school, they were ostracized by other youth and were unable to experience "the melting pot" of the playground. Moreover, fifteen-year-olds finding themselves "fastened in the lower grades . . . for several terms" were shamed into dropping out of school. "Common sense," Ira argued, dictated that it "would be far better to carry children of the Bungler type through the class as mere camp followers."[39]

If schools failed the Bunglers, churches served them even more miserably. Ignorance and "almost unbounded credulity" made such people "easy marks for the religious fakir." The orgiastic religion that enabled Bunglers who could not utter understandable English to become "expert in talking the unknown tongue" and that gave them solace in a hostile world featured snake handlers and preachers such as a husband-and-wife team consisting of a sixteen-year-old fourth-grade dropout and a fifty-year-old deranged widow. In Ira's estimation, however, such enthusiasts, mistaken as they were, bore less blame than "the leaders in the church" who could not "see clearly through the art glass windows." The enthusiasts were likewise less culpable than the conventional minister who preached against the sins of New York City and who ignored the families near his church "who were not sending their children to school, or to anything else except the cotton patch—and possibly the devil."[40]

Despairing, Ira hinted near the end of "The Bunglers" that selective sterilization might be in order—that, given society's refusal to help the Bunglers, there should be fewer of them. But he quickly passed over that suggestion and came back to what he knew best—the church, which "still has great influence over the lives of millions of people." Church leaders should "sense the situation"; ministers should "cease the warfare that they constantly wage against science"; "the fundamentalist and the modernist" should try to "understand the individual" and realize that "personality is the one thing of major importance." Were these developments to occur, "there would be far greater chance of appeal to the intelligent people in college and to the millions with fortunes." Could a revolution in thinking be effected, successful warfare might be waged against the forces—poverty, isolation, disease, and ignorance—that created people like the Bunglers.[41]

Nearly sixty years old when "The Bunglers" was published, Ira had devoted his life to the betterment of his fellow man. With little concern for a speech impediment, he had entered a profession that demanded weekly public speaking. With little thought of professional advancement, he had served his church throughout the South, often uprooting his family to do so. With little sympathy for the Calvinist doctrine of total depravity embraced by most members of his denomination, he had sought, by his focus on the importance of social environment, to undercut the theology of the church in which he had been raised.

Ira's reformist zeal generated opposition in Jefferson County, just as it had in other places. Some members of the Wrens church criticized him for the same behavior as had church members at Salem: devoting too much attention to the poor, who were not A.R.P. church members, and too little care to pastoral responsibilities such as visiting members' homes and conducting prayer and Bible-reading. Other ministers of the denomination likewise believed that he was too ardent a social gospeler. Townspeople generally, "sometimes thought him dogmatic" because "his championship of issues could be so spirited." A few accused him of being a socialist. One critic called him "a calamity howler . . . [who] viewed everything with alarm as he wanted to revoke the world." Ku Klux Klansmen in Wrens threatened to "run the goddam nigger lovin' S.O.B." out of town because his advocacy of fair treatment was ruining "every black bastard in the county." [42]

Nonetheless, admirers outnumbered detractors, especially among the young, who appreciated Ira's refusal to treat them condescendingly. A student who played on the athletic teams that Ira coached recalled that he "let the boys learn from the boys." Sometimes, that method meant letting young people make mistakes. "Ira didn't believe in discipline," that same student said; instead, he was convinced that "things would work themselves out sooner or later." [43]

If, as a child, Erskine had been "his mother's baby," as an adolescent, he was "his father's son." By the time the family moved to Wrens, he had become, as his mother put it, "set in his ways." A youthful acquaintance described him as a "very independent sort of a fellow" who attended church only rarely. Seldom mean but often mischievous, he, along with a few cronies, occasionally pulled pranks. Evidence of one of the more celebrated surfaced one Monday morning when teachers and students arrived at Wrens Institute to find the four-seater outhouse overturned. An excellent athlete but a mediocre student who went to school "whenever he wanted to," Red, as his friends called him, read voraciously, sometimes forgoing playing baseball to stay home with a book. Among the authors whose works had been assigned by his teachers were William Shake-speare, Oliver Goldsmith, and Charles Dickens, along with Edgar Allan Poe, James Fenimore Cooper, and Nathaniel Hawthorne. Erskine's pref-erences, however, were for works of history and geography that portrayed "the lives of people on this earth"—their habitats, occupations, aspira-tions, and cultures—for the dictionary, which he "read and re-read . . . with constant discovery," and for a series of volumes quietly given by his parents. *What a Young Man Ought to Know* dealt with the matter of sex.[44]

A reticent boy, Erskine often kept to himself and "didn't have many friends." A habit of acting independently and an insatiable curiosity led to many varied experiences in Wrens and its vicinity. According to a long-time resident of the town, he "lived differently from the rest of the people." Sometimes he would visit sawmills nearby to watch the machin-ery operate and to listen to the workers. Rough men, black and white, they were explicit in conversation, usually describing fights and sexual exploits. Occasionally, Erskine would travel to Augusta, where he would sit in the parlor of a brothel putting quarters in the piano so that he could remain and observe. Wrens men who patronized the establishment said that he "wouldn't take girls to bed; he'd just sit and listen" to the talk in the parlor. On Sunday afternoons in summer, he took cigarette makings to a sixteen-year-old black inmate at the chain-gang stockade who would regale him with jokes told by older convicts. For a brief period, he worked part-time on the night shift at the Wrens cottonseed oil mill, "the only completely democratic institution in town," he recalled, because in the mill "there was no intimation of racial distinction." While working there, he "got to know pretty well" members of a family that bore a marked resemblance to some of Ira's Bunglers and that soon left the mill to move to a nearby community through which ran a byway called Tobacco Road.[45]

Although a town of only a thousand people, Wrens had a full comple-ment of unusual characters: an albino who, according to what Erskine heard, had "superior abilities in many fields"; an indigent woman whose presence on the streets blocking store entrances was such a nuisance that she was sent to the county pauper farm, where men, as she later ex-claimed on the town's streets, "fucked me and didn't give me no money"; the widow of a Methodist minister, "a special character" with a deformed nose who from under her ever-present Bible would pull a cap pistol, fire it, and say to passers-by, "I'm shooting the devil out of you." After marrying a man much younger than she, this woman began to preach at a holiness church nearby whose members worshiped with frenzied emotion. For transportation she bought an automobile from a Wrens dealer who charged the amount of money she had on her, which was more than the car was worth. Ira was disturbed that a member of his congregation would fleece a customer.[46]

As Erskine was storing up impressions that would later be of great use in his writing, he was also developing an awareness of social injustice. Traveling around Jefferson County with his father or serving as driver for a doctor who made time to visit sharecroppers who he knew could not pay for his services, Erskine saw poverty so desperate that it made a lasting impression. The head of one family was so hopeless that Ira likened him to "a toad in a posthole." Like the frog, no matter how hard the man tried, he would never get out without help. Moreover, there was the case of a black boy at the county stockade serving a two-year sentence for the theft of an iron washpot that was too heavy for him to have moved. Finally, there was the influence of his socially conscious father, whose tolerance of youthful inquisitiveness enabled Erskine to witness things that a preacher's kid was not supposed to see. His concern for the lowly and his fascination with the lewd would last for the rest of his life.[47]

When Erskine left high school without a diploma but at the same time as classmates his age, the principal, who had spent many moments tracking him down while he was playing hooky, completed a certificate of admission for the use of college officials. While pointing out that Erskine's work was deficient in mathematics, he wrote: "I believe he will make good. . . . He has the elements of a good strong man." Notwithstanding Erskine's departure for college in September 1920, his connection to Wrens and its environs remained strong for twenty-five more years, until his mother left the town in 1945, a year after Ira's death.[48]

The matter of insufficient high-school credits was resolved through his father's intervention. Erskine College, Ira's alma mater, agreed to admit young Caldwell. The matter of insufficient money, though the costs were low, was resolved by Ira's borrowing. Soon after Erskine's arrival on campus, he discovered that some of the students there, many of whom were preachers' sons, could be brutal. One hazing incident involved a beating so severe that he was unable to walk for days.[49]

As had been the case at Wrens Institute, Erskine proved to be a lackluster student. His highest grades, C's, were in history and literature; his lowest, resounding F's, were in Bible and German. A classmate recalled, however, that he "read a lot." Much of the reading seems not to have been assigned by his instructors. When a history professor explained that he was omitting textbook passages dealing with the Civil War because the northern author "did not present the South's history in a favorable light," Erskine read them anyhow. Then, he read all the books on the subject that he could find in the college library.[50]

During the two and a half years that Erskine spent at the college, he earned credit in only half the courses he took. The habit of missing class persisted from high-school days, sometimes causing his grades to be lowered because of absences. Finding the college, with its requirement of daily chapel attendance, and the tiny town of Due West too restrictive, Erskine, sometimes alone and sometimes with a friend, would escape to visit towns nearby. On one occasion, the eve of a midterm examination, he and the friend walked four miles to the town of Donalds, where they boarded electric cars to Greenwood, eighteen miles away. Arriving there around midnight, they went to the all-night Busy Bee Cafe, where they met a couple of girls and "were entertained." Three hours later, they caught a train to Abbeville, fourteen miles distant. From there, they walked the twelve miles to Due West, reaching the college mess hall in time for breakfast. They reported for the exam—and failed it.[51]

A more extended trek resulted in Erskine's missing the spring semester of 1922. Early that year, he and a classmate, Andrew Murphy, secretly left school, bound for New Orleans. Once there, their attempt to ship out on a tramp steamer having been thwarted, Murphy returned to campus. Erskine, however, found a job selling magazine subscriptions in Bogalusa, Louisiana. When his crew chief skipped town, Erskine was left unemployed and broke amid people who had succumbed to the antiradical hysteria of the early 1920s and who feared that bolsheviks were knocking on their doors. He was arrested for loitering and was jailed. According to his account of the episode, Bogalusa authorities released him after he smuggled a letter to Ira with the help of a young black boy. Arriving back home in Wrens, he was greeted by his father, who showed not "a trace of displeasure" and asked him what he thought of Louisiana.[52]

Whatever Erskine lacked as a student, he tried to make up for as an athlete. Football was his love; for three seasons he played center for the

Erskine Seceders. Although he was six feet tall and weighed 170 pounds, he was much smaller than some of his teammates. But he was fearless. His finest hour came in November 1921, during a game with Clemson College, South Carolina's land-grant institution and a much larger school than Erskine College. When the Seceders' starting center, an all-stater, was knocked unconscious near halftime, Erskine, one of two substitutes, was sent in. A teammate expressed the unease that many of his fellows felt: "Here comes that goddam freshman . . . and we'll sure as hell get beat now." The fears proved groundless. As the teammate described events, "that long legged, shut mouth freshman did his full share. . . . On defense he acted like he was all we had, made tackles from end to end, threw 'em for losses dam near every play." The Seceders won, 13 to 0.[53]

Not only did Erskine excel in football, but also, as in Wrens, he proved to be quite willing to play pranks with other students: placing the president's buggy in a classroom and his horse in the chapel; printing a large banner that denounced the president; and rifling an opposing team's locker room. The locker-room incident, which took place in the spring of 1923, involved switching the clothing and other effects of members of a visiting baseball team. College administrators mistakenly believed that theft had occurred, because the report supplied to them was inaccurate. Erskine and his accomplice were asked not to return to campus once the 1922–23 term ended.[54]

Erskine's parents were, no doubt, exasperated by his behavior at college. Yet his father could not have objected too loudly, given his belief that young people should be allowed to make mistakes, from which he hoped they would learn and thereby develop stronger character. Moreover, Ira was aware of his son's admiration of him. Erskine liked the same food as he, engaged in the same adolescent prank of overturning outhouses, and played the same position on the same college's football team nearly thirty years later.[55] If the steady father was perplexed by the behavior of the wayward son, he nonetheless knew that the son had also begun to share his concern for the welfare of the South's poor.

CHAPTER TWO

The Making of a Writer

Well before Erskine College gently expelled Erskine Caldwell, he had tried to transfer to another school. In the summer of 1922, he corresponded with officials at the University of Virginia, an institution warmly praised by his mother. Although the university was willing to admit him, it could not offer him a scholarship, and his parents, who had always lived in genteel poverty, lacked the money to send him. Over the course of the next year, with the help of his mother, Erskine arranged financial aid. The United Daughters of the Confederacy awarded him a scholarship based upon the Civil War service of a maternal ancestor. In September 1923, he departed Wrens for Charlottesville.[1]

The University of Virginia accepted seventeen credits, most of them in history and English, for work done at Erskine College, only half the number awarded by the South Carolina school but enough to give Caldwell sophomore standing. To supplement his scholarship and the small sums his parents could afford to supply, Erskine worked in a poolroom near campus six hours a night, six nights a week, all for six dollars. His poverty and his lack of sophistication made him unwelcome among the elitists who set the tone of student life at Thomas Jefferson's university. He was often lonely.[2]

Although Erskine did not play football at Virginia and seems to have caroused less than he did at Erskine College, he again performed poorly in the classroom. To receive credit in a subject, a student had to complete satisfactorily a three-quarter sequence over the course of a year. The former football player took only one quarter of physical training, in which he made a grade of 31, forty-four points below passing. Two other courses, geology and psychology, he took for the entire year, but he failed them

23

also. The only subject that he passed—with a point to spare—was English literature, the first quarter of which dealt with William Shakespeare, the second with eighteenth-century essayists such as Jonathan Swift, Joseph Addison, and Samuel Johnson, and the third with the modern short story, including works by Robert Louis Stevenson and Rudyard Kipling. He did his best work in the short-story segment, which required "the writing of brief sketches or stories." [3]

When the academic year ended, Caldwell, after a visit to Wrens, headed north to Philadelphia where he enrolled for the summer at the University of Pennsylvania's Wharton School of Economics. Although wanderlust may have been part of the impetus for that move, he wanted also to try to understand how the American business system manipulated the southern poor. He supported himself with various jobs: clerk at a lunch counter; bodyguard for another Penn student; and stagehand at a burlesque theater where, it was rumored, he fell in love with a stripper, who did not return his affections. Because he passed two of the three credit hours he attempted, he felt that the summer "wasn't wasted entirely." [4]

Caldwell knew, however, that he had been squandering the opportunity to get a college education. In a long letter to his parents written near the end of the summer, the guilt-ridden, twenty-one-year-old sophomore informed them that he had decided not to return to the University of Virginia because he could no longer "take the money you both need." Instead, he would remain in Pennsylvania and work for a year. He assured Carrie and Ira that he was not "staying here to have a good time or to keep from going to school." His intentions were to save the money that he would earn that year, return to college and get his degree, and land a well-paying job. He implored his parents to work no more "than necessary for yourselves—leave me entirely out of it for a year and see what I can do to help you by not asking a cent from you." [5]

Two months later, having moved from Philadelphia to Wilkes-Barre, where he failed to earn a place on the roster of the city's semi-professional football team and instead took a job in a department store, Caldwell was ready to return to the University of Virginia. "I wanted to go back in Sept," he wrote his parents, "but couldn't as it ment you going into debt, so now if its possible I would rather be there than here." Homesick, he wanted to come to Wrens for Christmas. He lacked train fare, but he pledged "to economise and also to save" so that he could pay part of the thirty-dollar cost. [6]

Back at the University of Virginia for the winter quarter of 1925, Caldwell, having noted on his registration card that he intended to pursue a career in business, enrolled in three courses in economics. He failed one because of excessive absences, and he dropped the other two. The cause of his disastrous record that term was not the usual caprice but Cupid. At a concert in January, he met Helen Lannigan, who was four years younger than he but was already in graduate school studying French. The precocious and pretty daughter of the university's track coach and the tall and handsome yet lonely and insecure Caldwell were immediately attracted to each other. Soon sleeping together, they eloped early in March and were married in Washington amid the fanfare of Calvin Coolidge's inauguration. Fearing that Helen might get pregnant, Erskine wanted "to make an honest woman of her." [7]

Suspended from the university for the next year because of his "informal withdrawal" the previous spring, Erskine, with Helen, spent the summer of 1925 in Mt. Vernon, Maine, in a house that belonged to her family. In the fall of that year, he landed a job as a reporter for the *Atlanta Journal* that paid twenty dollars a week. Although Erskine had worked briefly for the *Jefferson County Reporter,* it was Ira's contacts that brought about the appointment. Erskine held the position through the following April. [8]

While working for the *Journal,* Caldwell met another reporter, Frank Daniel, who became a lifelong friend. Daniel introduced him to a manuscript of a novel written by another member of the *Journal'*s staff. Caldwell admired *The Hard-Boiled Virgin,* by Frances Newman, a native Atlantan whose talent and avant-garde views had earned the praise of H. L. Mencken. Caldwell's greatest admiration, however, was reserved for another *Journal* staffer whom he met once during his stint with the newspaper. He was deeply impressed by Margaret Mitchell's decision to give up her job at the *Journal* so that she could devote full time to writing a novel. [9]

In addition to writing obituaries, news stories, and special articles about the activities of the chamber of commerce that carried no byline, Caldwell reviewed books for a syndicate based at the *Charlotte Observer,* which he would continue to do after he left the *Journal.* Many of the works he reviewed were novels. His taste ran toward realistic stories rather than those in "the 'forever after' category." Of one novel, he wrote, "it is far fetched and unconvincing . . . a trifle too out of the ordinary;

the unusual element is too overdone to be even speciously possible." Not
only did Caldwell prefer realistic subject matter, he admired a straightfor-
ward style. Because the author of a collection of short stories he reviewed
was "never concerned with his method of telling it he tells his story well.
His style is simple and direct, not at any time self-conscious." [10]

Among Caldwell's reviews of works of nonfiction was one dealing with
a study of theological modernism, a philosophy that rejected the idea that
the Bible was infallible and advocated the application of scientific findings
to the interpretation of scripture. Like his father and unlike the funda-
mentalists common to the South, Caldwell endorsed modernism, contending that there was no inherent conflict between religion and science.
"Intolerance of any creed," he wrote in another review, "is the result in
every case of bigotry and a limited point of view." A book entitled *The
Red Web,* a hysterical account of radical efforts to subvert the government, he attacked as irresponsible. To the author's allegation that Moscow was raising an army in Mexico to invade the United States, the reviewer responded: "He failed to state whether his prophecy was a threat
or a promise." What struck Caldwell most about a volume dealing with
postwar Germany was its portrayal of the hunger and sickness suffered by
the people, especially the children. Poverty so desperate, he maintained,
threatened to undermine "the moral fibre of a nation." The young journalist enthusiastically commended a work coauthored by Howard W.
Odum of the University of North Carolina, who was emerging as the
South's preeminent social scientist. In *Systems of Public Welfare,* Odum,
believing that municipal and county systems were inadequate, argued for
the development of bigger and better departments of welfare at the state
level to solve the "problem of the unequal places and unequal folk." Caldwell considered the volume to be "authoritative . . . convincing . . . enlightening." It was "a distinct asset to the south" that should be studied
by everyone who held public office. [11]

Caldwell's warmest praise went to two studies of black life. Newbell
Niles Puckett's *Folk Beliefs of the Southern Negro* was without peer
among "recent books presenting a treatment of the southern negro."
Based upon his doctoral dissertation at Yale University, Puckett's book
was intended to serve not only scholarship but society as well. The more
that whites knew about black culture, the better the chances, Puckett
maintained, "of establishing more cordial relationships" between the
races. Caldwell admired the work because it was authoritative—and en-

tertaining. It would appeal, he believed, to the general reader, "who has more brains than he has been given credit for having." Moreover, Puckett's book should especially command the interest of southern whites because black folklore was part of their culture, too. "We read our lives and thoughts" in the book, he wrote, "as well as [those of] our neighbors.[12]

Caldwell was even more enthusiastic about *The Negro in American Life*, by Jerome Dowd, a sociologist at the University of Oklahoma. Of Dowd's 650 pages, which attempted to treat the totality of the black experience in America, Caldwell focused his analysis on the author's discussion of inferior housing, which, Caldwell said, was "one of the grave social and economic causes of the negro's present status." The reviewer mentioned the author's description of residential segregation in the nation's cities and the inequality that resulted. Then, Caldwell went further: "It is easy, in the south," he wrote, "to drive through the countryside and observe without effort cabins and shacks which are provided to house families ranging in number from three to four up to ten and twelve. When such a number of persons are forced to live in one or two rooms, or even three, the result of such practice is not far to seek." Near the conclusion of the review, Caldwell emphasized his sentiments: "No one who is interested in the advancement of society can afford to be without . . . [Dowd's] book."[13]

Following his departure from the *Journal*, Caldwell, with his wife and their infant son, Erskine Jr., who was born in Atlanta early in 1926, spent the summer of that year in Maine. That fall, Caldwell registered again at the University of Virginia. Of the four courses in which he enrolled, he seems to have stopped attending classes in Social Philosophy and in Nineteenth-Century English Literature. In his sociology course, Practical Problems in Public Welfare, which included fieldwork, he did well. His best performance came in Literary Composition, a course open only to students with "proved aptitude" who had obtained the professor's consent to enroll. That course and its instructor, Atcheson Laughlin Hench, would have a profound impact on Caldwell's development.[14]

In the fall quarter the coursework included evaluating contemporary essays. Caldwell turned in brief assessments of essays totaling more than 1,600 pages of reading matter. Like his reviews for the *Observer*, these evaluations reflect the developing cast of Caldwell's mind. He liked essays that denigrated the conservative American Federation of Labor and endorsed striking unionists, forlorn folk in the 1920s. He praised articles that emphasized environment over heredity as a factor in an individual's development, that rejected the idea of racial superiority, that promoted scientific farming, that advocated birth control, that made an intellectual argument for agnosticism, and that attacked the enthusiastic religion and business boosterism of the South. Among the essays he panned was one that defended Prohibition and called for its stricter enforcement and another that cited examples of progress in Georgia, attributed the state's backwardness to its rural tradition and large black population, and pleaded for sympathetic understanding of its circumstances.[15]

In the winter quarter, Professor Hench had his ten students write sketches and short stories, which often would be read and criticized in class. The "conversations," he said, "were lively." Although Caldwell's stories have not survived, Hench's evaluation of a few of them have been preserved. "The Promised Land," a story of seven pages, displayed an "abnormal style of writing—strong but unpleasant & unlikable." In the four-page "God's Children," Caldwell, Hench wrote, "attempts by staccato style to force attention, but forces *too* much attention." Generally, Hench thought, Caldwell's prose was "strip stark naked of words, pictorial words. He had a style in which he used nothing but stark nouns."[16]

The young Georgian's compositions, Hench recalled, often dealt with the effects of poverty. "He was something of a missionary. He was sort of a preacher and poverty-striken and had a very highly developed sense of social obligation. Had he been a more pious man and a man of a different nature, he might have been a preacher, or a social worker, because he was very much interested in the conditions of the poor."[17]

Never pious, Caldwell had, by the time he enrolled in Hench's class, lost his religion, even though the titles of the stories "The Promised Land" and "God's Children" indicate his interest in the subject. At registration for the 1926–27 term, for the first time he failed to record his religious affiliation, and he noted that he was not a church member. Moreover, he falsely listed his father's occupation as "newspaper editor." Disenchanted with what his mother called "the politics of the church," notably the opposition of some A.R.P. church members to Ira's work, Caldwell also believed more generally that the evangelical Protestantism that dominated the South, with its otherworldliness and intolerance, constituted a major regional problem. The change in his attitude toward religion reflected to some degree the evolution of his parents' thinking. By the 1920s, Carrie, her disillusionment with denominational politics having increased over the years, seldom attended church services; Ira, long a critic of the kind of Christianity that he perceived as narcotic, had become "more a sociologist than a minister," devoting most of his time to teaching, writing, and promoting charitable works.[18]

Religion figures as the most prominent topic in Caldwell's first publication, an essay submitted to Hench but probably written before he enrolled in the class. Published in a Kansas magazine that the editor described as "a weapon of war . . . on the enemies of Truth"—which included "the conspirators of organized religion"—"The Georgia Cracker" contains many of the themes that Caldwell would later treat in fiction—orgiastic religion, racial injustice, political demagoguery, social irresponsibility, and cultural sterility. Although the essay shows traces of the ribald humor that characterized some of his later work—a holy roller stripped to her underwear, "using her stomach and hips to great advantage, . . . sported herself like a hoochy-coochy teaser"—"The Georgia Cracker" is the work of an angry young man. "So this is Georgia," he concluded, a state "whose inhabitants do cruel and uncivilized things; whose land is overrun with bogus religionists, boosters, and demagogues; whose politics are in the hands of Klan-spirited Baptists; and yet whose largest city boasts of being the 'greatest city in the greatest state in the world.'"[19] H. L. Mencken would have described matters more cleverly but no more passionately.

Caldwell credited Hench with putting him "on the road to writing," and after two quarters of work in Hench's classes he was sustaining a B average. Even so, in April 1927, shortly after the birth of his second son, Dabney (whose delivery, like that of his brother, had been paid for by his grandparents), Caldwell formally withdrew from the university. Since his initial enrollment in September 1923, he had earned a total of three hours credit.[20] His blemished career as a student over, he knew now what he wanted to do with his life. That life would be devoted to writing, and the best of the writing would be devoted to attacking social injustice in his native region.

As Caldwell knew, the South of his youth and young manhood was a wretched place for many of its inhabitants. The root of their misery, which provided the nourishment for many other social ills, was intractable poverty. In the late nineteenth century, thousands of southerners, most of them white, began to flee impoverishment on the land in search of the golden opportunity to work in factories, particularly the textile mills that had been built throughout the Piedmont since the 1870s. Many of the farm-to-town migrants found that the opportunity was only gilded. Years after the industrial boom began, entire families, including children under ten years old, went to work in the mills for long hours—twelve a day for many adults as late as the 1920s—for wages so low that, even in the flush year of 1919, they were little above two dollars a day for many workers.[21]

Despite the good intentions of the southern humanitarians and politicians who participated in the Progressive Movement of the early twentieth century, millions of the region's industrial workers led desperately poor lives. Shortly after the Great War and again in the late 1920s and early 1930s, thousands of those workers, believing they had suffered enough, expressed their frustration by going on strike. Almost always, the strikes failed. The fortunate strikers were able to return to work under conditions that either had not improved or had worsened. The unlucky ones were often blacklisted, sometimes jailed, and occasionally killed. The killers went unpunished because many of the more affluent southerners justified any means of controlling labor unrest, which, they believed, was fomented by subversive radicals.[22]

Many of the southerners who remained on the land through the industrial expansion that began in the 1880s and continued intermittently into the 1920s suffered more than those who had moved to the mill villages. Except for brief periods of prosperity, such as during the Great War, when even tenant farmers could afford to buy Model T Fords, southern agriculture from the Civil War to the Second World War was mired in depression. C. Vann Woodward's poignant description of the travail of southern farmers in the 1890s, when Caldwell's father was a young man, might justly be applied to their condition in the 1920s, when Caldwell himself was a young man: "The annual defeat of the crop market and the tax collector, the weekly defeat of the town market and mounting debt, and the small, gnawing daily defeats of crumbling barn and fence, encroaching sagebrush and erosion, and one's children growing up in illiteracy—all added up to frustration."[23]

By 1930, the proportion of southern farmers that had to worry about the tax collector had been much reduced. Since 1880, the rate of tenancy had risen by almost 20 percent. As of 1930, nearly three of every five southern farms were operated by tenants. In Georgia, the rate statewide was two of three; in Caldwell's part of the state, the proportion was four of five. Farmers who owned no land did not have to pay taxes on real property. Instead, they suffered something worse than the annual defeat of the tax collector—the annual accounting of the landlord and furnish merchant, to whom they paid rent either in cash or in a share of the crop they had grown. Often, tenants found that not only had they not made any money but that they were deeper in debt. By the early 1930s, many southern tenants believed, as had oppressed southern farmers in the 1890s, that only collective action could ameliorate conditions so foul that thousands of the rural poor lacked outhouses. Only by organizing could tenants hope to bring to bay landlords who believed that "all that a share-cropper needs is a cotton patch and a corn cob."[24]

Like their fellows who attempted to unionize workers in southern factories in the 1920s and 1930s and who failed to improve industrial conditions, the farmers and others who tried to organize agricultural laborers were not able to effect significant improvement of the situation on the land. The agricultural unionists, too, met with violent treatment. Planters and their henchmen, like the townsmen who terrorized industrial unionists, feared the growth of radicalism that sought to provide economic security to people who were often little more than peons.[25]

The brutal treatment of blacks by whites had a much longer history than class violence among whites—from slavery through Reconstruction to the outbreak of an epidemic of lynching in the 1890s. In the economic depression of that decade, many white men could not provide for their families. But they believed that they could protect their families by lynching black men who, they thought, were bent on ravishing white women. Twenty-odd years later, in the immediate aftermath of the Great War, white men's fears rekindled in a blaze, this time without the fuel supplied by hard times. In 1919, more than eighty lynchings occurred in the South. Some of the victims were veterans still in uniform, men who, according to a Mississippi senator, had been "French-woman ruined." The violence against blacks continued into the 1920s, although by then the incidence of lynching had diminished and by then there were proportionately fewer blacks to be intimidated. The push of oppression and the pull of opportunity during the war years had caused hundreds of thousands of black people to leave the South for the North. The millions who stayed behind found that they continued to be victims of segregation, disfranchisement, and violence.[26]

In the 1920s, blacks, political radicals, Jews, Roman Catholics, and other presumed miscreants such as divorcees and northerners felt the wrath of a reborn Ku Klux Klan. Although the Klan of that era was a national curse, it was especially strong in the South, where it was headquartered until 1925. In the South, the Klan numbered among its members more townsmen than countrymen. Among the urban members were ministers, doctors, businessmen, lawyers, and an occasional governor and congressman. Because community leaders often belonged to the Klan, intolerance, hatred, and violence became respectable. Some Klansmen demonstrated their good citizenship, their commitment to "100 per cent Americanism," by boycotting Jewish merchants, by attempting to throw Catholics off of school boards, by flogging labor organizers, divorcees, and philanderers, and by terrorizing blacks. In the South, as in the rest of the country, the Klan began to lose strength after a prominent leader in Indiana was convicted of murder in 1925. Yet a Klan-like mentality, which both reflected and inspired the bigotry and violence endemic in southern society, lost none of its influence.[27]

In the South of Caldwell's youth and young manhood, cruelty reigned. Moreover, amid the brutality there flourished a business boosterism that encouraged the wanton exploitation of the South's poor. The chief locus of the booster spirit was Atlanta, which was also the home of the Ku Klux Klan. It took courage for southerners who were part of polite society, as Caldwell and his father were, to challenge what the Carolina journalist W. J. Cash later called "the savage ideal." As the elder Caldwell had learned and as his son would discover, publicly to criticize the inequities grounded in class and race in southern society and publicly to question the claims of boosters who said that all was well in southern society could bring not only vilification but also threats against one's life from the defenders of the status quo.[28]

By the summer of 1927, Erskine and Helen, with their sons, had returned to the Lannigan house in Mt. Vernon, Maine. The rage evident in "The Georgia Cracker," in which Caldwell had shown no reluctance to disparage the rich and powerful, had intensified. One of his first acts upon getting settled was to fire off a letter to the *Nation* that blasted the First Lady, whose seventy-year-old uncle, a day laborer for a railroad, "died near here recently." Grace Coolidge did not attend the funeral, Caldwell said, because her "social inclinations," in conjunction with "politics," had caused her to "disown . . . her uncle because he was a laborer."[29]

While he was struggling to write, Caldwell was also continuing to read avidly. In Hench's class at Virginia, he had been introduced to stories by Ernest Hemingway and D. H. Lawrence, which he considered first-rate. He also liked Theodore Dreiser's novels, Carl Sandburg's poems, and Ambrose Bierce's stories. His main interest, in fact, lay in the short story. The book that impressed him most was Sherwood Anderson's collection of stories, *Winesburg, Ohio*. In a letter to a friend, written late in 1932, Caldwell expressed his admiration for Anderson and in doing so made some telling comments about his own literary credo. "Story-telling," he told Alfred Morang, is "what fiction is." Anderson was "the best writer in America" because he was "a story-teller." "What else is there to matter?" Caldwell asked rhetorically. "The best story-teller is he who tells his tale the most convincingly and beautifully. That's why God made words. Words are to tell stories with. They are delicate; we ought to handle them with the love and care a mother does her baby." [30]

Although the craft of composing short stories appealed most to Caldwell's sensibility, he continued to experiment with the writing of poetry, which he had begun at the University of Virginia. Lackluster efforts for the most part, the unpublished poems, many of which deal with nature, beauty, and love, sometimes evince an ear for the rhythmic cadences that would characterize some of his later prose. Moreover, a few of the poems presage themes that would become staples of his fiction: the shortcomings of organized religion, economic deprivation, and racial injustice. The most memorable of the poems is about a lynching. In "The Face Beneath the Sky," the dying black victim describes to the narrator, who has discovered him hanging from a tree, the horrible acts of the members of the white mob:

> they fought, he said, in passion for his ears,
> his blood they drew with gruesome pride
> and took his hands away for souvenirs. [31]

Living on whatever subsistence their parents could spare, the Caldwells suffered lean times; even their typewriter was rented on credit. As Erskine soon discovered, the Lannigan house, designed to be a summer retreat, afforded poor protection against the Maine winter. Cold winds blew through cracks in the walls and floors. He also learned soon that food, plentiful in summer, ran dangerously low in winter. As he struggled to provide for his family, he struggled also to write amid cold, hunger, and the distractions of two small children. Sometimes, as Helen wrote to Carrie, Erskine did not want "to have any one around him at all." At those times he would go to a cottage half a mile from the house, where he would write all day and, by kerosene lamp, into the night, sometimes staying there overnight.[32]

In November 1928, having lived for a year and a half in Mt. Vernon, the Caldwells, seeking to support themselves without their parents' help, moved seventy-five miles distant to Portland. There, with capital supplied by their parents, they opened a bookshop, which was stocked partly with copies of the volumes Caldwell had reviewed without pay for the *Observer* syndicate. While Helen ran the shop, Erskine continued to write. Doing so was difficult. As he told his father, "I have been trying to write for a long time and it is becoming discouraging. . . . If I could only get one piece accepted by an important magazine or publisher possibly it would be easier to have hopes." As the economy collapsed in the fall of 1929, so did the bookshop soon thereafter. The following spring, the Caldwells returned to Mt. Vernon, leaving debts in Portland of one thousand dollars, a daunting sum in the Great Depression.[33]

By the spring of 1930, Caldwell's fiction had begun to be published— five stories and a novella since June 1929. All of the short stories appeared in little magazines, a medium that he had discovered at the University of Virginia. Operating on shoestring budgets, able to pay contributors only a token if anything at all, usually short-lived, the little magazines nonetheless exerted a profound influence on American literature by encouraging experimentation in form and content. Caldwell was one of many important writers whose creative work first appeared in their pages. Not confined to the intellectual centers of the Northeast, little magazines existed all over the country. In the South during the 1920s, Richmond was home to *The Reviewer,* New Orleans to *The Double Dealer,* Nashville to *The Fugitive.* By 1929, Mississippi's State College for Women was publishing a little magazine, *blues,* which brought out one of Caldwell's earliest stories.[34]

In these early works, Caldwell displayed a wide range of style and subject. The first story published, "Midsummer Passion," is a hilarious farce with a New England setting. Another, "The Strawberry Season," poignantly describes the awakening sexuality of two southern adolescents. Two others, "Tracing Life with a Finger" and "Inspiration for Greatness," are highly experimental pieces, hardly conventional stories. Impressionistic, surrealistic, dreamlike, they record, in first person, the reflections of the nameless young narrator. In these partly autobiographical prose poems, whose overriding topic is loneliness, social injustice provides a minor theme. "In the fall after all the crops had been gathered, some men lynched a negro boy. When they were ready to go home they cut off his ears and fingers and toes and put them into their pockets."[35]

The strongest of the early stories is the shortest. "Joe Craddock's Old Woman," a 750-word snapshot of the life and death of a cotton farmer's wife, illustrates Caldwell's rage over conditions in the poverty-stricken South. It shows, too, the gift for conveying emotion in simple language, tightly constructed, that would characterize his best work of the following decade. Dead at thirty-five, toil-worn Julia Craddock, through her married life, had never been "pretty and charming." The undertaker, however, had turned her into "a beautiful young girl" who looked like the image captured in the photograph that she had given to her fiance. Caldwell's sensitivity to the travail of poor southerners, women and men, shines in his succinct portrayal of the Craddocks' lives.

> Death was . . . [Julia's] compensation . . . for the ugliness of her face and body, and of her life. She had been miserable while she lived—eleven children, fourteen cows, and a flock of chickens.—And eight stinking hogs. Not once had Julia left the farm in over ten years. Work, work, work, from four in the morning till nine at night; never a vacation, a trip to town, nor time to bathe all over. Joe worked all the time, too. Yet his labor returned nothing but an aching back, heartbreak, and poverty. The harder he worked the poorer he became. If he made twenty bales of cotton in the fall the price would drop to where he could barely pay for the fertilizer—usually not even that. Or if the price went up to thirty cents a pound he would, by the curse of too much rain or not enough rain, have no cotton to sell. There with Joe and Julia life wasn't worth living very long.[36]

The observations and experiences that had figured large in many of the early stories provided the basis for some aspects of Caldwell's first extended work, a novella begun when he was a student at the University of Virginia. The fly-by-night publisher that issued the work late in 1929 entitled it *The Bastard*. Set primarily in a town named Lewisville in an unnamed southern state, the story traces the life of Gene Morgan, illegitimate and illiterate son of a prostitute and carnival stripper, who earns his living in a cottonseed oil mill, a sawmill, and a poolroom. Rife with violence, graphically portrayed, and with sex—adultery, miscegenation, implied incest—never depicted in the act itself, the novel gratuitously piles horror upon horror. There is hardly a flicker of the social conscience that would inform Caldwell's later novels. Even so, the author hints that the protagonist is someone who has been brutalized by a hellish environment.[37]

The Bastard was more than Portland could stand. The city banned it and brought charges of obscenity not only against Caldwell for writing the book but also against his wife for selling it in the shop. Caldwell leaped to defend Helen, himself, and the novel. In March 1930, "In Defense of Myself" was printed and distributed. An impassioned defense of the integrity of his work, the broadside also defended the people portrayed in the story, who lived in an environment that was "realistically uninhibited." The Gene Morgans of the South, Caldwell pointed out, were hardly a part of polite society; they did not play golf, had no social club, and were ignored by the churches. His rage unrestrained, Caldwell went beyond the story to defend other poor people in the South: "Here is a woman, a girl in years, who has no friends with whom she can play bridge. She works in a cotton mill. She is a lint-head. She earns eleven dollars and fifteen cents from one Saturday to the next. The mill lays her off six weeks. Neither her mother, nor her father, if either she has, can afford to give her money to buy a pair of stockings and a hat. Somebody else can. A man. She goes with him and he buys her the clothes she wants so much. A week later he is in New Orleans, in Chicago, in Detroit. She gets along the best way she can. We all do." He summed up the "Defense" by saying, "I did not write this novel with obscenity, lewdness and immorality in mind. I wrote the book because I have a deep sympathy for the people in it. I know them . . . and I love them. . . . This story belongs to them even more than it does to me."[38]

The novel and the stories brought very little cash—the "bastards" who published *The Bastard,* Caldwell wrote to a friend, "vamoosed with all the copies and the money"—but much satisfaction to the fledgling writer, whose dedication, hard work, and talent had produced a published author.[39] Fortunately for southern literature, Caldwell would soon abandon in his long fiction the experiment in sensationalism that characterized *The Bastard.* And the skillful handling of short fiction evident in "Joe Craddock's Old Woman" and "The Strawberry Season" would only get better.

CHAPTER THREE

The Godforsaken South:
The Fiction of the Thirties

The essay "The Georgia Cracker," published in 1926, and the short story "Joe Craddock's Old Woman," published in 1929, foreshadowed much of Caldwell's southern work of the 1930s. In that decade, virtually all of his strongest writing, fiction and nonfiction, dealt with the millions of poor southerners who, as his father had observed, would never escape the posthole of destitution without help. No other major southern writer of the thirties portrayed as extensively and as forthrightly as Caldwell the inequities growing out of discrimination based upon class and race. "The masses in the South," he wrote in the summer of 1931 as he applied for financial assistance to enable him to write a novel, "have always been undernourished, uneducated, and without a spokesman."[1] He would be their voice.

By the spring of 1930, the Caldwells had departed Portland and returned to Mt. Vernon, where Erskine was "working like hell" but "not writing stories for money primarily." Despite having published some of his work, Caldwell continued to receive publishers' rejections of his manuscripts. An editor of a little magazine in Portland advised his colleagues: "Under no circumstances print Caldwell." The *Bookman*, an experimental journal published in England, disdained the "sawdust and blood" of his fiction.[2]

Despite those rejections, Caldwell received steady support from Richard Johns, the editor of *Pagany*, a Boston little magazine that published four of his stories in 1930. To Johns, Caldwell described his theory of composition, which had been developing since his days at the University of Virginia. The litmus test of a creative work was whether it possessed "the utmost in vitality." Moreover, he believed that a writer was obligated to make his work accessible to the reader. Praising *Pagany* because "the contributions are intelligible," he expressed his conviction that "any man who consciously covers up his work in difficult technicalities is robbing himself and his readers. The easiest way the reader's emotions can be reached (the hardest way to write however) is the perfect way. The work leaves a deeper and more sincere impression on the mind." [3]

Two of Caldwell's published stories had deeply impressed an important figure in the literary establishment. Near the middle of February 1930, Caldwell received a letter from Maxwell Perkins, senior editor at Charles Scribner's Sons. Instrumental in launching the careers of F. Scott Fitzgerald, Ernest Hemingway, and the young southerner Thomas Wolfe, Perkins had read Caldwell at Fitzgerald's suggestion. The editor asked Caldwell to consider submitting his work to the company's magazine. The chance to appear in *Scribner's* was hardly an opportunity to ignore, and Caldwell responded immediately. Although his first submission was rejected, the June number carried two of his stories, both of which were set in New England. And he was richer $350. [4]

Shortly before those stories came out, Scribner's offered to publish a collection of stories in the winter of 1931 and asked Caldwell to write an additional thirty thousand words to fill out the proposed volume. Although Caldwell promised to try, he stipulated that he would "much rather have the privilege of doing a few good stories than writing a lot of rotten stuff." He asked Perkins which stories he thought were more successful, the ones about Maine or those dealing with the South. Perkins replied that the southern stories were better because they revealed more, went deeper, had more meaning, and dealt with fresher material than those about New England. [5]

Editing the manuscript of the collection—to be published as *American Earth*—was placed under the direction of Perkins's conscientious and capable associate, John Hall Wheelock. Praising Caldwell's "natural talent for understanding people . . . and a talent for writing which is not surpassed by any of the younger men," Wheelock, echoing Perkins's judgment, said that Caldwell had "only one serious artistic failing and that is the quite natural and rather hopeful one of over-emphasis." Experience and discipline, Wheelock felt, would correct that flaw. In a number of stories, Wheelock's suggestions made significant improvements by revis-

ing details that rang false. Yet, if Caldwell had followed the spirit of all
the changes his editor proposed, two of the stories—the strongest in the
collection—would have been eviscerated. Wheelock's aversion to "the pil-
ing on of horror upon horror and brutality upon brutality" caused him
to diminish the importance of "Savannah River Payday" and "Saturday
Afternoon." Fortunately, Caldwell's minor revisions did not weaken the
impact of those powerful stories.[6]

The first two paragraphs of "Savannah River Payday" address the myth
of the Sunny South.

> A quarter of a mile down the river the partly devoured carcasses of five
> or six mules that had been killed during the past two weeks by the heat
> and overwork at the sawmill lay rotting in the mid-afternoon sun. Of the
> hundred or more buzzards hovering around the flesh, some were perched
> drowsily on the cypress stumps, and some were strutting aimlessly over
> the cleared ground. Every few minutes one of the buzzards, with a sound
> like wagon-rumble on a wooden bridge, beat the sultry air with its wings
> and pecked and clawed at the decaying flesh. Dozens of the vultures
> glided overhead hour after hour in monotonous circles.
>
> The breeze that had been coming up the river since early that morning
> shifted to the east and the full stench of sun-rotted mule-flesh settled over
> the swamp. The July sun blazed over the earth and shriveled the grass and
> weeds until they were as dry as crisp autumn leaves. A cloud of dense
> black smoke blew over from the other side of the river when somebody
> threw an armful of fat pine on the fire under the moonshine still.[7]

Closely kin to southwest humor—with which Caldwell was not familiar—but without the condescending narrator present in many stories of
that antebellum genre, "Savannah River Payday" records an afternoon's
antics of two sawmill workers who "don't [intend to] work all week and
let payday git by without tankin' up good and plenty." While they are still
sober, Jake and Red, fast friends, knock the gold teeth from the mouth of
a dead black man, try to rape a mulatto girl, and commit various other
gruesome acts of violence, most of them upon each other. Throughout
the horror, described matter-of-factly, Caldwell deftly sustains an under-
tone of humor. To Wheelock, the story was "unrelieved brutality." To
Caldwell, such a judgment would have no meaning to Jake and Red.[8]

The finest story in the collection, and among the best of the many powerful stories that Caldwell wrote, is "Saturday Afternoon." With brutal
irony, the action of the story undercuts the title, which suggests a week-

end's diversions. Instead, Caldwell leads the reader in a descent into hell. The story opens in a meat market where "lazy, stinging, fat and greasy flies" light on the butcher, Tom Denny, who is trying to relax on the meat block. His head rests on " a hunk of rump steak" flecked with the tobacco juice that he had tried to spit into a nearby sawdust box laden with offal.[9]

Tom is good at his work. If a customer wanted pork, "Tom turned the hunk of beef over two or three times businesslike and hacked off a pound of pork." If a customer wanted veal, Tom "slammed the hunk of beef around several times making a great to-do, and got the veal. . . . He pleased everybody." [10]

Irrationality reigns outside the butcher shop as well. That Will Maxie, who is getting on in years, is "a pretty good Negro . . . minding his own business, stepping out of the road when he met a white man, and other-wise behaving himself" only infuriates the whites who envy the success that his hard work has brought. In their eyes, he is "too damn good for a Negro. He did not drink corn whisky, nor make it; he did not carry a knife, nor a razor; he bared his head when he met a white man, and he lived with his own wife." [11] To white savages, good habits among blacks are threatening.

When the butcher hears that Will has "said something" to a white girl, he grabs his shotgun and joins the mob pursuing him. After burning Will alive, the mob "filled him so full of lead that his body sagged from his neck where the trace chain held him up." All the while, the druggist's son was busy selling Coca-Colas to the crowd of onlookers, which, although smaller than usual at such events, bought six cases at double the regular price. The butcher could not stay to help the rest of the mob tie Will's body to a limb for display. He had to hurry back to his shop and quarter a cow so that he could hang that meat in the icehouse before the late afternoon rush of customers arrived. In Wheelock's opinion, "over-emphasis on horror . . . in connection with the lynching takes away its reality." In Caldwell's much more realistic view, horror defined lynching.[12]

Among the other southern stories in *American Earth* in which regional setting figures significantly in the action are two that vary widely in tone and content. In "Molly Cotton-Tail," the narrator, a young boy, ulti-mately rejects his visiting aunt's belief that "to be a real Southern gentle-man" he must first hunt and kill game. Poignantly told, the story not only challenges a deeply entrenched regional custom but also undermines stereotypical views of the South. Hunting as a rite of passage is rejected by some southerners, including not only the narrator but his father as well. "A Swell-Looking Girl," a burlesque of masculine vanity and feminine inscrutability, tells how Lem Johnson, the owner of a two-horse farm, gets his come-uppance. Excessively proud of his good-looking bride and her dainty underthings, Lem, goaded by a doubting neighbor, intends to show the "pink little things" to the young men who have gathered at his house. To his great amazement his bride wears nothing under her dress. The only passage that serves no function in the telling of the tale reveals that Lem, as a bachelor, lived in a four-room house. His black tenant, with a wife and six children, had only a cabin.[13]

Throughout the South, from Richmond to New Orleans, reviewers extolled *American Earth* as the work of an extraordinary writer. Other newspapers agreed with the assessment of the *Louisville Courier-Journal:* "One feels this young man's power as something to be reckoned with." Reviewers praised the simplicity of Caldwell's style, although some felt that it needed polish. One perceptively noted that the brief stories suggested "a dramatic action continuing beyond the confines of a related episode" and illustrated the point with "Joe Craddock's Old Woman": "Here in three and a half pages we are given a simple picture of the burial of a toil-worn farm woman. But the author has suggested also the early love affair, thwarted hopes, years of toil, ugly friction with her worked-down husband—a whole life story is revealed, and by the simplest means."[14]

A glowing and thoughtful review by Aaron Blum Bernd in the Macon, Georgia, *Telegraph* noted that the New England stories were less vigorous and less successful than the southern ones. Among the latter, the comic tales were reminiscent of the sketches in Augustus Baldwin Longstreet's *Georgia Scenes* except that Caldwell shunned Longstreet's "preaching and . . . educating," letting "no moral conventions limit his themes or his language." After commending the humorous stories, Bernd singled out "Saturday Afternoon" for special praise. Although some other reviewers characterized the story as "highly improbable" and exaggerated—one wanted "to see affidavits" supporting it—Bernd found its "vivid reporting of such horrors . . . bleak and revolting and . . . convincing." Informing readers of Caldwell's place of birth and contending that he would soon gain national attention, Bernd urged Georgia "immediately [to] stake out its claim" for ere long other southern states in which he had grown up "will be claiming the man as their own." [15] Thirty years would pass before Bernd's prediction would begin to come true.

Before reviews of *American Earth* had begun to appear in the spring, Caldwell had completed a novel. By early May he had mailed to Scribner's a manuscript entitled "Tobacco Road." [16]

"I have finished the book," Caldwell wrote to Richard Johns in April 1931, that "I've been doing these long, sometimes hungry, most of the time painful [ten] months. . . . It's not sensational, experimental, nor important; it is just human. Maybe it's not so good; but I have a sympathy for the people in it." Despite his doubts of the manuscript's quality, he expressed confidence that Scribner's would want to publish it. [17]

Maxwell Perkins was not so sure. Although he thought that "Tobacco Road" was "well-nigh perfect within its limits," he feared that it would not sell. The Great Depression, he told Caldwell, made it difficult to sell any kind of book, particularly a novel that lacked any character that "any reader could possibly identify himself with, with any sort of pleasure." [18]

Caldwell responded immediately to Perkins's objection. With an observation that tellingly reflected his theory of writing, he replied: "The sympathy of a reader—in my mind—is won and held by the intense reality of a story, not by its pleasure-pain. And I do not believe the sympathy of any reader is worth the holding thereof if the winning was not at first difficult." Because he knew "the trueness of . . . [the book's] people," he could not believe "that it should be thrown away unread with the published trash of yesterday." To his friend Johns, he confided, "The real trouble is that it is a story of a Georgia family . . . who are starving of malnutrition and pellagra because the absentee landlord has stopped giving them credit for food and seed." [19]

Perkins likewise responded immediately to Caldwell's defense of "Tobacco Road," saying that Scribner's had decided to publish the manuscript the following spring. The question of sales remained an important concern, not only because of the Depression but also because a vice president stressed the damage the novel might do to sales of the company's textbooks in the South. Nonetheless, Perkins and Wheelock, who also encountered objections that the story was offensive, had so strongly recommended publication that the company's president agreed. [20]

Perkins still believed that the "trouble" with the novel "is there is no one in it that it is pleasant to read about." But he admired Caldwell's "absolute artistic integrity . . . which flinches from none of the facts, how-

ever unpleasant or tragic." Other writers had described "in naturalistic
manner" conditions of "awful degradation" such as those in "Tobacco
Road," but only Caldwell "fully and sympathetically understood the
people," causing the reader to realize "that what is wrong with them
comes from their situation."[21]

After Caldwell made some slight revisions suggested by Wheelock, *Tobacco Road* was published in February 1932. As Perkins had feared, sales
were slow. Not only was the Depression a formidable barrier, so was
Scribner's sales department, which failed to push the book enthusiastically.[22]

"Down there on the tobacco road," the authorial voice notes fairly
early in the novel, "no one ever laughed." Yet the story's humor, black
though it is, makes the novel emotionally bearable and saves the characters from being merely objects of pity. The humor heightens after Sister
Bessie Rice, an evangelist, buys an automobile, ostensibly to help her
carry on her ministry. Thenceforth, Sister Bessie and the poor-white Lesters who travel with her—Dude, a sixteen-year-old boy whom Bessie intends to turn into a preacher and who soon becomes her husband in a
ceremony that she performs, and Jeeter, Dude's sixty-year-old father—are
lambs in a world of wolves. The automobile salesmen fleece Sister Bessie
and while doing so laugh at her deformed nose. The county clerk who
issues the license to allow the illiterate Bessie and Dude to marry com-
plains about having to write her name, which he "don't get paid for." In
an Augusta flophouse, which Jeeter, who has never before spent a night
in a hotel, thinks is "a fine place," men guests shunt Bessie from room to
room. Even though the humor in that scene derives from Bessie's, and the
Lesters', ignorance of the men's intentions, it highlights the moral superiority of the people on Tobacco Road. They engage in illicit sex with a
will—and they do not conceal their designs.[23]

The humor in *Tobacco Road* is sometimes tied to religion. On one
occasion, Jeeter reminds Sister Bessie that while praying for the family
she failed to mention Dude, who is "as big a sinner as the rest of us Lesters." Bessie then prays for Dude, but Jeeter considers it "a durn short
prayer for a sinner like Dude" who "cuss[es] his Ma and Pa like he does
other people." Later, when the county clerk's refusal to issue a marriage
license to Bessie and Dude because Dude is under age prompts Bessie to
pray, the clerk quickly gives in. He prefers to grant a license "than listen
to that." In the funniest passage in the novel, wherein Caldwell tellingly

satirizes the irrelevance and narrow moralism of socially conservative Christianity, Jeeter is baffled by the topic of Dude's initial sermon—black shirts. To Jeeter's query, "Is he going to preach for black shirts, or against black shirts?" Bessie responds, "Against them." Mystified, Jeeter says, "I ain't never heard of nobody preaching about men wearing black shirts—against black shirts, at that. I ain't never seen a man wearing a black shirt, noway." Sister Bessie then enlightens Jeeter: "Good preachers . . . always preach *against* something."[24]

If the humor interspersed through *Tobacco Road* saves the story from sentimentality, the novel is nonetheless, as its editor Wheelock said, "a profoundly compassionate work." Perkins's observation that Caldwell was not "primarily interested in the story per se" is confirmed by the structure of the novel. The plot—what little there is—is hardly conventional, consisting merely of a series of episodes that occur over a week's time. Likewise, characterization is of secondary importance; only Jeeter receives any degree of development. What is central is setting. Caldwell's depiction of an environment that is so brutal it can crush all decency from its victims gives the novel its great power. So strong was his desire to emphasize the omnipotence of environment that he included in *Tobacco Road* something absent from much of his other work: an account of the impact of the past on the present. Trying to portray the force that history possessed, he interjected chapters at appropriate points in the story that contain little but social commentary and that advance the plot hardly at all.[25]

Like Ira Caldwell's Bunglers, the Lester family has not always been destitute. On the eve of the Civil War, Jeeter's grandfather owned many acres of land, which he was able to hold until his death. Having inherited half of his father's plantation, Jeeter's father replaced tobacco with cotton. Poor soil and high taxes soon caused him to lose half of his land. At his father's death, Jeeter inherited "what was left of the Lester lands and debts." The debts far outweighed the value of the land. Within two years of his father's death early in the century, the remaining land having been sold to satisfy claims against the estate, Jeeter has become a sharecropper for Captain John Harmon, who has purchased the land. Each passing year brings to the Lesters "poverty more bitter than that of the year before." Realizing that his operation was a failure, Captain John gave up farming early in the 1920s and moved to Augusta. With him went Jeeter's source of credit, although the absentee landlord allowed Jeeter and his family to live rent-free in their shack. As did thousands of other white southerners caught up in the hard times since the Civil War, the Lesters have fallen from prosperous landowners to impoverished tenants in three generations. Attributing the plight of the Lesters and other of Captain John's tenants to his failure to practice scientific farming, Caldwell offered an alternative to the South's wasteful system. "Co-operative and corporate farming," he wrote, "would have saved them all."[26]

Unlike many of the thousands of white southerners reduced to tenancy who fled the farms to seek a living in the cotton mills of the South, Jeeter refuses to leave. The inertia that has rendered him incapable of acting in virtually all of the other affairs in his life has little to do with that decision. Irresolute in all other matters, he is firm in his determination to stay on the land, for which he has "an inherited love." Farming, he tells his son-in-law, Lov Bensey, is "in my blood. . . . My Pa and his Pa before him was the same kind of men." In a novel that hardly calls for lyricism, Jeeter's recollection of planting season approaches poetry. "When the winter goes, and when it gets to be time to burn off broom-sedge in the fields and underbrush in the thickets, I sort of want to cry. . . . The smell of sedge-smoke this time of year near about drives me crazy. Then pretty soon all the other farmers start plowing. . . . When the smell of that new earth turning over behind the plow strikes me, I get all weak and shaky."[27]

Although Jeeter believes that his condition is a "man-made calamity," he nonetheless contends that "God sees fit to make me poverty-ridden," because "God is got it in good and heavy for the poor." Even so, God, "a wise old somebody," intended that Jeeter stay on the land where He put him. Were Jeeter to move to Augusta and work in a mill, God might strike him dead or hound him "all the time with little devilish things."[28]

Because farming is in his blood and because he fears divine retribution if he leaves the land, Jeeter stays. And the land is an indescribable hell. With no land of his own, no seed, no tools, no mule, no fertilizer, and no credit, a gumptionless Jeeter can only talk about tilling the soil. Crops cannot grow, but horror flourishes. In effect, Jeeter sells his twelve-year-old daughter to a suitor for quilts, "nearly a gallon" of cylinder oil, and seven dollars, all of which the Lesters desperately need. For years he has failed to get another daughter's harelip repaired. After that daughter has offered herself to her brother-in-law for a sack of turnips, her brother, disgusted by her deformity but not by her nakedness, covers her face but not her body. The Lesters shove Jeeter's mother out of the kitchen at mealtime because there is not enough fatback soup and cornbread to go around. Jeeter beats her for stealing snuff, the use of which eased her pangs of hunger. He and his pellagra-ridden wife, Ada, watch unconcernedly as Mother Lester lies dying after Dude has accidentally backed Bessie's car over her.[29]

Life for the Lesters has been reduced to an animalistic struggle to survive. The death of Mother Lester means simply that there is one less mouth to feed. When Dude leaves the Lester place for good with Bessie, only one child remains to be provided for. Jeeter wheedles Lov to take in the harelipped Ellie May after Lov's child bride runs away to Augusta. If Ellie May fails "to get a man somewhere," Jeeter tells Lov, "there won't be nobody to watch after her" after he and Ada are dead. Jeeter's fear that the "niggers would get her in no time" unwittingly underscores his family's degradation, for the blacks along Tobacco Road had shown no interest in her or any of the other Lesters, having always viewed them with derision. When Ellie May leaves for Lov's house on her father's orders, Jeeter instructs her to bring food back to the Lester place because "Lov makes a dollar a day . . . and he's got rations."[30]

With only himself and Ada left at home, Jeeter again prepares to plant a crop. The fire that he sets to burn off the broom-sedge, fanned by the wind overnight, blazes out of control and consumes him and Ada as they sleep in their shack. The land that Jeeter loved so much has at last ended his suffering.[31]

Caldwell's keen consciousness of social injustice is expressed not only through the authorial voice but also by Jeeter, illiterate and isolated though he is. Having been swindled by chicaning moneylenders who leave him three dollars in debt after a year's labor, Jeeter erupts: "You rich folks in Augusta is just bleeding us poor people to death. You don't work none, but you get all the money us farmers make." Returning from the ill-fated trip to Augusta during which he failed to sell a load of wood, an angry Jeeter discards his cargo and tries to burn it. "If the rich people in Augusta won't buy my wood," he fumes, "I ain't going to let it lay here so they can come and take it off for nothing." To get money for food in Augusta, he succeeds in selling, with Bessie's consent, the spare tire of her automobile. Amazed by the three "pretty and new" dollar bills that he receives as payment, he recalls that the little money he had seen on Tobacco Road "was just about ready to fall apart, it was that worn out. Up here in Augusta the people has got good money." Later, during a furious argument with Bessie, Jeeter orders her "to get off my land." To her retort that the land is not his, he responds: "It's the old Lester place. . . . Them rich people up there in Augusta come down here and take everything a man's got, but they can't take the land away from me." [32]

After Jeeter's death, Lov ponders the one long frustration that was his life. The "raising of a crop . . . was all that he wanted," Lov reflects; but, as Lov further observes, "There ain't no sense in . . . raising crops. . . . [Farmers] can't make no money at it, not even a living. If they do make some cotton, somebody comes along and cheats them out of it. . . . I can't figure out how . . . [rich people] got hold of all the money in the county, anyhow. Looks like it ought to be spread out among everybody." As had Jeeter, Lov suspects that the poverty along Tobacco Road is partly the result of God's neglect. The "Lord don't care about crops being raised . . . or He would be more helpful to the poor. He could make the rich people lend out their money, and stop holding it up." [33] To people who lived by the credo "The Lord will provide," divine neglect was the final abandonment.

Sister Bessie might have been right; Jeeter may have been "a powerful sinful man in his prime." But Jeeter was certainly right when he said of himself: "I ain't no sinner by nature." Nor was anyone else, in Caldwell's view of humanity. [34]

Although *Tobacco Road* sold poorly—only five hundred copies in 1932—it received widespread critical acclaim in the South. Seldom did reviewers mention the novel's comic dimension, focusing instead on the pathetic and the tragic. Occasionally, certain aspects of the story were deemed unconvincing, but most reviewers praised its "authenticity," its "genuine realism," its "savage realism." Fine craftsmanship had enabled Caldwell to produce "smooth, swift-running, limpid prose" and to record realistically the speech of his characters without resorting to dialect. So accomplished was his art, the *Baltimore Evening Sun* contended, it merited ranking with William Faulkner's and Thomas Wolfe's. Moreover, he had succeeded at the difficult task of eliciting the reader's sympathy for characters whose actions were often repulsive. "Absolutely bestial poverty," wrote one reviewer, had erased from the Lesters "the noble characteristics assigned by sentimental tradition to those who live close to the soil." Jeeter, in particular, was thought to have been strikingly drawn; "an authentic man," one reviewer called him, "victim of his own weakness, to be sure, but also victim of an economic system of whose very existence he was unaware." Another commentator extolled the novel's didacticism, calling *Tobacco Road* "an earnest appeal, a forceful sermon, a compelling argument for diversified farming." An adulatory review in the *Augusta Chronicle* defended "the truth of the book" but predicted that the author would be castigated by Georgians "whose loyalty is stronger than their eyes. Mr. Caldwell illustrates his points with extreme cases, and no good citizen will admit anything worse than average." [35]

A few months after the publication of *Tobacco Road,* Milton A. Abernethy, the editor of *Contempo,* a little magazine published in Chapel Hill, North Carolina, asked Caldwell to write a piece on a southern writers' conference—whose participants were "annoyed" by the realism of Caldwell and Faulkner—that had been held in the Carolina mountains. In declining Abernethy's offer, Caldwell demonstrated his tenuous connection to the southern literary renaissance, which by then was in full flower. He told Abernethy that if the conservative writers Allen Tate and Caroline Gordon had not been present in "the crowd" of conferees, who were more interested in the past than in the present, "they should have been." "I wish to God," he wrote in response to Abernethy's further entreaty, that "I were capable of writing the piece on the brotherhood of southern authors, but I know my limitations." He suggested that Abernethy himself write the essay, because "you know more about the situation than perhaps anyone else." Should Abernethy not be able to do the article, Caldwell recommended two other critics, Matthew Josephson and Stringfellow Barr. As editor of the *Virginia Quarterly Review,* Barr was "the better informed"; moreover, he was "a violent enemy of the Nashville school" whose comments might produce "a good dog fight." But Josephson, who had "a mind like God himself," had the advantage of not being a southerner. Such a perspective, along with "some outside help and observation," would enable Josephson to "do wonders with the article." [36]

Six months later, Caldwell offered to review for *Contempo* "a damn good 'Southern' novel" if Abernethy had one to send. "But," he continued, "none of your goddam Hervey Allens, DuBose Heywards, [Ellen] Glasgows, [James Branch] Cabells, etc. I swear I'll ship it back to you freight collect if it's by one of those sires." Although Caldwell disdained the writers of the Charleston-Richmond axis, he had earlier expressed admiration for William Faulkner's novel of poor whites, *As I Lay Dying.* The rest of the Mississippian's work was another matter, however. "I just could not bring myself to read any of the other novels," he told Abernethy; "I just didn't care for the scare-head ballyhoo, for one thing." Nor had

Faulkner's stories impressed him. "I can't see his short stories," he wrote Abernethy, "not with a telescope."[37]

Notwithstanding Caldwell's rejection—wrongheaded as it sometimes was—of much contemporary southern writing, he was optimistic about the region's literary future. "Listen," he wrote Abernethy in September, 1933, "the South . . . is the place where the best writing is going to come from during the next several years. The rest of the country hasn't any life. . . . A writer in the South has everything to gain, nothing to lose; therefore he can cut loose and write like a damn fool."[38]

Less than three years later, responding to queries from a scholar of southern literature, Caldwell reiterated his conviction that the South was laden with life. The "character of the Southern people," he wrote to William Stanley Hoole, "provides the richest fiction-mine in America." Southern writers had mined that material successfully because they had been isolated from the schools of Paris and New York. The literati stressed "form"; the southern writer knew that "content" was more important. As long as the southern writer stayed home in his imagination and produced work that was "loaded with reality, people, and story," he would be "more fortunate" than writers elsewhere.[39]

Because Caldwell's social conscience pushed his imagination to a concern for the South's dispossessed, he sometimes drew the fire of conservative writers in the region. The Arkansan John Gould Fletcher, a contributor to the Agrarian symposium *I'll Take My Stand,* had admired Caldwell's early prose poem "Tracing Life with a Finger." By 1934, however, Fletcher portrayed Caldwell in private correspondence as a proletarian writer and a "practitioner . . . of the flagrantly obscene and horrible" that "the public is now gone a-whoring off after." When Fletcher publicly blamed agitation by white northerners for the plight of nine black boys charged with raping two white women near Scottsboro, Alabama, and opined that under the South's system of white supremacy "the great majority of the [Negro] race are leading happy and contented lives," Caldwell disagreed sharply. In a letter to his agent, Maxim Lieber, that was published in the Communist magazine *New Masses* early in 1934, Caldwell declared that Fletcher represented "an obnoxious majority of the people in power. . . . The state of mind he makes articulate is common." But, Caldwell continued, Fletcher did not "represent a majority of the [South's] population. The Negro, the tenant farmer, and the mill worker have contributed, involuntarily, to the power of those holding the whip-hand; but the hand grows weak, the oppressed gain strength, and the outcome of the coming struggle cannot be in doubt." Neither was Caldwell's position in doubt. "I have taken my stand," he wrote, and "it is on the other side of the fence from Fletcher." [40]

Caldwell's peripheral connection to the southern renaissance was most tellingly illustrated in the perception of another Agrarian, John Donald Wade. In an overview of Caldwell's work through 1935, which he condemned considerably more than he praised, Wade nonetheless concluded that his fellow Georgian was a writer "of considerable power." Moreover, he considered Caldwell to be "a good Southerner still," but one who had sacrificed his art "to please the kind and class of people that he has come to be affiliated with—the detached, nervous, thrill-goaded metrocosmopolitans of his own day." [41]

Wade's erroneous perception was born of ignorance. Although Caldwell's response to Fletcher showed his naïveté about the possibilities of class struggle in the South, he certainly had not written his works to please the kind of audience that Wade described. In fact, the Agrarians—or at least some of them—did not know quite what to make of Caldwell. He did not seem to share their interest in the South's history, traditions, and myths. He wrote—sensationally and sentimentally, they felt—about people who did not fit into their schema of a pastoral South whose values were nobler than those of a grasping North. According to Donald Davidson, the most consciously theoretical member of the Agrarian school, writers like Caldwell who focused on conditions among poor whites demonstrated a mentality that was "not quite healthy." [42]

Back in the summer of 1931, shortly after Scribner's had accepted *Tobacco Road*, Caldwell had applied for a Guggenheim Fellowship to give him the time and the money to write a novel of "proletarian life in the South." Because he believed that the condition of tenant farmers, cotton-mill workers, "and all those living somewhere between those two occupations" had been treated only superficially by creative writers, he felt that it was time for someone "to go beneath the surface of the subject." Caldwell's application to the Guggenheim Foundation is so crucial to understanding his intent as a writer that it bears quoting at length.

I believe I have the necessary understanding of the white tenant farmer and the white textile mill operative to enable me to write the novel which would at least lay open the sore which is spreading to every man, woman, and child. I am a Southerner by birth, by inheritance, and by residence, and my sympathies lie with the millions who do not know what to do. Shall they continue a precarious existence, living from hand to mouth, always in debt, uneducated, and solemnly waiting for "a better day"? Or shall they be given an opportunity to become educated, independent, and self-respecting? The answers to these questions lie in an inclusive novel of proletarian life, purely creative, written perhaps from the point of view of the masses. There is no use in waiting endlessly for "better times." . . . There has already been too much of "romance," of "magnolia blossoms," of "Negro dialect"; it is time someone really wrote about "life" . . . to try to let "the poor whites," "the white trash," and "the lint-heads" present a different picture. I am confident that I have the material, my work in the past should show my ability to undertake the writing, and my seriousness of purpose will, I believe, give to the completed task the sincerity and significance that it requires. Outstanding, as in any creative work, should be the quality of the writing. I am confident that I can bring to it the best that is in my power.

The Guggenheim Foundation rejected his application. Caldwell wrote *God's Little Acre* anyhow.[43]

Scribner's, however, would not be its publisher. Dissatisfied with the company's failure to push *Tobacco Road*, with its editorial alterations of his work, and with its rejection of a novel dealing with rural Maine that he had written at its suggestion, Caldwell found another publisher. Viking Press brought out *God's Little Acre* in February 1933, without having insisted, Caldwell told William Carlos Williams, "on my changing words or anything else." As with Caldwell's previous books, sales were slow—until obscenity charges were brought.[44]

Sex, an important theme in a number of Caldwell's earlier works, is central to *God's Little Acre*. A passionate man who sometimes engaged in casual liaisons, Caldwell nonetheless felt that the conjugal act was the utmost manifestation of love. For one character in the novel, Darling Jill Walden, sex is merely attraction—to the albino, Dave Dawson; to her brother-in-law, Will Thompson; and obliquely to the fat politician, Pluto Swint. Yet for Darling Jill's sister-in-law Griselda, sex is love, as it often was for Caldwell. A woman like Griselda, however, can truly love only the kind of man whose desire for her is so overwhelming that, as her father-in-law, Ty Ty Walden, puts it, he "just ache[s] to get down and lick

something." Only three men in the novel understand passion like
Griselda's: Ty Ty, his black tenant Sam, and his son-in-law Will, a cotton-
mill worker. Significantly, only a "male man" like Will, who possesses
what Caldwell described elsewhere as "an animal-like instinct to love
someone," which Ty Ty and Griselda believe to be God-given, has the
courage to confront the mill company that workers are striking.[45]

Perhaps because the Maine novel written after *Tobacco Road* had redi-
rected his thinking, the "proletarian life" that Caldwell said in his Guggenheim application would be the focus of *God's Little Acre* makes up
only a small, albeit pivotal, part of the story. On strike for eighteen
months because management instituted the stretchout, whereby production quotas were increased and pay was cut, the workers in Scottsville, a
mill town in Carolina's Horse Creek Valley, are desperate. Subsisting on
fatback and flour distributed by the Red Cross, they are so malnourished
that pellagra is epidemic. The union that represents them, which is affiliated with what one millhand calls "that son-of-a-bitch A.F.L.," advocates
returning to work for wages that some strikers feel are too low. "I'll be
damned," Will tells Pluto, "if I work nine hours a day for a dollar-ten,
when those rich sons-of-bitches who own the mill ride up and down the
Valley in five thousand dollar automobiles." Led by Will, the strikers resolve to take over the idle plant and run it themselves.[46]

Just after Will has decided to turn on the power in the mill and just
before he makes love to his sister-in-law Griselda, he says repeatedly: "I'm
as strong as God Almighty Himself is now." Avenging god and Christlike
deliverer though he considers himself to be, Will is not strong enough to
overcome the forces of oppression. His death at the hands of mill guards
is a failed martyrdom. Conditions in the valley's mills will not change; the
men who carried Will to his grave will return to the mills "to card and
spin and weave and dye"—and eventually to die from breathing the lint
that causes them to spit blood.[47]

Will's death, the climax of the story, ushers in more violence. Brother
kills brother when Ty Ty's rich son from Augusta, Jim Leslie, comes to
take Griselda away with him and is shot by her husband, Buck. When Ty
Ty realizes that one son has been killed on the acre that he has tithed to
God, he wills "that God's little acre follow Buck, stopping when he did
so that he would always be upon it." But again, God fails. At the novel's
end, Buck, shotgun in hand, walks into the woods to take his own life.[48]

As in *Tobacco Road*, a major theme in *God's Little Acre* is the disintegration of family. Yet the causes of the destruction are strikingly different. The Lesters are victims of brutalizing poverty; the Waldens are not desperately poor. Ty Ty owns the hundred-acre arm near Augusta that he refuses to work, and he employs two black tenants who cultivate twenty-five acres. Also unlike the Lesters, the Waldens have plenty to eat—although their tenants do not—and an automobile that runs. That Ty Ty spends much of his time digging for gold may not be as foolish as many of the other characters think. Doing that could be as profitable as growing cotton.[49]

Unlike *Tobacco Road, God's Little Acre* is not concerned primarily with portraying economic conditions. Ty Ty's explanation of the Waldens' domestic tragedy places blame on the sexual possessiveness of men. Unlike the women of his household, who "are willing to live like God made them to live," the men "go off and hear fools talk and they come back here and try to run things counter to God." The fools are preachers who encourage the stifling of God-given emotions that cannot be quelled. "When you try to take a woman or a man and hold him off all for yourself," Ty Ty tells his family after Jim Leslie's death, "there ain't going to be nothing but trouble and sorrow the rest of your days."[50]

How much Ty Ty's explanation reflected Caldwell's thinking can only be conjectured. The self-professed skeptic evinced, as he had in *Tobacco Road,* an abiding interest in God and His whimsy. Ty Ty's creator has him say: "There was a mean trick played on us somewhere. God put us in the bodies of animals and tried to make us act like people." The maverick preacher's son displayed, as he had in *Tobacco Road,* contempt for the conventional emissaries of Christianity. Ty Ty defines the cause of the family's disintegration thus: "A man has got God in him from the start, and when he is made to live like a preacher says to live, there's going to be trouble." The husband whose prenuptial association with his wife spanned only three months demonstrated a fondness for other women; by the time he wrote *God's Little Acre,* seven years into his marriage, he had engaged in at least two extramarital affairs. Like Rosamond, Ty Ty's daughter who tolerates her husband Will's infidelity, Helen Caldwell had endured her husband's dalliances. And she had had an affair herself.[51]

Whatever else *God's Little Acre* is about, it is not about digging for gold. Some idea of Caldwell's intention can be gained from the perceptive commentary by William Soskin in the *New York Evening Post,* a review that Caldwell appreciated. Soskin recognized that behind the "comedy and . . . hilarious antics" lay "an essentially ominous note." He saw, too, that Ty Ty was "something more than a clown. He is something like the [D. H.] Lawrence hero who puts the hard, self-seeking commercial world behind him and goes off on dark exploits." As Soskin observed, Ty Ty's digging for gold provided a way "to satisfy his own emotional urge that will not be denied." [52]

The protean nature of *God's Little Acre* befuddled southern reviewers who were sensitive, thoughtful, and sympathetic to Caldwell's works but who did not know quite what to make of his latest effort. Was it social commentary, domestic tragedy, or bawdy comedy? Had Caldwell tried to incorporate disparate themes and, though striving mightily, failed? Labeling him "a Georgia Rabelais," A. B. Bernd in the *Macon Telegraph* expressed the view that the novel's strength lay in its "vast fun and humor." Caldwell's clumsy inclusion of the theme of social injustice, Bernd felt, sounded an ominous note that produced discord in the telling of a tale that should have been exclusively comic. [53]

To Barry Bingham of the *Louisville Courier-Journal, God's Little Acre* was a novel with "big virtues" and "big faults." As long as Caldwell kept his focus on the agrarian Waldens, whose lives reflected "a reality that demands acceptance," he crafted a story that possessed "solid bone-deep merit." But when he introduced Will Thompson, a "product of the strange, new industrial South," he destroyed "the pattern of his book." At that point, the "admirable naturalness " of his description "of people close to nature" gave way to a "peculiar poetic frenzy that is one of the distinguishing marks of the very modern American novel." That frenzy had caused Caldwell "to do violence to his characters" in an attempt to present "a curious thesis on the meaning of passion." [54]

More perceptive than the reviews by Bingham and Bernd was the commentary by Jonathan Daniels in the *Raleigh News and Observer.* Like Bernd, Daniels praised the humor of the story, which, he believed, grew out of Caldwell's deft handling of character—such as that of Pluto Swint—and situation—such as Ty Ty's feverish efforts to avoid giving the fruits of his labor to the church. Like Bingham, Daniels admired Caldwell's portrayal of the Waldens, who, unlike the Lesters of *Tobacco Road,* were "moved by some vigor of desire." Unlike either Bernd or Bingham, Daniels came closer to recognizing the unity of the story and thus to identifying its strength. "It would be a mistake," Daniels wrote, "to consider Mr. Caldwell a grim realist. Behind his grim, sometimes shocking, details he is a poet, . . . whose sensitiveness to life is made strong and whole by a vigorous sense of humor." [55]

The novel's poetry, Daniels believed, derived from Caldwell's ability to render in lyrical language the plight of the South's plain folk. Nowhere was that ability more evident than in the description of mill workers in Carolina's strife-torn Horse Creek Valley, which Daniels quoted at length.

> The men who worked in the mill looked tired and worn, but the girls were in love with the looms and the spindles and the flying lint. The wild-eyed girls on the inside of the ivy-walled mill looked like potted plants in bloom.
>
> Up and down the Valley lay the company towns and the ivy-walled cotton mills and the firm-bodied girls with eyes like morning-glories and the men stood on the hot streets looking at each other while they spat their lungs into the deep yellow dust of Carolina. . . . In the mill streets of the Valley towns the breasts of girls were firm and erect. The cloth they wove under the blue lights clothed their bodies, but beneath the covering the motions of erect breasts were like quick movements of hands in unrest. In the Valley towns beauty was begging, and the hunger of strong men was like the whimpering of beaten women.

In Daniels's estimation, there were few descriptions of industrial conflict in American literature that were "so simply, so directly, and so accurately done." [56]

Daniels's only misreading resulted in his denying what Bingham believed was frenzied and what Bernd contended was clumsy. Daniels had rightly praised Caldwell's art in both its humorous and poetic dimensions. He had rightly called *God's Little Acre* a "strong story of forgotten lives." Then he ignored Caldwell's argument in the very segment of the novel that he believed had been so skillfully executed. "Never once," he wrote near the end of the review, "is Mr. Caldwell pointing a finger at injustice." [57]

Caldwell had done his job too well. Discerning readers sympathetic to his work—Daniels, Bingham, and Bernd—could not envision the totality of the most complex novel that he would ever write. The complexity begins at the beginning—with the title. An acre is an acre, so why is God's acre "little"? Is the interjection of the adjective evidence only of Caldwell's ability to write rhythmically? Or, is Ty Ty returning to God what God has given to him? The complexity continues with the matter of sex, which suffuses the story. Is the emphasis on sex gratuitous, reflecting merely Caldwell's interest in the subject and an intent to shock his read-

ers? Or does his treatment of the matter demonstrate his skill with characterization? Significantly, sex is most compellingly presented in scenes that
involve Will. Might not Caldwell have been aware of the possibility that
a man broken by society will show his prowess in whatever way he can?
Although Bernd, Bingham, and Daniels had read *God's Little Acre* sensi-
tively, none was able fully to understand that it is at once a bawdy novel
of domestic tragedy that attacks social injustice in language that is sometimes poetic. Each of those reviewers, however, asserted that the novel
was not obscene.[58]

Many other journalists throughout the South seem not to have been so
sure. It is safe to conjecture that editors' fears that *God's Little Acre* might
be considered prurient caused it to receive much less attention than had
Tobacco Road. From Richmond to New Orleans, many newspapers ignored the novel, including significant ones in Georgia such as the *Augusta
Chronicle,* which had praised *Tobacco Road,* and the Atlanta papers. Ap-
parently, not even Caldwell's tireless champion, Frank Daniel, could persuade his editor to run a review in the *Journal.*[59]

If editors' misgivings diminished the number of reviews in southern
newspapers, the action of New York's Society for the Suppression of Vice
enhanced the book's sales nationwide. Helped by the publicity of an obscenity trial, which was decided in the novel's favor, *God's Little Acre* had
sold 5,700 copies by mid-June 1933, four months after its publication.
That figure exceeded the combined sales of Caldwell's four previous
books. Even so, his family, with another child on the way, was still so
badly in need of money that, in May, Caldwell had made the difficult
decision to accept an offer to write for Metro-Goldwyn-Mayer Studios.
He asked Helen to join him in California, but her condition caused her
to remain in Maine. When he learned that his parents had not arrived in
Mt. Vernon in time to attend Helen in the birth of their daughter Janet,
he was "griped as hell."[60]

In Hollywood from May until August, Caldwell labored at work he
loathed, occasionally seeing Clark Gable walking around, "trying to
show off," and finding rare satisfaction in the company of fellow southerners Lynn Riggs and Paul Green. But the pay was good—two hundred
fifty dollars a week. By the time his three-month contract expired, he had
paid off all his debts, some of them long outstanding, and was three hundred dollars in the black. "We can live on that," he wrote a friend, "till
kingdom comes if necessary."[61]

Although writing movie scenarios paid richly and writing serious fiction paid poorly, Caldwell knew where his artistic strength lay. During his free time in Hollywood, he was busily engaged in making selections for a forthcoming collection of short stories. There was disagreement between author and editor, however, over the contents of the proposed volume. Caldwell wanted twenty stories to be included; his editor, Marshall Best, a kind and generous man whom Caldwell liked, wanted only sixteen. Caldwell's selections differed slightly from Best's. Late in September 1933, Viking Press published, in a limited edition, *We Are the Living*. The collection contained twenty stories, all but one of which Caldwell rightly thought should be included.[62]

Of the stories in the volume, most of which had first appeared in little magazines after the publication of *American Earth*, fewer than half depend upon a southern setting for their distinctiveness. In most of those seven, humor figures prominently and usually lends emphasis to a serious theme. "Meddlesome Jack," a folk yarn about the aphrodisiac effect of a jackass on women, shows that appearances can be deceiving and that a husband who ignores his wife might lose her. "The Medicine Man" features a con artist who gets a dose of his own medicine from a seemingly innocent and naive small-town maid who turns his attempt to seduce her into a shotgun wedding. "The People's Choice" satirizes a one-party politics that values personalities above issues and a religious system that prizes larger church membership and full collection plates above all else. "Picking Cotton," a ribald account of adolescent sexuality, portrays white boys' fears of the carnal superiority of black boys. Two somber stories, "The Picture" and "Yellow Girl," depict the insecurity white women feel about the allurements of mulatto women.[63]

By far the most striking southern story in the collection is "August Afternoon." A year before *We Are the Living* was published, Caldwell had offered the story, which he claimed was "not a shocking piece at all," to *Contempo*, telling its editor that his agent "didn't have hope of selling it." Within a few months, however, a new magazine—"some god damn contraption called Esquire," as Caldwell called it—bought the story and published it in its first issue, which also featured work by John Dos Passos and Ernest Hemingway.[64]

Perfect in its raunchiness, "August Afternoon" features Vic Glover, a lazy white farmer; his fifteen-year-old wife, Willie; his black field hand, Hubert; and Floyd, a drifter from Carolina who shows up at Glover's

Georgia farm. Enervating heat sets the context of the story. Avoiding the noontime sun, Vic is asleep on the porch of his house when Hubert wakes him to say that there is a stranger sitting under a water-oak watching Willie—a girl with city ways, according to Hubert—who is wearing only a "skimpy outside dress." Sitting atop the porch steps, she is "showing her pretty," and soon the switchblade-flaunting Floyd has "got his pecker up." After Hubert prudently refuses Vic's order to disarm Floyd, the drifter takes Willie off into the woods. Before going back to sleep, Vic tells Hubert to awaken him when the lovers return. Hubert lets him sleep.[65]

"August Afternoon" is a masterfully told story in which pace, tone, and dialogue perfectly fit the situation and in which the action is funny yet potentially deadly. It is the black character who has prevented a killing, and, throughout the story, it is he alone who shows any sense of decency. Although the story is comic, Hubert is not a comical darky. He will not step and fetch for the white boss; he will not allow Vic to make unreasonable demands. Like other of Caldwell's blacks, he possesses a strength of character that many whites lack. To Caldwell, sex was serious—and so was race.

The inclusion of "August Afternoon" was doubtlessly the reason that *We Are the Living* was published in a limited edition. Perhaps because of such publication, the collection went unnoticed in the southern press.[66]

Like Caldwell's previous books, except for *God's Little Acre*, *We Are the Living* sold poorly. Even so, Caldwell would soon become a man of means. Early in December 1933, the play *Tobacco Road* opened in New York, where it would set a record by running for seven and a half years. With road productions and periodic revivals, one with a black cast, the play would remain a phenomenon and a curiosity until the 1950s. Caldwell's role in the production was to watch rehearsals of the dramatization written by an Arkansan, Jack Kirkland. "The show is fine," Caldwell wrote his Portland friend, Alfred Morang. "Kirkland has made a tight drama, and the only slip [possible] will be . . . in direction and acting. It surprised me a lot. I was looking for a mess."[67]

Kirkland did make a tight drama—and a mess of the novel. Given the strictures of stage performance, Kirkland perhaps could not have dramatized such episodes as Sister Bessie's purchase of the automobile and the trip that she, Dude, and Jeeter made to Augusta. Even so, the play transmogrified the novel: the black characters, although minor, do not appear at all; Mother Lester simply wanders away, and Jeeter's wife, Ada, is the one run over and killed by Bessie's car; the Lesters' daughter Pearl, never seen in the novel, figures prominently; new characters are introduced; Bessie's nose is not deformed; the dialogue is more profane; Jeeter merely falls asleep as the curtain rings down. Considering Caldwell's intent in the novel, the most serious alteration resulted in the virtual elimination of social commentary. Yet, paradoxically, Kirkland's dramatization is not as humorous as Caldwell's novel. To theatergoers from New York to Los Angeles, however, the play was little other than a comedy. Unfamiliar with the novel, they could hardly have thought otherwise, because generally the actors played for laughs—197 of them, according to a "careful check." The author of the novel was perplexed by the excessive laughter.[68]

Although the novel upon publication had elicited little outrage against Caldwell in the South, reaction to the play rained torrents of vilification on him. Few were the voices raised in his defense, such as that of an Augusta woman who confessed her impatience with a false pride "that takes offense at any allusion to the existence of possible imperfections within a certain area." If the novel *Tobacco Road* "be propaganda in the interest of humanity," wrote Marguerite Stefan, "it has nevertheless enough literary merit to stand on its own feet as a piece of naturalistic fiction distinguished by some very good characterization, description, and even a certain kind of pathos." Many commentators discussed novel and play interchangeably, and some attributed authorship of the play to Caldwell.[69]

Laughing at the antics of Tobacco Road's denizens, Yankees ignorant of the South considered the Lesters typical of the region—such was a common complaint from southerners. Georgians led the chorus of denunciation. "Erskine Caldwell's pot boiler and Georgia disgracer, . . . perhaps the filthiest story that was ever written about human beings . . . was typical of nothing—except depraved imaginings," the *Macon Telegraph* editorialized. The *Atlanta Georgian* defended the condemnation of the novel by the state's clubwomen "because they have the best interest of their state at heart." *Tobacco Road,* the writer continued, had caused "the most dreadful abuse of Georgia, whose good name is more important than any literary gem!" On the floor of the United States House of Representatives, a Georgia congressman denounced the novel as an "untruthful, undignified, undiplomatic and unfair sketch of Southern life." After Chicago banned the play, Georgia's governor, Eugene Talmadge, commended the mayor for preventing "misrepresentation" of the South. A Tennessean who had seen the play in New York agreed with the Georgians. In a letter

to the *New York Times* that was reprinted approvingly in southern newspapers, he expressed resentment of northerners' beliefs that the drama
was "an accurate picture . . . of the conditions in the South." He proceeded to describe the horrible sights that he had witnessed on the streets
of New York and added that such conditions were "no more a true picture of New York as a whole" than *Tobacco Road* was of the South.[70]

When, more than four years after the play's debut on Broadway, a road
company brought the production south for the first time, the furor
reached an unprecedented level. Not only was the play a calumny on the
South, many southerners contended, it would also corrupt public morals,
particularly those of the young and impressionable. Few had the temerity
publicly to defend the play as had W. J. Cash earlier. "I defy anybody
with a grain of grit," Cash had written in the *Charlotte News*, "to read
Caldwell's book or see his play [*sic*], and still believe that it might conceiv-
ably move any youth not a raving lunatic to imitation—or that it would
do anything but goad him to headlong flight away from anything which
reminds him of it. The thing, indeed, is a terrific sermon—and in other
senses than the social one Caldwell intends." Heedless of such remon-
strances, some southern cities refused to book the play, and in many
places where it was performed—even in New Orleans—it was heavily
censored.[71]

Georgians were especially uneasy. When word arrived that the play
was scheduled to be performed in Augusta, the police chief in Wrens
asked the sheriff of Richmond County to ban it because "the Caldwells
have created a great deal of excitement with their books and writings in
reference to Richmond and Jefferson counties." Despite the objections of
lawmen, clubwomen, churchmen—from Baptist to Catholic—newspaper
editors, and other defenders of decency, *Tobacco Road* came to Georgia
and played to overflow crowds in Savannah, Augusta, and Atlanta. Everywhere, the audiences laughed—loud, long, and often. In Augusta, tenant
farmers from Tobacco Road, brought by Caldwell's father, shared the
mirth. Ira also took the play's cast to Tobacco Road; subsequently,
the actors sent a portion of their salaries to him to help provide for the
needy.[72]

Here and there over the South, some viewers protested that the play
distorted the novel. A Georgian lamented that "the love-of-the-land
theme is subordinated and the comedy emphasized." A Tennessean deplored "the excess of filth and the total lack of any redeeming purpose"

as well as the failure to probe "the deeper human implications of the tenant farmer problem." An Alabaman pointed out that though the novel's "primary aim" was "to portray the miserable plight of the tenant farmer in all its hopelessness," the play had made "lewdness the most striking quality of the work."[73]

Occasionally, critics who held the novel in high regard felt compelled to defend the play as well, or at least its right to be performed. In doing so, they demonstrated that the novel *Tobacco Road* had made the kind of impact, at least on some southerners, that its author had intended. Believing that the play was an extension of the novel, Caldwell's friends Earl L. Bell of the *Augusta Herald* and Frank Daniel of the *Atlanta Journal,* who admired him as a person and who esteemed his work, wrote moving defenses of both the novel and the play. To Bell, it was salutary that Augustans, who had been "busy building polo fields and checking golf scores," should witness "the tragedy of the lowliest white agricultural element struggling against crushing odds because of their love of the land." Granting that *Tobacco Road* was "untypical," Bell nonetheless insisted upon its veracity. "As for this reviewer," he concluded, "who has seen Richmond County sharecropper children so famished that they snatched raw beef liver off the kitchen table before it could be cooked and ran off with it like so many little wolves—well, it is not for him to hurl the ugly word at Jeeter Lester's Boswell."[74]

To Daniel, who believed that Caldwell was the greatest writer in Georgia's history, *Tobacco Road* was "a work of great power and great beauty." The stage version had impressed "on the minds of millions of people" the shocking conditions of the South's rural poor and for that reason alone had served "an admirable purpose." For the first time, Daniel said, a writer had spoken for people—the Lesters of the South—"who cannot speak for themselves." In an impassioned rebuke of his fellow southerners who contended that *Tobacco Road* was not typical of conditions in the South, Daniel responded that those making the charge never seemed "to make any effort to determine just how frequent such conditions are." Furthermore, he asked, "how general must starvation and degradation become before it may permissibly be deplored? If there is even one instance in the world of a condition like that presented in 'Tobacco Road,' isn't that single case too general? . . . How can anyone who has lived through the past decade deny that need is everywhere, with its consequences to body and mind and soul?" The erudite Daniel also asked his readers to decide whether the situation in *Tobacco Road* was more rare than circumstances portrayed in works by Sophocles, Shakespeare, Goethe, and Chekhov.[75]

The South Carolinian J. H. Marion Jr. also ringingly defended *Tobacco Road*, as novel and as play. In an article published in the *Christian Century* early in 1938, Marion averred that Caldwell had "impressively brought to light" the "scabrous horrors" that lay "beneath the surface of cropper life." To the critics who cried that "Caldwell's pictures of poor-white life are caricatures, his characters grotesque," Marion responded: "One could only wish they were!" Caldwell's grimly realistic portrayal of rural poverty, he concluded, had the effect of "not letting southerners live in a world that is only a painted lie."[76]

Caldwell did not want merely to confirm the converted such as Bell, Daniel, and Marion. By his account, he hoped to awaken people of good-will, especially southerners, to the reality of such destitution as *Tobacco Road* portrayed. To the incessant charge that such conditions were not typical of the South, he responded, "perhaps the great error of my life was in not appending a preface to 'Tobacco Road' stating that the story did not pretend to typify the entire South, but that it was my purpose merely to sketch a representative family among five million persons who are actual residents on Tobacco Road, who are likely future residents there. As it is, we have the spectacle of a man entering a room full of people, crying 'Thief,' and seeing nearly every person present in the act of running away." If the story *Tobacco Road* told was exceptional, it was nonetheless legitimate, Caldwell insisted. The actions of the characters, he told a newspaper interviewer, "are not mere imagining on my part. They grow out of the environment." Nor did he consider the story obscene, because the characters "do not live consciously in a lurid or dirty way."[77]

Caldwell contended that *Tobacco Road* could have been set in any part of the cotton belt from the Carolinas to Arkansas, where "economic slavery, subtropical climate, and depleted soil . . . [had converged] upon a group of people over a long term of years." Throughout that time, little had been attempted to alleviate a worsening situation. Politicians, whose "static ignorance . . . is a thing to marvel at," bore much of the blame. So did the church. With the exception of a few socially conscious ministers, preachers for the past fifty years had been unduly concerned "to save the heathen" elsewhere in the world, although their "own people were being subjected to the economic blood-sucking of the landlord-elders and the politician-deacons." The result of this unholy alliance of church and state was that "the South has not only produced a coolie serfdom but, more than that, has turned around and deliberately kicked it in the face." Precisely because he loved the South, Caldwell wrote, "I insist upon such a story as 'Tobacco Road' as a means of exposing the shame of its civilization." The play, wherein, according to Caldwell, "sex and profanity are incidentals," was bringing much-needed attention to the South's decay, whose "stench is a complacent nation's shame." He hoped that "with the help of science, economics, sociology, and common humanity" the expansion of Tobacco Road could soon be halted and that "eventually it could be wiped completely off the map."[78]

When *Tobacco Road* concluded its record-setting run on Broadway in the spring of 1941, the *Montgomery Advertiser,* in an editorial reprinted in other southern newspapers, assessed the reasons for the "phenomenal appeal of Erskine Caldwell's play [*sic*]." Not its sociological aspects or its libel of the South but its "unique humor" was the source of the play's popularity. "Its lusty, often lewd, lines evoked gales of laughter North, South, East and West." Yet the *Advertiser* admitted that *Tobacco Road* had dramatized "some very real problems which we Southerners have been slow to face." Nearly three years before, the same newspaper had credited the play with a social achievement that was more concrete—inspiring the Rosenwald Foundation to fund a study of sharecropper conditions that had produced "considerable good." Other southern newspapers agreed that the play, and the novel, had been socially constructive.[79]

Back in December 1938, the fifth anniversary of the play's debut, Caldwell had shown that he was not as confident of the salutary effects of the production as were its southern supporters. The optimism that he had expressed two and a half years before had given way to doubts about whether "the condition of tenant farmers in the South has improved during the last five years." Such stagnation should hardly be considered the fault of a dramatic production, he argued to critics who asked what good the play had accomplished. What the Tobacco Roads needed, he maintained, was a broad federal program to reeducate the rural poor in the skills needed to conduct scientific, mechanized farming. If the government failed to deal adequately with the conditions that produced the Jeeter Lesters of the South, then such people might become the "manpower of Fascism."[80]

Caldwell's father agreed that more aggressive federal action was imperative. Amid reports that *Tobacco Road* was to close on Broadway, Ira Caldwell, pushing seventy and suffering from failing eyesight, went to Washington in August 1940 to try to persuade Georgia Congressman Carl Vinson and Secretary of Agriculture Henry A. Wallace to work toward establishing "a rural rehabilitation community" on Tobacco Road. The elder Caldwell envisioned a farm modeled on the Pine Mountain Community, a New Deal settlement across the state near President Franklin D. Roosevelt's retreat at Warm Springs, whose residents lived in "neat, white clapboard houses" and were taught how to farm scientifically. He hoped that the government would be convinced that Tobacco Road was "an ideal proving ground for the theory that those who live on the land will profit from the land if they are given the right opportunities."[81]

The following year, Tobacco Road was absorbed into a sprawling army compound.[82] What the Caldwells could not remedy and what the New Deal would not rectify had been obscured by the Second World War.

In the same year that the stage version of *Tobacco Road* closed in New York, the film version was released in Hollywood. Based on the play rather than the novel, the movie mangled Caldwell's intent even more thoroughly than had the play. The playwright Kirkland—who, like Caldwell, was not consulted by the filmmakers—had at least left intact the spirit of the novel's unhappy ending, adulterated though it was. Among other travesties, the screenwriter Nunnally Johnson, a Georgian who knew better but who followed the directives of the producer, imposed a happy ending wherein landlord saves tenant from destitution. As William L. Howard has observed, Hollywood transformed the travail of tenant farming "into an American Dream story." The millions of Americans who saw the movie did not know that Caldwell abhorred it, especially its "absurdly falsified happy ending."[83]

While the play *Tobacco Road* was still in rehearsal and before his share of royalties from the production made him a man of means, Caldwell had again considered changing publishers. Viking Press showed little enthusiasm for a novel that he had completed by the fall of 1933. Tempted by a two-thousand-dollar advance offered by another publisher, he was forced to remain with Viking when the other publisher, Harcourt Brace, withdrew the offer after reading the manuscript. A year later, Viking agreed to issue the novel, but only conditionally. Fearing that the work would not enhance Caldwell's reputation and that it might be charged with ob-

scenity, Viking offered to publish the manuscript in a trade edition only
if he softened it. Should he refuse, the publisher would issue only a limited
edition. Having worked extraordinarily hard on the story—"This damn
novel takes the blood out of me," he confessed to a magazine editor while
writing it—he stood firm. "I told . . . [Viking] to go to hell before I'd
change it," he wrote to his friend Morang. Early in 1935, Viking brought
out *Journeyman*—in a limited edition.[84]

Caldwell's integrity as an artist impelled him to resist censorship. Yet
his taste as an artist caused him to doubt the quality of *Journeyman*. Writing to his wife, Helen, from Hollywood in the summer of 1933, he asked
her to read the manuscript again to see if she "could find something
wrong with it." He confided to her, "I can't decide whether it's any good
or not." Helen liked it; Morang liked it; Caldwell's agent, Maxim Lieber,
liked it. But his own doubts, like those of his publisher, were legitimate.[85]

Journeyman recounts the horrors committed upon the villagers of
Rocky Comfort, Georgia, by Semon Dye, an aptly named demonic picaro
who incorrectly describes himself as a journeyman preacher. He is instead
a master at his craft of duping the gullible. In the name of God, he does
the work of the devil. Over a period of only five days, the elapsed time of
the story, Dye attempts to bed an unwilling black woman; shoots her
protesting husband; pimps for one of the wives of his host and later
pistol-whips her; seduces his host's other wife, a fifteen-year-old girl;
cheats his host out of nearly everything he owns in a crooked crap game;
drinks corn liquor by the gallon; and climaxes his stay by mesmerizing
Sunday worshipers into a leaping, wallowing, clothes-rending frenzy that
is transparently orgasmic.[86]

The grotesqueness is unrelieved and unconvincing; even the humor is
mean-spirited. Unlike Caldwell's earlier novels, *Journeyman* fails to portray the economic environment. Unless Semon Dye and the other major
characters are motivated by innate depravity, an idea that, like his father,
Caldwell rejected, their actions are insufficiently accounted for. Caldwell
was undoubtedly sincere when he said that he wrote *Journeyman* to "hold
Semon Dye and all he represents up to such ridicule that this form of
religion would lose its dope-like grip on the South." Yet the eruption of
the rage over the irresponsibility of otherworldly religion that had long
festered in the minister's son produced something new in the Caldwell
canon—a dirty book.[87]

Some southern reviewers thought that *Journeyman* was "an amusing

book," "delightful reading," "sheer humor." Others recognized the grim
nature of Caldwell's subject and his "exasperation" with his characters.
When the short-lived play adapted from the novel met stinging reviews
from New York critics, Caldwell's steady champion came to his defense.
In addition to providing entertainment, "the theatre has a teaching role,"
Ira Caldwell wrote to the *New York Post*. Therefore, "the theatre ought
to portray to what depths the church has fallen in many quarters. Stream-
lined, well-to-do churches have, to a large extent, ignored poverty-
stricken people. Religious charlatans are exploiting millions of people
who are shut out of the average church." [88] *Journeyman* failed, however,
to educe compassion for those millions.

The year 1935, in which the disappointing *Journeyman* appeared, also
brought the publication of the best of Caldwell's many books. Ever since
he had begun writing, Caldwell had attacked racial injustice and had
fashioned black characters who elicited the reader's sympathy as men and
women. Only rarely had he dealt in caricatures and stereotypes; seldom
had he succumbed to "darky humor." The skill and the sensitivity with
which he explored race reached their apogee in *Kneel to the Rising Sun*.
A collection of seventeen tales previously published in periodicals, the
volume contains a few humorous pieces, but most of the stories are the
work of an angry man. Occasionally, the anger escapes Caldwell's control, as in "Blue Boy" with its brutish white landlord who forces a black
idiot to masturbate for the amusement of holiday guests. More often,
Caldwell controlled his rage, and the result was such masterful stories as
"Candy-Man Beechum" and "Kneel to the Rising Sun." [89]

In language that is so rhythmic it approaches poetry, "Candy-Man
Beechum," in just 1,500 words, issues a powerful indictment of racism.
A week's work done, the giant Beechum, a sawmill hand in the swamps
along Georgia's Ogeechee River, is going to see his woman on a Saturday
evening. Along the way, he intends to stop and eat catfish in "the white-
folks' town. " His friend Little Bo warns him to be careful passing
through town because "white-folks is first-come." "Me and white-folks
don't mix," Candy-Man replies, "just as long as they leave me be. I skin
their mules for them, and I snake their cypress logs, but when the day is
done, I'm long gone where the white-folks ain't are." But a white policeman, "tired of chasing fighting niggers all over town every Saturday
night," attempts to jail him on presumption of guilt. When Candy-Man
objects—"I never hurt a body in all my life, white-boss"—the lawman

shoots him. Unvanquished, Beechum struggles to rise; "White-boss, I sure am sorry you had to go and shoot me down. I never bothered white-folks, and they sure oughtn't bother me. But there ain't much use in living if that's the way it's going to be." Big, strong, and mysterious, Candy-Man is, according to the erroneous perceptions of whites, the quintessential "bad nigger," violent, conscienceless, and contemptuous of society's rules. Because the white establishment is wrong, it cannot down him; it can kill his body, but his spirit is unconquerable.[90]

Caldwell was justly proud of "Candy-Man Beechum"; it is a tour de force. So is "Kneel to the Rising Sun," a story that *Harper's Magazine* rejected because an editor who knew "all about *crop-sharers*" thought that it was "too cruel and sadistic." Considerably longer than virtually all of the other stories Caldwell had written, "Kneel to the Rising Sun" is a portrait, rather than a snapshot, of racial—and economic—injustice. Lonnie Newsome, a white man, and Clem Henry, a black man, share the misfortune not only of being trapped in farm tenancy but also of being sharecroppers for a satanic landlord. Arch Gunnard enjoys inflicting pain. His hogs are fat, his tenants gaunt from short rations. His hobby is collecting dogs' tails, which he delights in amputating while showing off to the crowd at the crossroads store. As he cuts off the tail of Lonnie's dog, Lonnie says nothing, but Clem is silently restrained by the other black men present. After Lonnie's father, Mark, deaf and starving, wanders off in the night looking for food and stumbles into Arch's hogpen, where the swine kill and mutilate him, Lonnie hesitates to awaken Arch. Clem insists that Arch be roused. "A man who short-rations tenants," he tells Lonnie, "ought to have to sit and look at that till it's buried." Aware that Clem, not Lonnie, is his antagonist, Arch is enraged. Because Clem stands his ground as they fight, Arch telephones his neighbors. The mob that gathers at Arch's place can find the fugitive Clem only if Lonnie tells where he is. Reminded by the mob that he is a white man, a distraught Lonnie, who "could not figure out how a Negro could be braver than he was," discloses Clem's whereabouts. Clem is lynched, shot from a tree by the mob.[91]

> Lonnie did not remember how long the shooting lasted. He found himself running from tree to tree, clutching at the rough pine bark, stumbling wildly towards the cleared ground. The sky had turned from gray to red when he emerged in the open, and as he ran, falling over the hard clods in the plowed field, he tried to keep his eyes on the house ahead.

> Once he fell and found it almost impossible to rise again to his feet.
> He struggled to his knees, facing the round red sun. The warmth gave him
> the strength to rise to his feet, and he muttered unintelligibly to himself.
> He tried to say things he had never thought to say before.[92]

Caldwell's characterization of Clem belies his assertion elsewhere that planters preferred black tenants because they were more tractable than white ones. Black Clem knows that to resist Arch is to court death, yet his moral sense will not let him accept the horror of Mark Newsome's fate. White Lonnie, for whom the consequences of resistance would not be swift death, has lost nearly all vestiges of self-respect, but at least he is not "a nigger-lover." Because race consciousness conquers class interests, victim betrays victim. The tyranny of race helps to sustain a socioeconomic system that permits the brutal exercise of absolute power.[93]

Caldwell's sensitivity to the plight of forgotten people such as Clem Henry and Lonnie Newsome called forth some of his most bitter writing. "Daughter," first published in the proletarian magazine *Anvil*, describes the agony of a sharecropper who kills his daughter to keep her from starving. Cheated out of his entire share by his landlord, the cropper refuses to "go around begging after I'd made enough to keep us." His neighbors free him from jail, believing he has suffered enough. "Masses of Men" depicts the desperation of a homely widow so deranged by the hunger of her children that she sells the services of her ten-year-old daughter to buy food. The company for which her husband had worked for twenty-five years and in whose service he was accidentally killed had refused to provide a pension. "Slow Death," first published in the Communist magazine *New Masses*, tells the story of two friends, out of work and out of luck, who live in a Hooverville along the Savannah River. After the older man, Dave, a widower who has lost his family to hard times, earns fifty cents from a pick-up job, he and the younger Mike walk to Augusta barefoot in near-freezing weather to buy food. Despite Mike's insistence that Dave spend the money on himself, Dave intends to split it. After a reckless driver hits him and then refuses to take him to the hospital because "the dirty bum's faking," Dave dies in the street. The policeman who rushes up to disperse the crowd clubs Mike unconscious because he refuses to leave Dave's body. Subsequently, Mike is helped to safety by another "bum." The down-and-out receive succor only from one another.[94]

Notwithstanding the catastrophe of the Great Depression, America's shame, Caldwell believed, was not that the country *could* not help the

destitute but that it *would* not. He understood the rage born of desperation expressed in Dave's remark to Mike: "As soon as the people know
what to do, and how to do it, we can . . . run hell out of those fat bastards
who won't give us our jobs back."[95]

In "The Growing Season," Jesse English does not know what to do. If
people in the cities are looking for jobs that do not exist, he has more
work than he alone can handle. With a sick wife and without a single
black hand on his farm, Jesse is waging a losing battle with the wire grass
that is destroying his twelve acres of cotton. "Jesse could see the wire
grass choking the life out of his crop of cotton. He ran to the far end of
the yard and out into the field and began kicking the cotton plants and
grass. . . . Even then the wire grass sprang back like coils in a bed-
spring. The cotton plants he had kicked from their roots began slowly
to wilt in the noonday heat." Frustration, overwhelming heat, and the
rattling chain of Fiddler, a creature leashed to a tree in the yard, push
him to madness.[96]

Returning from the field, Jesse, as his wife screams in protest, drives
Fiddler to a gully, where he kills him with a shotgun and an ax. Returning
to the house, trying "to stop the burning of his eyeballs by digging at
them with his knuckles," Jesse files his hoe knife-sharp and, "bareheaded
in the hot sun," heads back to the field, feeling that "he might be able to
save his crop." From the palpable irony of its title to the poignant pathos
of its conclusion, "The Growing Season," as Randall Jarrell said, is an
"extraordinarily ingenious" story. Art serves argument as Caldwell challenges the agrarian idyll that was so lovingly embraced by some southern
intellectuals. Unlike Jesse English, most agrarian intellectuals were spared
the reality of working in the field, of fighting weeds under a blazing sun,
and of trying to make a living by the sweat of their brows.[97]

Of the remaining stories in *Kneel to the Rising Sun,* many are humorous in tone but serious in theme. In "Maud Island," Caldwell returned to
a favorite subject, the false religiosity that allows a self-appointed
preacher to use his calling as a ruse for carousing. Miscegenation provides
the leitmotif for "Honeymoon," wherein a poolroom loafer, accustomed
to copulating with black women, cannot conceal his amazement the
morning after his wedding night when he realizes that he has been "sleeping in bed with a white girl." "A Day's Wooing" strips away the veneer of
southern hospitality to reveal the viciousness of a family bent on driving
away their daughter's suitor. Although Toy Shaw, the marshal in "The
Shooting," does his duty, albeit with understandable reluctance, the

townsfolk deride him anyway because the person he disarms, at great risk to himself and without anyone's getting hurt, is a woman. After the woman surrenders her .45-caliber revolver, the marshal expects the plaudits of the citizens, not one of whom had ventured to help him. Instead, he hears one man say: "You'd better hurry home and rest up awhile now, Toy. . . . I know you must be all wore out after taking a gun away from that thin little girl." Relishing that remark, the other cowards "broke out in laughter." [98]

Kneel to the Rising Sun contains Caldwell's best writing. Many of the stories in the collection feature the kind of characters that he had seldom fashioned earlier. With greater frequency than before, he created characters who resist being victims. Candy-Man Beechum, Clem Henry, Dave and Mike, the sharecropper who kills his daughter, and Jesse English fight the forces that oppress them. That they lose illustrates Caldwell's recognition of the ruthlessness of environment. But at least they fight. In many of the stories, the art is so accomplished as to appear artless. Continuing to use the unadorned style that at once could be poetic and could reflect the lives of the plain people that he wrote about, Caldwell portrayed the uncommon experiences of common people. Some of the stories possess overwhelming power. No matter how hard one might try, one cannot forget the title story, "Candy-Man Beechum," or "The Growing Season."

While reviewers in New York and Chicago were condemning *Kneel to the Rising Sun*—the *Chicago News* said that Caldwell had "hit . . . an all-time low"—southerners were generally lavish in their praise, although a Tennessean called the title story "a vile caricature." From Richmond to Jacksonville and across the Appalachians, reviewer after reviewer extolled the collection, particularly the title story. The Louisiana writer Hamilton Basso considered it "one of the finest short stories any American has written." As he unwittingly commented on the ordinariness of lynching, Basso perceptively observed that "Kneel to the Rising Sun" "is bitter and merciless in its indictments, but it also has that quality of tenderness that so few critics who have tried to assay Caldwell have remarked upon; and a strength, a rightness, derived from its idealness which, if taken away, would make it no more memorable than the report of a lynching in a newspaper." Other reviewers praised the craftmanship not only of the title story but also of the collection as a whole, commending the strong, spare style, the appropriateness of the language, "the classic, Greek purity of his narrative organization." The *Nashville Tennessean* contended that, unlike

William Faulkner, Caldwell possessed "the commendable attribute of being willing to let his audience in on what he is talking about." [99]

Although one reviewer, whose comments betrayed a failure to read
closely some of the stories, lamented that Caldwell, in the service of reform, had "sacrifice[d] his art on the altar of horror," many others applauded the social purpose of the collection and believed that the author
had effectively fused art and argument. One wrote that the stories "establish beyond dispute the author's mastery of the short story form as a ve-
hicle of sociological criticism." The stories, wrote another, "bite into the
memory like an acid, disturbing the complacency of the reader and
pricking his social consciousness." Each new disclosure of the desperation
of the South's rural poor, contended another, "makes Caldwell less the
figure of a cynical young man, out to shock his readers, and more the
truthful, sincere observer that he is." Caldwell's fiction, argued yet another, "indicates that . . . [he] is fully aware of a sociological problem
faced as yet by only a few governmental experimenters." There were, it
seems, a number of thoughtful, articulate southerners who perceived not
only the skill of Caldwell's art but also the worth of his social goal. [100]

By 1935, after six intensely creative years, Caldwell had published
three collections of stories and five novels. Then, for the next three years,
his interest turned primarily to writing nonfiction. His objective in making the change was twofold: to provide factual evidence of the suffering
of the South's poor and to prove the legitimacy of his fictional rendering
of that suffering. He did not, however, abandon the writing of fiction. As
he traveled over the South collecting material for the nonfictional accounts *Tenant Farmer* and *You Have Seen Their Faces,* he found time to
compose short stories. [101]

In June 1938, Viking Press brought out its third collection of Caldwell
stories, all but two of which had appeared in periodicals since the publication of *Kneel to the Rising Sun.* Notwithstanding the title of the volume, *Southways,* some of the stories could have been set virtually anywhere and are not distinctively southern. Of the southern stories, one, a
hilarious yarn about a wrestling bear, is purely entertainment. Humor
also figures significantly in some of the other tales, again, as in most such
Caldwell stories, highlighting a serious theme. The rest are not intended
to amuse at all. [102]

Southways includes a few stories that introduce a thematic departure.
The previous collections had contained a number of stories, some of them

southern, that dealt with the victimization of women, either by general social forces or by specific men. Although one earlier story, "The Medicine Man," shows a woman outwitting a man, she does so with the help of her brother, and her object is to force the man to marry her. Here and there in *Southways*, however, Caldwell presents sympathetically drawn women who act alone to preserve their dignity and self-respect or to protect the defenseless. "Carnival," set in a small town near Birmingham, depicts the satisfaction gained by a woman who has suffered for two years the open philandering of her man. After she throws a game of chance so that his carnival stand will become the property of someone else, she walks out of town, alone and relieved. In "Runaway," an assertive black woman refuses to return a nine-year-old black girl to her white employer, the proprietor of a boardinghouse, because she has beaten the girl and worked her to exhaustion without paying wages. Scathingly denouncing such treatment, Aunt Gracie tells the proprietor's husband: "When you get home . . . tell your wife I've got Lessie, and that I'm going to keep her. Tell her to come down here herself after her, if she dares to, but I don't reckon she will, because she knows what I'll say to her will make her ears burn red."[103]

Gracie's actions take nerve; so do Daisy Lane's in "A Small Day," a seriocomic attack on masculine arrogance. The sixtyish landlord and former governor for whom Daisy's father farms assumes that the young woman will welcome the chance to marry him. Without proposing to her, he instructs his lawyer to secure a license. To her father's warning that Daisy is "just about as wild as they come," Governor Gil responds with assurance: "I've yet to know the wildest one of them that wouldn't tame when the time comes to handsel." Governor Gil wants to use Daisy that evening, even though the marriage license will not be ready for another two or three days. When her father reminds her that marriage to Governor Gil will insure her material comfort, Daisy goes to the big house for the handseling. The ill-fed, ill-clad tenant girl then sends the lecherous landlord into a frenzy—of agony—by biting "the daylights out of him." Amid his yells, Governor Gil instructs his houseboy to send for his doctor—and his lawyer. Daisy has escaped handseling—and marrying.[104]

The dimension of class, ancillary to gender in "A Small Day," provides the focus of three stories in *Southways*. All of those stories deal with the desperation of young married couples—two malnourished, one starving; two homeless, one threatened with eviction. All of the couples are victims not only of hard times but also of the callousness of those who are better off. In "Man and Woman," an expertly crafted and beautifully written story, husband and wife are walking more than forty miles to visit the grave of their infant daughter, who died after having been taken to her aunt's house when her father became sick and lost his job. The starving husband and wife stop at a house to ask for food. Although she has enough for both, the woman of the house, thinking the travelers are tramps, offers to feed only the wife. When the wife declines to eat if her husband cannot, he refuses to go any farther unless she accepts the woman's offer. As the wife eats in the kitchen under the gaze of her shrewish host, who berates the husband waiting outside, she surreptitiously slips food into her clothing. Later, as she and her husband continue their journey, he having hungrily consumed the smuggled food, emotions overwhelm her. As she grieves over her dead child, she realizes that the stranger's professed generosity was actually selfishness, that the woman shared her food in order to demean and taunt two unfortunates who had already suffered enough.[105]

"Wild Flowers," even more grim than "Man and Woman," deals with the eviction of a tenant couple by a landlord who "couldn't help it" even though the wife is far advanced in pregnancy. The husband "had pleaded to be allowed to stay in the house a little longer so Nellie would not have to go like that. The only answer he had got, even after he had explained about Nellie, was a shake of the head. There was no use in begging after that. He was being put out, and he could not do anything about it. He was certain there should have been some money due him for his crop that fall, even a few dollars, but he knew there was no use in trying to argue about that, either." As the young husband and wife search desperately for a house to take them in, she dies in childbirth.[106]

As with other of Caldwell's stories, the title of "A Knife to Cut the Corn Bread With" hides the content of the piece. In that tale, a young tenant farmer, paralyzed from the neck down after a bale of cotton has fallen on him, watches his seventeen-year-old wife chop cotton every day so that they can remain in their shack and receive their meager rations of corn bread and coffee. If not for her labor, their conspicuously religious landlord would evict them. The landlord's refusal to advance them a slab of bacon pushes the husband into a delirium in which he imagines cutting "a slice out of his numb legs" to furnish meat for him and his wife. Awaking, he asks his wife to bring "the sharpest knife to cut the corn bread with." [107]

The characters in these three stories are not subhuman trash. They are instead sensitive people who love the smell of flowers and the majesty of the sun and who care more for their mates than they do for themselves. Moreover, in these stories, Caldwell struck a raw nerve: the inability of men, through no fault of their own, to provide for their women. Despite the flaw in technique—could a paralyzed man cut anything?—and despite the bathos—would anyone evict a woman eight and a half months pregnant?—in the light of Caldwell's mission, the stories work.

In "Wild Flowers" and "A Knife to Cut the Corn Bread With," the only characters who try to help the destitute protagonists are black people who themselves have very little. When circumstances are reversed, compassion is withheld. A bitterly humorous story, "The Negro in the Well" shows that the camaraderie of hunters, something cherished by many southern men, cannot bridge the chasm of race. On a cold January night, white Jule Robinson, who has left his two frightened daughters home by themselves to follow his foxhounds, discovers that someone has fallen into his unmarked, twenty-foot well. His demands to know "who's down there muddying up my well?" go unanswered until the man in the well hears him call to his dogs. Recognizing the "Whoo-way-oh" of another fox hunter, black Bokus Bradley, Jule's neighbor, identifies himself. Expecting rescue, Bokus instead hears Jule demand two of his hounds as the price of help. After pondering Jule's proposal for five minutes, Bokus, who has removed his shoes in a failed attempt to climb out of the well, replies: "I just naturally couldn't swap off two of my hounds." Covering the well with boards to muffle any cries for help that the black man might utter, Jule leaves Bokus, standing barefoot in well water in January, to follow his hounds.[108]

Underlying the humor of the story, which derives from each man's obsession with the hunt, is a symbolic indictment of racial inequality. The white man is on top, the black man on the bottom. Were Bokus on the ground instead of in it, he might show that he is as good a hunter as Jule, maybe better, because his dogs, as Jule well knows, are "mighty fine foxtrailers." Abandoned in the well, Bokus has no chance to prove his mettle. At story's end, the departing Jule calls again to his hounds, and the echo is "a masterful sound to hear." Although Jule is master of his dogs, he cannot master a man who will not be broken.[109]

Caldwell's continuing interest in black culture is reflected in other stories in *Southways*. The strength of "Nine Dollars' Worth of Mumble" and "The Fly in the Coffin" lies in his ability to write from the perspective of poor, rural blacks unpatronizingly and without sentimentality. A slight tale of conjure gone awry, "Nine Dollars' Worth of Mumble" features excellent dialogue that is free of dialect. A far more significant story, "The Fly in the Coffin" is a hilarious, yet serious, tall tale in which Dose Muffin, sawmill hand and lifelong hater of flies, rises from the dead to swat a fly so that he can rest in peace. The humor of a preposterous situation conveyed through the sensibility of an exasperated dead man highlights the underlying gravity of the story. So poor that they cannot raise the twenty-five-dollar down payment on a coffin, Dose's family and friends build a pine box, dig a grave, and wash, starch, and iron the jumper that he is buried in. These are people of dignity whose sense of community gives them the strength to accept the naturalness of death.[110]

The vitality portrayed in a tale about dying is glaringly absent from another story in *Southways* that deals with race. "Return to Lavinia" explores a subject examined in a few earlier stories: the perception among white men that dark women possess superior passion. The story is leaden because the characters, a genteel mulatto woman and a white shopkeeper, are middle-class townspeople, the kind of folk that did not adequately engage Caldwell's imagination. The striking contrast between "Return to Lavinia" and "The Fly in the Coffin" provides further evidence that Caldwell's gift lay in depicting the rural poor, be they white or black.[111]

The great chorus of praise from southern reviewers that had greeted *Kneel to the Rising Sun* was much muted in response to *Southways*. In a review that indicated that he had not read, or else had forgotten, half of the stories in *Kneel to the Rising Sun,* Jonathan Daniels of the *Raleigh News and Observer,* earlier a perceptive critic, lamented Caldwell's shift "from comedy to pity." Praising only two stories in *Southways,* both of them comic, Daniels contended that Caldwell "seems to be becoming . . . an American moralist"—something he had in fact always been. Moreover, "as a Southern patriot," the Carolina journalist objected to the implication of the book's title that the ways depicted were uniquely southern. A variation of that opinion found expression in the *Memphis Commercial Appeal,* which noted defensively that not only were "cruelty and sheer horror" part of the South's ways, so, too, were "things sweet and things clean, things honest and things good." The *Nashville Tennessean,* while admitting that "A Knife to Cut the Corn Bread With" and "Wild Flowers" possessed "a creeping horror which etches them in one's

memory," dismissed "The Fly in the Coffin" as a "lame, futile tale" and
"The Negro in the Well" as "just an anecdote." "Half this collection," the
Tennessean concluded, "might well have been left buried in the periodicals in which it was first published," a judgment with which the *New
Orleans Picayune* agreed. With no basis in the stories to support such a
statement, the *Nashville Banner* contended that Caldwell had attempted
to write dialect and had failed. One of his great strengths, the writing
of dialogue, the *Banner's* reviewer dismissed as a "lack of facility with
conversation." "Caldwell is not an artist," the *Banner* opined. "He is a
sociologist and a propagandist; he has the consuming desire to treat social
questions in fiction." [112]

The *Durham Herald* disagreed. In a laudatory piece that reflected inat-
tention to detail in some stories, the reviewer asserted that "*Southways* is
no social dissertation." Likewise, the *Atlanta Constitution* commented
approvingly that the collection was "more entertaining than we might
expect from the bitter pen of the author." A more perceptive review in
the *Macon Telegraph* noted that within the stories, whether "tragic or
humorous, . . . lies Caldwell's unspoken, but gravely implied, social comment." The author, the reviewer continued, had come "a long way from
the sexual aberrations that once discolored his meanings." An even more
discerning review, written by Caldwell's old friend at the *Atlanta Journal,*
Frank Daniel, recognized his intent to comment on class and race in stories such as "A Small Day" and "The Negro in the Well." All of the stories,
Daniel concluded, were fundamentally real and poetic and compelling,
serving to "remind us that Mr. Caldwell is a master at employing simplicity for eloquence, and under-statement for poignancy, and inarticulate-
ness for conveying the most significant emotions." Although Daniel over-
stated his case—some of the stories do not justify his glowing
assessment—on balance, his evaluation was sound. At his best, Caldwell
was indeed a master of the aspects of writing that Daniel described. [113]

Two of Caldwell's finest stories appeared after *Southways* was published. Although "The People *v.* Abe Lathan, Colored" and "The End of
Christy Tucker" came out as the country began to recover from the Great
Depression, both reflect Caldwell's continuing concern with themes that
had held his attention throughout the 1930s, the twin evils of economic
dependency and racism. Past sixty but still able to grow cotton, Abe Lathan is ordered off the land he has worked for forty years by a landlord
who can no longer keep his elderly tenants. During Abe's forty years of

tenancy, he has received as payment not a share of the crop but only food, lodging, and clothing. Baffled by the proposed eviction, Abe cannot bring himself to leave. The next day, lawmen haul him away, along with his wife and their belongings. After leaving his wife and possessions beside a road near some Negro houses, the deputies take Abe to jail. Locked up on the false charge of threatening his landlord, Abe cannot retain the services of a lawyer; one after another refuses to take the case of a man who is not only indigent but who is also black. As the story ends, Abe sits hopelessly in his cell waiting for the system of justice to send him to the chain gang.[114]

The title, "The People *v.* Abe Lathan, Colored," suggests that Caldwell is not scoring an unfeeling individual but rather is indicting a heartless society that permits the humblest of its members to be cruelly wronged. The one white character who displays a whit of sympathy for the Lathans is powerless to help them. A lifetime of back-breaking toil has earned the utterly helpless Abe, who is as much a slave as was ever any antebellum chattel, another kind of forced labor that, the reader feels sure, will kill him.

Unlike the elderly Lathan who would have been content to live out his days on his landlord's place, Christy Tucker is young and energetic. But he, too, is black. His race and his ambition are his undoing. Because of his initiative and his desire to avoid debt, Christy is considered "one of those biggity niggers" by his landlord and furnish merchant, a tan-shirted, black-booted tyrant aptly named Crossman. When Christy refuses Crossman's order to undress, kneel, and submit to a whipping, the landlord shoots him dead. "Open up the . . . [store] door," Crossman tells his brother at story's end, "and let those niggers out in the back see what happens when one of them gets as biggity as that coon."[115]

That many southern planters bore little resemblance to Lathan's and Tucker's landlords hardly diminishes the force of these stories. The target of Caldwell's attack is a system so flawed that it allows the admirable traits of fidelity, diligence, and drive to be mocked and the innocent to be punished.

Published in June 1940, "The End of Christy Tucker" was the last of Caldwell's 1930s stories. A few months before, his final 1930s novel had appeared. The punishment of innocence that characterizes "The End of Christy Tucker" likewise provides the theme of *Trouble in July*. Moreover, the novel expands and dramatizes some observations that Caldwell had

made five years earlier. In a brief document that accompanied a 1935 art
exhibit in New York that dealt with lynching, he forthrightly attacked the
common justification of the practice, that it was "necessary in order to
protect the honor of Southern womanhood. . . . This is merely an excuse,"
he charged, "to cover up the true intent and purpose. Rape is not confined
to any one race." Condemning the barbaric treatment of the black victims
of lynching, Caldwell was equally concerned with the effect the practice
had on whites. "Social deterioration is the payment extracted for a
lynching," he wrote. "The community surrounding a lynching scene loses
all trace of progress and civilization." No one escaped the contamination.
Even the children "practice brutality just as if they were learning to fish
and hunt." Because southern states had demonstrated by "a policy of in-
action that they will not take the necessary steps" to punish lynchers,
Congress should do so. Federal legislation should be passed soon, for
"each day of delay will force millions of people towards further descent
into the slough of barbarism."[116]

Such legislation had not been passed by February 1940, when *Trouble
in July* was published. Figuring peripherally in all of Caldwell's previous
long fiction, the matter of race is central to this novel. Within the brief
time of the story, forty-eight hours, the author weaves around the center
of race a web of sex, "honor," and guilt.[117]

The eighteen-year-old black boy, Sonny Clark, who is done to death
by a lynch mob, is the victim of forces beyond his comprehension: the
desire of a fifteen-year-old white girl who is motherless, unloved, and pro-
miscuous; the fanaticism of a religious enthusiast; the cowardice of politicians who care more for their offices than for the life of someone who has
been unjustly accused. Sonny's innocence of the machinations of whites
renders him as helpless as the rabbits he keeps and loves dearly. So thoroughly has he internalized the doctrines of white supremacy that he does
not even try to escape from an unarmed white farmer who leads him to
his doom.[118]

Sonny's terror at the advances of Katy Barlow stands in sharp contrast
to the desire for interracial sex shown not only by Katy but also by certain
other white characters. More than once, Sheriff Jeff McCurtain warns his
deputies to stop bringing black women to the jailhouse. "If you can't stick
to white gals," he tells one, "you've got to go somewhere else to do your
laying-out with the nigger ones." "I ain't going to stand," he says a little
later, "having this jail turned into a whorehouse every time I turn my

back." When the sheriff, innocent in this instance, expresses to the lynch mob his embarrassment over being discovered in a cell with a black girl, one member of the mob replies: "Nobody cares about that." Later, the omniscient narrator implies that a few of the lynchers, as they search for Sonny, will rape the attractive wife of a young man absent from the Negro quarters. White women, too, instigate interracial sex. Upon learning of the alleged rape of Katy Barlow, Sheriff Jeff tells a deputy: "Some of those folks up there in those sand hills . . . raise girls that have never drawn the color line. . . . It's not an easy thing to say about brother whites, but it has always looked to me like them folks up there never was particular enough about the color line."[119]

Katy's father, however, is tragically particular. Shep Barlow's skewed sense of honor demands that the rumored assault on his daughter by a black boy be avenged. His neighbors, whose daughters may have been the girls that the sheriff described, agree. The men's fears of black-on-white sex is the linchpin of their distorted concept of honor. Moreover, the clannishness produced by their isolation makes them suspicious of outsiders who want to help. Sandhillers, they believe, should take care of their own.[120]

Yet when the lynchers realize that one of their own has deceived them—Katy having proclaimed Sonny's innocence when she came upon his bullet-riddled body—their anger over her duplicity, which has caused them to spill innocent blood, leads them to wreak a terrible vengeance. Like a biblical harlot, Katy is stoned to death. Notwithstanding the horror of the novel's climax, the guilt that the lynchers feel is a sign of hope. As Sheriff Jeff gazes upon the dead bodies of the white girl and the black boy, he tells his deputy that this incident "ought to put an end to lynching the colored for all time." Caldwell suggests that a sense of guilt—that of the lynchers, of the sheriff, and of the white farmer who had refused, after much emotional turmoil, to help Sonny—might produce a feeling of shame, which might, in turn, result in beneficent change.[121]

The guilt and the shame could provide much-needed ammunition for the saving remnant in white southern society that was fighting the continuing oppression of blacks. Among that minority were Katy's grandfather, who did not want her "mixed up in a shameful lynching"; "a handful of men and women" who had always insisted that Sheriff Jeff fulfill "his sworn duty to protect the life of a suspect until he could be taken to trial"; and a white tenant farmer who asked the sheriff, "How come you didn't lock up that nigger in the jailhouse? . . . How come you didn't stir around and catch him before that mob got on his trail?"[122]

Hard times and religious fanaticism negate the intentions of people of goodwill. Among the would-be lynchers, "the price of cotton was the most important thing in their lives." Having no control over that price, some white farmers angrily resent the occasional black man who has more money than they. "Hell, this is a white man's country!" says one member of the mob. "Ain't no nigger going to flash a bigger roll of money than I can, and me not do something about it." That Sonny Clark had never flashed a roll of money, large or small, made no difference.[123]

For all the blame that Caldwell places upon hard times to explain the actions of whites in the novel, religious enthusiasm is far more culpable. More than anyone else, the person responsible for Sonny's death is the fanatical Narcissa Calhoun. Outraged by the appearance of Black Jesus Bibles purchased by Julie County blacks from a Chicago mail-order house, Narcissa draws up a petition to be submitted to the President that urges him to send "all persons having any degree of Negro blood to the country of Africa without undue delay." The absurd petition is treated with derision by a number of white characters. Shielded by her race and her sex, Narcissa is, however, hardly just a laughable eccentric. To enhance the popularity of her petition, she, along with her companion Preacher Felts, who is also aptly named, fabricates the charge of rape against Sonny. The word of a white woman is enough to seal the black boy's fate.[124]

Occasional glimmers of hope and sporadic flashes of humor cannot conceal the intent of *Trouble in July*. The story indicts a brutal, violent society and does so all the more forcefully by portraying the lynching of Sonny Clark as a political conspiracy, not merely the visceral act of a mob of wool-hat boys. Even so, more than thirty-five years after the publication of the novel, Caldwell observed that part of its purpose was to show "that human kindness is struggling to prevail."[125]

Some white southern reviewers condemned *Trouble in July*. One called Caldwell "the personification of an earthworm," and another claimed not to "see much point" to the story. More often, however, the responses were temperate, if sometimes wrongheaded. Commending Caldwell for having "put his finger on many a recognized sore spot of southern life," the *Chattanooga Times* nevertheless maintained that "a reformer's zeal . . . causes him to overemphasize." Because the story's characters "are too exaggerated," said the *Durham Herald,* "the force of much that . . . [Caldwell] has to say is lessened." The *Charlotte Observer* agreed that the characters "are not quite human"; therefore, "we do not need to sympathize with them." The *Birmingham News* observed, however, that "the book is bound to increase the bitter distaste for lynching among Southern people. It will help the [antilynching] movement which is well under way." Although more than one review criticized the narrowness of Caldwell's vision and admonished him to include in his fiction yeoman farmers and middle-class urbanites, the *Atlanta Journal* recognized that such people failed to capture his imagination. Moreover, the *Journal* noted, "the compassion which impels" Caldwell, coupled with "his great skill," had produced "a stark and stunning tale," an "unforgettable, powerfully presented novel." [126]

Among the most perceptive commentaries on *Trouble in July* was one written by a black southerner. In the *New Republic,* Richard Wright, after praising Caldwell's "simple, melodious and disarming" language, pointed out that "fear is the pivot of the story." Everyone in the novel is afraid of some unwanted eventuality, yet, as Wright correctly noted, "the most poignant fear" is that of the white farmer, torn between morality and convention, who refuses to help Sonny escape the mob. Afraid that he will be branded a "nigger-lover," he cannot bring himself to do the right thing. Wright was so impressed with Caldwell's description of Sonny's inability to flee from the farmer—the result of Sonny's Jim Crow education—that he called the passage "some of the most laughable, human and terrifying pages Caldwell has ever written." In a postscript, Wright advised readers not to accept "as good Caldwellian fun Narcissa Calhoun's idea of shipping the Negroes back to Africa. Caldwell was serious, no matter how fantastic it sounds, for such notions are being aired in the halls of Congress today." If some white southerners thought that *Trouble in July* was exaggerated, a black man victimized by "the ethics of living Jim Crow" knew that Caldwell's account was all too believable. [127]

Richard Wright was not the only black person who applauded Caldwell's treatment of race. In December 1940, ten months after the appearance of *Trouble in July, Opportunity,* a journal of black life published in New York, ran a review of *Jackpot,* a newly published anthology of Caldwell stories. The reviewer, Ulysses Lee, was extraordinarily perceptive. He expressed admiration for many aspects of Caldwell's writing: its "passion for truth," its "profound comedy," and its ability "to convey the flavor of [characters'] speech" without resort to dialect. He conferred his highest praise on Caldwell's handling of black-white relations. No other writers—not the white T. S. Stribling or William Faulkner or the black Arna Bontemps—had matched Caldwell's "accuracy in picturing the actualities of life in the South." Lee cited example after example from *Jackpot* to illustrate that "Caldwell's eye picks out many a meaningful action which finds its way into a story where it may have little surface relevance." Moreover, Lee contended, the work of a white southerner "is showing the way for Negro creative effort. . . . If the half-dozen or so capable Negro practitioners of fiction were ever to discern as many possibilities in Negro life as Caldwell has already seen, all fears that having to write of Negro life is a restricting force would disappear."[128]

Over the course of the 1930s, Caldwell had published four novels and more than forty stories that were distinctively southern. To all of the short stories he brought a transparent sincerity, to many a rollicking and righteous humor, and to some—those that dealt with social ills—an uncompromising sense of justice. In a genre wherein he had few equals, he fused a paucity of words and a wealth of emotion to expose the genteel insensitivity, flagrant callousness, and outright brutality that sometimes characterized the South of the 1930s. The novels, with the exception of *Journeyman*, illustrated his deep sympathy for people, black and white, on the margins of southern society. Whether, like Jeeter Lester, they were too poor to be decent, or, like Ty Ty Walden, they attempted futilely to find emotional escape from the travail of existence, or, like Sonny Clark, they failed fully to comprehend the forces that oppressed them, such southerners were the victims of a social system that denied them full humanity. Both novels and stories often depicted a godforsaken land of desperate poverty, pervasive ignorance, and pernicious traditions. Caldwell's dark vision was brightened, however, by a reformist impulse that was present in much of his fiction. Because human beings were moral creatures, social improvement was possible. His social concern insured that his best work would oppose whatever stood in the way of that improvement.

1. Caroline Bell Caldwell, Erskine
Caldwell's mother, ca. 1901. Copyright ©
1987 Erskine Caldwell.

2. Ira Sylvester Caldwell, Erskine
Caldwell's father, ca. 1930. Copyright ©
1987 Erskine Caldwell.

3. Erskine Caldwell, Prosperity, S.C., ca. 1911. (Courtesy of Dartmouth College Library)

4. Erskine Caldwell on Tobacco Road, 1936. (Photograph by Margaret Bourke-White by permission of Jonathan and Roger White)

5. Ringgold, Georgia. "Those poor people walking all the way from Florida looking for a job, and hungry every step. It's a shame they have to walk so far, but they've got to go somewhere—they can't stay here." (Photographs and caption from *You Have Seen Their Faces* [1937]; photographs courtesy of Syracuse University Library by permission of Jonathan and Roger White)

6. Marion Junction, Alabama. "No place to plant me a little garden when the white-boss says to plow the cotton in right up to my front door." 7. Scotts, Arkansas. "And so the fairy godmother in the storybook touched the little white girls with her wand and they were all turned into little princesses." (Photographs and captions from *You Have Seen Their Faces* [1937]; photographs courtesy of Syracuse University Library by permission of Jonathan and Roger White)

8. Sweetfern, Arkansas. "Poor people get passed by." (Photograph and caption from *You Have Seen Their Faces* [1937]; photograph courtesy of Syracuse University Library by permission of Jonathan and Roger White)

9. McDaniel, Georgia. "Snuff is an almighty help when your teeth ache." (Photograph and caption from *You Have Seen Their Faces* [1937]; photograph courtesy of Syracuse University Library by permission of Jonathan and Roger White)

10. Locket, Georgia. "I've done the best I knew how all my life, but it didn't amount to much in the end." (Photograph and caption from *You Have Seen Their Faces* [1937]; photograph courtesy of Syracuse University Library by permission of Jonathan and Roger White)

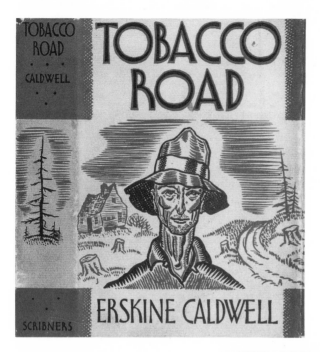

11. Dust jacket of first edition of
Tobacco Road, 1932. (Courtesy of
Dartmouth College Library; reprinted
with permission of Simon & Schuster)

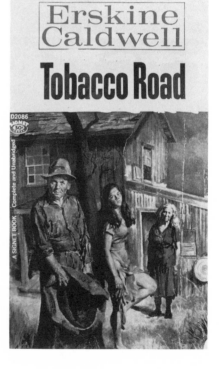

12. Cover of paperback edition of
Tobacco Road, ca. 1963. (By
permission of Penguin USA)

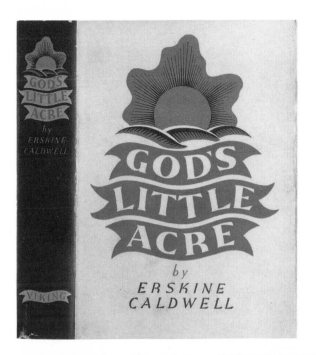

13. Dust jacket of first edition of *God's Little Acre*, 1933. (Courtesy of Dartmouth College Library by permission of Penguin USA)

14. Cover of paperback edition of *God's Little Acre*, ca. 1963. (By permission of Penguin USA)

15. Erskine Caldwell, Dunedin, Fla., 1971. Copyright © 1987 Erskine Caldwell.

CHAPTER FOUR

Radical Activism:
The Nonfiction of the Thirties

The 1930s brought profound changes to Caldwell's life. At the beginning of the decade, he lived a hardscrabble existence in rural Maine. At the end of the decade, he enjoyed the comforts of suburban Connecticut. In the interim, he made big money from the play *Tobacco Road* and from screenwriting, became famous—and notorious—and left his wife for another woman. Amid the vicissitudes of his personal life, Caldwell produced significant work, not only fiction but also nonfiction. Notwithstanding his growing affluence after 1933, his anger at social injustice remained intense, and his attacks on it increased.[1]

At the beginning of the 1930s, in a review of *American Earth,* the Communist poet and critic Norman Macleod, after perceptively describing Caldwell as "a hardboiled idealist," concluded: "He should go left." Caldwell already had, and occasionally in the early 1930s he considered joining the Communist party. "Some day," he wrote a friend, "I'll probably join the party if for no other reason than to be able to say, and say proudly, that I am a Communist." Although he did not become a member of the party, he did participate in front organizations such as the League of American Writers and the New Theater of Action. Moreover, he supported the Communist ticket, which included a black vice presidential candidate, in the campaign of 1932, and he wrote occasionally for Communist publications. He did not, however, consider himself a proletarian writer. Nor was he; for seldom in his work do the deprived band together and succeed in overcoming social injustice.[2]

Caldwell's radicalism was tied to southern realities, not to the party

line. Moreover, party intellectuals believed that the characters in his fiction, in Macleod's words, were "un-class-conscious proletarians in the
sticks." Although Caldwell's characters possess a keener sense of class
inequities than the Communists recognized, Jeeter Lester, Ty Ty Walden,
and others lack the highly developed class consciousness of urban
Marxists.[3]

American Marxist thinkers in the 1930s were not aware of the tradi-
tionalism of rural southern radicalism. Steven Hahn has observed that the
Populist revolt of the 1890s was not "a proletarian movement." Instead,
"Populism spoke for the men and women of 'small means' who faced
and sought to resist the specter of proletarianization." Southern farmers,
whether in the 1890s or in the 1930s, embraced a producer ethic. They
wanted the opportunity to maintain or to regain the independence that
land ownership offered. Communist intellectuals could not understand
an ideology so foreign to the thinking of industrial workers in the North.
Significantly, the welfare of the South's rural poor remained on the periphery of Communist concerns in the 1930s.[4]

Caldwell's sense of social justice, the product in great measure of his
father's influence and of his own observations, owed more to 1890s Populism than to 1930s Communism. Like the Populists, Caldwell was an
agrarian rebel. During a trip to New York shortly after the publication of
American Earth early in 1931, he visited with his friend Mike Gold, editor of the Communist weekly *New Masses*. Gold, who had recently returned from the Soviet Union and who was, according to Caldwell, "still
full of it," constantly harangued him about his "special brand of Communism." In addition to differing ideologically with Marxist intellectuals,
the individualistic Caldwell knew that writing was "a lone-wolf job . . .
even though the American soviets say otherwise."[5]

If Caldwell was not a card-carrying Communist, he was, no less than
the Communists, outraged by "the barons of coal and steel, wheat and
cotton" who had "imposed upon America" an "unhealthy, squalid, painful environment" and by "the gut-rotting disorganization of unplanned
society." His stints in Hollywood in the summers of 1933 and 1934 deep-
ened his outrage. There, where Clark Gable strutted about and Robert
Montgomery behaved like an ass, where "money was spent on nothing,
while the rest of the country was down and out," he met a writer—someone who should have known better—who insisted that the farmers' revolt
in his home state of Iowa was the work of "a handful of Communists."

"He's completely capitalistic," Caldwell wrote to his wife, Helen. "He's made a lot of money ... out here, and he's all against admitting that people in his own country are starving." The movie moguls, Caldwell wrote to a friend, "are afraid to recognize poverty, or that there are people in America who don't have enough food to keep them alive." At the age of thirty, Caldwell was more than ever his father's son.[6]

Although the Georgia boy feared that southern California Communists would "try to make me out as something that I'm not," he knew that American Communists provided an alternative to the major political parties, whose response to the Depression, he believed, was woefully inadequate. Moreover, the Communists gave him an outlet to vent his rage. The *Daily Worker* commissioned him to investigate conditions in Detroit's automobile industry, and *New Masses* published "Slow Death," his angry story about abuse of the destitute.[7]

Early in 1934, *New Masses* ran two reports that Caldwell submitted on "A Story That Got Lost." During an extended Christmas visit to his parents' home, Caldwell learned of racial unrest near the town of Bartow, twenty-five miles south of Wrens. At considerable risk—"I came pretty close to getting my neck stretched," he wrote to a friend—he discovered that three black men had been killed. One, trying "to protect his life," had been shot by a policeman. Another, whose identity could not be established, had been riddled with gunfire and nearly decapitated with a knife. The other, who had objected to being called "a son-of-a-bitch" by a group of white men, had been beaten to death and thrown into a well. A witness to the beating, himself seriously injured, was being held in the Jefferson County jail for his protection.[8]

These incidents, Caldwell erroneously wrote, had gone "unreported in the daily press" because Georgia newspapers did not consider newsworthy the deaths of a few blacks. His mistake does not seem to have been intentional. Two days before his first article appeared in the weekly *New Masses,* the daily *Atlanta Constitution,* aware that he was investigating the matter, had carried a brief story about the killing of two black men in Bartow, one of whom had been slain nearly two months before and the other two weeks earlier. Caldwell may have filed his story before the *Constitution* report was published, or he may not have been aware of it. Whatever the case, the publication of his articles, which received the editorial endorsement of the *New Republic,* brought a level of attention to the Bartow incidents that they would not otherwise have received in Georgia. During the last week of January, the *Constitution* ran four long stories, two of them on the front page, that dealt with the Bartow killings.[9]

Those articles show that most of the officials with jurisdiction in the matter believed that Caldwell's charges were unfounded. The solicitor general, who said that he knew the writer personally, described the reticent Caldwell as "just a fellow who likes to talk if he can get anybody to listen to him." Moreover, that officer, unwittingly substantiating Caldwell's argument, described the killings as "nothing out of the ordinary." The superior court judge denigrated Caldwell's charges and stated, "There is not the slightest suggestion of a wave of crime . . . or intolerance in Jefferson County." Governor Eugene Talmadge expressed confidence that local authorities were handling the matter properly.[10]

One of those authorities, however, was not as sure as the governor. Admitting that the "affair looked powerful bad," Sheriff J. J. Smith requested that a special session of the grand jury be convened "to clear up the whole thing." When the judge dismissed Smith's request on grounds of insufficient evidence, the sheriff offered "to furnish the evidence necessary for an immediate grand jury investigation."[11]

Spurred by Caldwell's exposé, the Atlanta-based Commission on Interracial Cooperation sponsored an investigation conducted by Arthur F. Raper, a member of its research staff and a sociologist whose specialty was the study of lynching. The commission commended Sheriff Smith's offer to place evidence before a grand jury, and it endorsed his call for an immediate investigation. Muting Caldwell's language, the commission substantiated his claim regarding the perpetrators. The "identity of white participants in these affairs is well known," its report charged, and "not one of them has been indicted, or even put under arrest." Moreover, in addition to the killing of three black men and the severe beating of another that Caldwell had described, the commission cited other instances of white vigilantism that he had not related; fifteen months earlier, two blacks had been flogged, one of them a girl who had been "accused of stealing clothes."[12]

In some ways the commission's findings regarding the trouble of late 1933 differed from Caldwell's. He had mentioned the beating of five men; the commission reported that only two had been beaten. He had not mentioned that whiskey was an ingredient in some of the violence; the commission found that some of the blacks and whites involved had been drinking. He had implied that fourteen houses had been burned as a result of racial unrest; the commission, hinting that the motive was arson so that the owners of the vacant houses could collect insurance, found that the fires had occurred before "the recent interracial troubles." The commission's findings nevertheless supported Caldwell's contention that a "reign of terror" existed in Bartow. The "negroes of the community are living in a state of fear," its report said, because "these tragedies so far have gone unchallenged by the courts and the white citizenship." So serious was the trouble that Bartow blacks were afraid to patronize the two institutions most dear to rural black southerners: school and church. A "negro night school at Bartow has been virtually abandoned," the commission reported, "and night church attendance has been reduced almost to the vanishing point."[13]

Caldwell had excoriated the press for not reporting the Bartow matters; the commission denounced the judicial system, with the exception of the sheriff, for having "taken no steps to investigate these crimes and bring the guilty to justice." In its indictment, the commission included "the law-abiding citizens [who] cannot be excused for permitting a few irresponsibles to terrorize the negro population with impunity." The commission concluded that "vigorous legal steps are imperatively demanded by the circumstances," and it urged Bartow's citizens to support the sheriff's demand for an immediate grand jury investigation.[14]

The defensiveness of the prosecutor and the judge and the affirmation of the Interracial Commission had been elicited primarily by Caldwell's first report to *New Masses*. His second, published a week later, was much longer, less reportorial, and more revealing of the anguish that he felt. An interview at the county jail with the man who had been badly beaten when his friend was killed left Caldwell "feeling uncomfortable" because he was white. He suffered a racial guilt, he implied, because the victim was "an accusing finger pointing at the white men of . . . [my] country who butcher hogs with more humaneness than they kill Negroes." When he revisited Bartow after the interview, the feelings of guilt were intensified. Near midnight, he met a black boy on the road. Seeing the white man, the boy dodged; hearing his greeting, he darted off into a swamp. The unidentified victim whose body had been mutilated "lies buried in an unmarked grave in an abandoned field. Nobody knows his name; nobody cares." Standing in Bartow's main street, Caldwell attempted to understand what he could not comprehend. "I was trying to reason why three Negroes could be put to death in such a quiet, peaceful town by white

men who were at that moment in their homes asleep. Nobody was walking around in the dark with a flashlight trying to find evidence to convict
the killers. Nobody was abroad offering protection to Negroes who
wished to come out of their cabins. Bartow was as calm as any Georgia
town at midnight. Georgia was as peaceful as any Southern state in January." The piercing incongruity became all the more painful when Caldwell passed by a drugstore whose window featured "a seven-color card-
board poster displaying three naked girls and the name of a perfume
manufacturer." The odor from the drug store "filtered through my senses
and I turned away wondering if I could ever forget the association in my
mind of perfumed women and brutal men." [15]

In Augusta a couple of hours later, a still introspective Caldwell
stopped by a drugstore to buy a pack of cigarettes. The "startling odor
of perfumes and cosmetics does something to me," he wrote. "The clerk
thinks that I am drunk; I am unable to ask for what I wish, and I have to
cling to the tobacco counter for support." Ushered out by the clerk into
the reviving air of the early morning, Caldwell realized that "after a night
spent in the Ogeechee [River] swamps, perfumery and brutality will ever
plague me." [16] The epiphany rightly disturbed him. As white men killed
black men, white men wanted their women not only to act as though
nothing had happened but also to enhance their attractiveness. For Caldwell, however, no amount of perfume could conceal the foulness of southern racism.

In the *New Masses* articles, Caldwell charged that the identity of the
killers was widely known. Quoting a statement by a witness to one of the
killings, he named one of the suspects. Back in Maine by the middle of
February, he told a friend that "the Bartow business isn't over yet by a
long shot. . . . Some of the bastards have started civil suit against me. If
they all go through with it, I'm going to raise hell sure enough this time.
I can break a few heads in Georgia." The suit was dropped, as was prose-
cution of a victim of the violence who had been charged with assault.
There was, however, no immediate grand jury investigation of the matters
that Caldwell had publicized. [17]

A year after the exposé in *New Masses*, Caldwell turned again to journalism to examine life among the oppressed in Georgia. In February
1935, the *New York Post* ran a series of four articles dealing with conditions among tenant farmers in the area around Augusta. Hard times and
inadequate relief, Caldwell charged in those pieces, were forcing former

sharecroppers into day labor at wages averaging thirty-five cents—when they were lucky enough to find work—pushing them off of tillable soil "into the swamps, the stony acres, the waste land," and reducing them to destitution so deep that they were compelled to eat "snakes and cow dung." The Federal Emergency Relief Administration (FERA), Caldwell further charged, denied that such wretchedness existed and failed to provide assistance to the neediest people, who were isolated in the country-side, "unknown and unseen." Governor Eugene Talmadge, the suspenders-snapping "wild man" who called himself "everybody's friend," was, Caldwell observed, a vehement opponent of relief who used federal funds to enhance his political position. Although Caldwell failed to point out—because he probably did not know—that Talmadge's politi-cization of relief had caused President Franklin D. Roosevelt the year be-fore to remove federally funded programs from the governor's control, his indictments of Talmadge and of the inadequacy of relief were accurate. So, too, was his gut-wrenching account of an incident that his father and two of his father's friends had witnessed. In a tenant shack near a Tobacco Road community, two babies lay nursing at a dog.[18]

Had Caldwell's report of eviction, starvation, and unspeakable destitu-tion—all worsened by official neglect—not been excerpted in *Time* mag-azine early in March, it might have escaped notice in the South. Amid what *Time* described as shouts of "Libel!" from the southern press, the editor of the *Augusta Chronicle* decided "to call Caldwell's hand." Con-ducting its own investigation, the *Chronicle* played with a stacked deck. At the outset, an editorial declared: "We do not believe such condition [*sic*] exists as described by Erskine Caldwell, for some of the good people of . . . [Jefferson County] would have heard about and corrected them." At the conclusion, an editorial headnote to the reports of the two journal-ists sent to Tobacco Road maintained that their "true picture of condi-tions will clear once and for all the name of our good neighbors in Burke and Jefferson counties."[19]

Guided by Caldwell's father to "the worst afflicted dwellings," the *Chronicle* reporters found "dull, stolid, stupid people, seemingly unaware of all their ills save hunger," who "seem in their ignorance fairly satisfied with their lot," and who, upon receiving food, ate it quickly, foolishly failing to conserve it. Displaying contempt more than compassion, the *Chronicle* articles were also stridently defensive. A child who Caldwell said had died of anemia had actually perished of "a violent hookworm infestation, influenza and pneumonia." Ironically, the reporters seem not to have realized that the prevalence of hookworm provided a harsher indictment of official neglect than the occurrence of anemia. The reporters found no evidence of Caldwell's "most piquing description"—the dog suckling the babies. The poor that Caldwell described had been poor for a long time and were "victims of their own shiftlessness and ignorance." Again and again, the reporters emphasized the small number of the destitute: "from 10 to 12 to 35" families; "from 10 to 35 . . . individual cases"; "but a minute part of the whole population." And there were similar examples of destitution elsewhere in the nation, they pointed out.[20]

Always his son's champion, the elder Caldwell responded to the *Chronicle*'s implications that Erskine had written the *Post* series for financial gain by noting that his son sent money home for relief of the poor. Although Ira commended the *Chronicle* for conducting its investigation, he contended that "conditions are worse and poverty has a wider spread" than its stories indicated. In a passionate, though diplomatic, rebuke of the *Chronicle*'s assertion that the poor had only themselves to blame for their condition, Ira wrote: "Thoughtful people are beginning to realize that every individual is to a large extent the product of his environment, of the institutions that men have set up, of the social forces that society lets loose. No man is self-made and no man is self-unmade."[21]

Caldwell had other defenders as well. An east Georgia farmer thanked him "for an effort to open our eyes" and urged "good sympathetic Christian people" to join together to bring about change. An east Georgia sharecropper stated in *Time* that he knew "only too well what thieving, gouging, 'chiseling,' browbeating, bulldozing landlords do to us [tenants]." In a bitingly sarcastic commentary, a Virginian warned that people "better not starve in the South because the Chamber of Commerce don't like it, and smart alecks like . . . Erskine Caldwell write stores about it." Sarcasm likewise informed the observation of the *Charlotte News*, which noted the *Chronicle*'s "sympathetic feeling for the neighbors of the better classes pained by thus being held up to the national horror." Citing instances of suffering found by the *Chronicle*'s reporters, the *News* reckoned that Caldwell "is not greatly upset over the 'true picture' which set out to refute him."[22]

Outrage surpassed defense, however. The chairman of the Jefferson County Commission, after making "a comprehensive inspection tour of his county" in one day's time, denied the existence of conditions described by Caldwell. "Were the entire country in as good shape as Jefferson County," that official declared, "the relief rolls would soon banish [i.e., vanish]." Another east Georgian asked the *Post* to "inform Caldwell that Georgians would prefer that he cease referring to Georgia as his birthplace." "Such silly stuff as he writes about," that citizen maintained, "will make excellent copy for Russian newspapers." Scolding *Time* for not "presenting . . . the bright side" of Georgia, a Savannah newspaperman described Caldwell's articles as a "crackpot version of conditions" and reminded the magazine's editors that "he gets paid to write that tomfoolery." Another journalist, from faraway Indiana but who had "six years' intimate familiarity with Jefferson County," defended it as a place with a "low . . . percentage of social injustice" and condemned Caldwell as one who could take "a single stink and . . . create a magnificent hog wallow." From Arkansas, a planter disturbed by the activities of the recently founded Southern Tenant Farmers Union contradicted Caldwell's "horrible stories" by asserting that thirty years' experience had convinced him that "the share cropper is a pretty happy individual. . . . He has many opportunities for bettering his condition and increasing his income." [23]

Caldwell responded to the *Chronicle*'s charge that his description of conditions was exaggerated by writing that the *Post* series had understated the enormity of the problem: "I could tell of families thrown out of their homes, plodding along the public highways of Georgia and dragging their possessions on the ground behind them. I could tell of men, with tears in their eyes, begging fruitlessly while their children starved. I could tell of teen-age girls, without job or home, offering "french dates" for a quarter on the streets of the editor's home city. . . . I could tell of these and many more, and to illustrate the point I can take pictures with a camera that will drive the nail home." [24] And that is what he did.

Two months after the February series in the *Post*, another four-part article appeared in that paper, with photographs taken by Caldwell. In the latter part of March, he and his father had traveled through Mississippi, Alabama, and Georgia gathering material to confirm the picture that he had drawn in the initial series. Events that Caldwell did not describe in the *Post* testify that the trip was hazardous. He and Ira were chased out of a county in Alabama, and in Georgia, Erskine had to restrain a knife-toting man who was angered by reports in the *Chronicle*, while his father "talked him down." [25]

In the hills of north-central Mississippi, the Caldwells found white ten-

ant farmers who had been driven from rich river-bottom lands by landlords who preferred more tractable black labor. For "a long time before
1930," these desperate whites had been trying "to woo, entreat, beg,
curse, and flail a living" from sterile soil that could be productive only
with liberal applications of fertilizer. Should the tenant be able to purchase any, he was "forced to drill it so thinly that its effect is barely worth
more than the effort of hauling it from the nearest town." Even those
tenants farming government-rented land received annual incomes of less
than two hundred dollars.[26]

Mississippi blacks were worse off. Reduced by stages from sharecropping to renting to laboring by the day, the black tenant, "doing the same
work he has always done, finds that his condition is even worse than it
was ten, twenty, fifty years ago." Always under the thumb of the white
man, blacks were earning only ten dollars a month as seasonal farm-
hands. On FERA projects they worked with picks and shovels as whites
supervised and received higher pay. Food supplied by FERA was commonly sorted into two classes, "the good and the bad, and the Negro
receives the worse." Blacks on plantations sometimes were charged for
clothing furnished by relief agencies that was supposed to be distributed
free. Makeshift relief measures were hardly adequate, Caldwell contended. The federal government, he suggested, should establish a program
to relocate Mississippi tenants to better land that they could purchase,
along with stock and implements, "on terms that could be met." Such a
program would provide these poor, hardworking people "a start in life
they never had to begin with."[27]

Moving eastward into Alabama, a state rich in natural resources whose
"human beings are among the most exploited of any in America," the
Caldwells found illiteracy, peonage, and landlord brutality. In Tuscaloosa
County, the site of the state university, they met, in an hour's time, eleven
white children of school age who had "never attended for a day any kind
of educational institution." In Dallas County, the heart of the state's black
belt, a tenant told them that he had received nothing for his labor in 1934.
"By any fair means of accounting," wrote Caldwell, "this Negro tenant
should have received not less than $150 in cash." In Macon County, home
of the citadel of black self-help, Tuskegee Institute, the Caldwells heard
reports of tenants who had been beaten or killed for requesting better
treatment from their landlords.[28]

Conditions in Georgia, a state "busy telling the world about its natural assets and tricky golf courses," were, if anything, worse than those in Mississippi and Alabama. Whereas Caldwell's focus in the two other states had been on black tenants, in Georgia he highlighted the plight of whites who had been pushed off of fertile land to "gully-washed hills" by landlords who preferred more easily defrauded black tenants. "It is astonishing," he wrote, "to find in this Jim Crow State that the economic condition of this class of white tenant is lower than that of the Negro." Isolated, illiterate, disfranchised, and dirt poor, such tenant farmers sometimes supplemented their diet of meal and molasses with clay, practiced incest, suffered from social diseases, and fell prey to religious excitement. On the occasions that these tenants' eligibility for federal relief had been "forcibly proved to the administrators," assistance came not in money with which to rent land or buy seed and stock but "in the form of mattresses, which can neither be eaten nor made to pull a plow." Such practices, he concluded, were "disgraceful [and] misguided." [29]

The major cause of the tragedy on the land was the Agricultural Adjustment Act (AAA). Caldwell charged that local administration of this measure, passed in the spring of 1933 and designed to control farm production, raise crop prices, and increase farmers' purchasing power, was permeated with fraud in the states he visited. In some counties, subsidy payments to which tenants were entitled were not given to them but were deposited to the credit of landlords. He could not understand "how such widespread thieving continues month after month, in county after county, without detection in Washington." Because of the AAA, sharecroppers were being reduced to cash renters and then to day laborers as landowners realized the benefits of fewer risks and greater profits. Caldwell concluded that "the tenant-farming system must be abolished." He suggested two alternatives, both of which would involve "the discarding of the landowner": collective farming or the distribution of land in "small parcels for intensive cultivation." [30]

Following the publication of the second installment of the second *Post* series, Ellison Durant Smith, senator from South Carolina, had had enough. A planter himself, "Cotton Ed" told his colleagues that Caldwell's reports of conditions among southern sharecroppers were "vicious propaganda and gross exaggeration." What the senator ignored was Caldwell's distinction between sharecroppers and other tenants. Although Caldwell would hardly have agreed with Smith's portrayal of the happy life of the sharecropper, he had taken pains to show the differences between sharecropping on the one hand and renting and laboring by the day on the other. With sharecropping, landlord and tenant shared the profits, if any, and the risks. With the other arrangements, especially after implementation of the AAA, the tenant and laborer saw much risk and little profit. According to "Cotton Ed," however, these people were "just as happy and contented as the share-croppers." Only a southerner, Smith maintained, could be trusted to report conditions accurately.[31]

A month after the *Post* ran Caldwell's second series, a radical house in New York published his thirty-page pamphlet, *Tenant Farmer*. The pamphlet reprinted virtually intact both of the series in the *Post*. Most of the few changes were minor. Among the significant revisions was the replacing of the *Post*'s often sensational headlines by chapter titles that were less inflammatory and thereby stronger. Thus "Georgia Land Barons Oust Dying Girl and Her Father" became "God-forsaken—Man-forsaken" and "Starving Babies Suckled by Dogs in Georgia Wastes" became "Hungry People." Perhaps to keep the cost of the pamphlet low—twenty-five cents—the photographs from the second *Post* series were omitted. Responding to the *Chronicle*'s suggestion that sterilization was the only solution to the problems of the destitute, Caldwell added a paragraph in which he condemned the "superficial thought" behind such a proposal. Aware of the chorus of objections that the *Post* articles might be perceived as describing conditions typical of the South, he incorporated a suggestion offered by the *New Republic* in an editorial on the controversy: he included a paragraph that denied the typicality of the circumstances that he portrayed while insisting that they were representative of the plight of thousands of isolated families throughout the Deep South. The few revisions strengthened the indictment that had been presented in the *Post*. The Louisiana novelist Hamilton Basso asserted that the pamphlet should be read "by every Southerner who professed to be interested in the welfare of his section."[32]

The force of *Tenant Farmer* lay in its impressionistic quality, which highlighted Caldwell's anger at injustice and his compassion for the invisible poor. Yet, to one southern reviewer, the pamphlet's strength became its signal weakness. Caldwell was doubtless surprised by the response of William Terry Couch, the director of the University of North Carolina Press and a significant figure in the South's intellectual awakening. Like Caldwell, Couch knew firsthand the hardships of southern working people, and he wanted to call attention to social problems in the region.[33]

Back in 1932, Couch had asked Caldwell to contribute a chapter to a collection of essays that he was editing that would be entitled "Civilization Below the Potomac." Excited about Couch's assignment, which called for an impressionistic rather than statistical account of southern industrial workers, Caldwell accepted the invitation immediately. "I am wholly sympathetic towards the people who compose that portion of the population," he wrote to Couch. Three weeks later, however, he asked for an extension of the deadline for submission. When he had accepted the assignment, he explained to Couch, he had believed that he could put aside a novel that he was writing. He found that he could not interrupt work on *God's Little Acre,* yet he still wanted very much to write the chapter. "It's straight down my alley," he told Couch. The editor denied Caldwell's request for an extension even though he had initially given him considerable leeway and even though the book, retitled *Culture in the South,* did not come out until two years later.[34]

The correspondence of 1932 may have affected Couch's opinion of Caldwell and of *Tenant Farmer.* Couch considered the pamphlet to be unintelligent and meaningless, demonstrative only of "the remarkable confusion" that pervaded Caldwell's mind. Couch wanted evidence to support Caldwell's "bare statement" that times were harder in 1935 than they had been five years before; he rejected Caldwell's contention that the AAA should bear great responsibility for the suffering of southern tenants; and he ignored Caldwell's disclaimer that the people portrayed in the pamphlet were representative only of a certain class and were not typical of the South. Expanding his review of *Tenant Farmer* to include commentary on *Tobacco Road* and *God's Little Acre*—in the process showing considerable ignorance of what Caldwell had said in those novels—Couch declared that the degenerates Caldwell described were beyond redemption, a strange reaction by someone who the year before had praised artists who served argument and who had likened the rural poor to a stolid "peasantry."

One cannot help wondering if Couch was confused. Caldwell's impressionistic account, based largely on anecdotal evidence, confirmed the findings of social scientists who were either on the faculty of Couch's institution or whose work its press had published. Caldwell's perception of the effects of the AAA and other New Deal agricultural legislation was much closer to the mark than his. Moreover, it was precisely because Caldwell still had hope that he wrote *Tenant Farmer.* Yet Couch intimated that royalties—however grand they might be on a twenty-five-cent pamphlet published by an obscure house—outweighed reform in Caldwell's system of values. Couch likewise failed to note that *Tenant Farmer* had proposed systemic change to solve the crisis on the land. Using his keen editorial eye, he did make one valid point: Caldwell's writing was occasionally haphazard.[35]

Couch's most serious indictment of Caldwell went beyond the scope of the piece under review. "Nothing has been done," he charged, "and nothing will be done to improve the condition of the Southern tenant farmer, black or white, because of anything Mr. Caldwell has written." As of the spring of 1935, very little had been done to help southern tenants. Couch, however, failed to appreciate the perils of prophecy. Within the next few years, efforts would be made to alleviate tenant suffering, although with results far shy of those that Caldwell—and Couch—would have wished. Caldwell was very much a part of that enterprise. Moreover, it is likely that the publication of the *Post* articles and of *Tenant Farmer* was timed to call attention to the suppression of a government report that seemed to have been highly critical of the Agricultural Adjustment Administration (AAA).[36]

Back in January 1935, the Legal Section of the AAA had dispatched Mary Connor Myers, an expert in administrative law, to the strife-torn Arkansas delta to conduct a secret investigation of allegations of widespread fraud in the implementation of the administration's Cotton Contract. Myers gathered much evidence that showed that the contract was "being openly and generally violated" and that hundreds of sharecroppers were being cheated. When newspapers leaked word of the investigation, reports came to the AAA from Tennessee and Missouri that confirmed the existence of fraud in those states, too. After Myers submitted her report, the AAA director refused to release it to the press. Newspapers throughout the country, including the *Post,* demanded its publication. Admitting that the South "has special problems which may be beyond the power of any one Administration to solve," the *Post* argued that officials of the AAA "should see to it that their policies do not aggravate an already frightful situation." Not only was the Myers Report not published, it disappeared from AAA files.[37]

But Caldwell could not be made to disappear. Later in 1935, the pamphlet *Tenant Farmer* appeared again, under the title "Southern Tenant Farmers," in his book entitled *Some American People,* which Viking Press refused to publish because it feared slow sales. Southerners' reactions to *Some American People,* which usually focused on the section treating tenant farmers, were often favorable. Observing that "certain Georgians have already discovered [that] Mr. Caldwell's data are usually authentic," A. B. Bernd in the *Macon Telegraph* maintained that he had written "a true and accurate report of conditions in many parts of the South." The Kentuckian Elizabeth Hardwick agreed, and she thanked Caldwell for presenting "a great deal of honest-to-God living" rather than a "romanticized ode . . . to beauty." An unsigned review in the *Atlanta Journal* commended Caldwell's "sincerity and sympathy" and pointed out that his latest book showed "directly the sociological concern which evoked his earlier writings." [38]

Another Atlanta paper disagreed. Citing the tenant-farmer segment, the *Constitution* condemned not only the book but also its author, whose "hatred of the capitalistic state" had resulted in "the propagation of a ridiculous socialism." The signed review concluded by advising Caldwell to "hang your head in shame" for not "producing clean, decent works." The reviewer, Caldwell wrote to his friend Frank Daniel at the *Journal,* was "no mean critic. . . . There ought to be a yearly prize for the boys who know what they don't like. I'll be glad to donate a box car full of gophers, if you'll agree to unload them in his front yard." [39]

Caldwell's first book of nonfiction says much about the cast of his mind. In the first of many travel books that he would write, he demonstrated that his interest lay not in tourist attractions but in "people and their activity." For the third time, he stood by his account of southern horrors, including the much-doubted story of the babies nursing at the dog. Amid depictions of the Depression humor of westerners, the hardships of Detroit's automobile workers, and the lack of social conscience in the American business system, he demonstrated a deep love of the land, a desire that the soil be conserved and not ravaged, and a hope that the federal government would institute measures that would make the have-nots self-sufficient. Because the New Deal was not doing enough to bring about such self-sufficiency, collective action was necessary, action more forceful than that of the American Federation of Labor, a union that he considered little more than a tool of business. Doubtlessly with the Southern Tenant Farmers Union in mind, he rejoiced that "now at last" the "undernourished, undereducated, underpaid laborer" of the cotton states was "fighting to regain equal rights with his countrymen." [40]

Within a few months of the publication of *Some American People*, Caldwell was making plans for another trip across the South to investigate conditions on the land. Like the *Post* series of April 1935, this report would be illustrated, but this time with photographs taken by a professional, not by himself. In January 1936, he met Margaret Bourke-White. That meeting led to developments that profoundly affected his life.[41]

A few months younger than Caldwell, Bourke-White had begun to enjoy acclaim in her field at the same time that he began to receive recognition in his. At the outset of her career, she specialized in industrial photography, her pictures often being used in advertising. So accomplished was her work that, in 1929, Henry Luce invited her to join the staff of his new magazine, *Fortune*. She accepted the offer on condition that her responsibilities to the magazine be only part-time so that she could continue to pursue her own projects. Her rise in her profession was meteoric, the result partly of photographs that she had taken in Russia. Before the United States granted diplomatic recognition to the Soviet Union in 1933, she had made three trips there, had earned the distinction of being the first foreigner to bring still photographs of Soviet industrialization out of the country, and had published a book that was an admiring portrayal of economic growth in the adolescent Communist state. By 1935, many of her fellow countrymen knew her name, not only because of her photographs but also because of her public lectures, her participation in radio programs, and her endorsements of Maxwell House coffee. By that time, her professional interests had assumed a new focus. In 1934, a *Fortune* assignment to take photographs of the desolation in the Dust Bowl made her eager to continue to turn her camera "in the direction of something that might have some social significance."[42]

Bourke-White and Caldwell agreed to embark on their southern journey near the middle of June 1936. She arrived in Augusta long after the appointed date of departure. Caldwell, who had been waiting at his parents' home in Wrens, was so angered by the delay that he nearly canceled the project. Eventually, in mid-July, Bourke-White, Caldwell, and his secretary, Ruth Carnall, set out on their odyssey through the South. A few days later, the secretary parted company after the photographer and the writer became lovers.[43]

It is difficult to determine who initiated the affair. Bourke-White, an attractive woman who had had many lovers before, said that Caldwell did. According to Carnall and Maxim Lieber, Caldwell's agent, Bourke-

White did. Carnall called the matter a seduction; Lieber was more blunt—"She raped him." Caldwell himself did not write publicly about the matter until late in his life. Gentleman that he was, he refused to tarnish a lady's name. He said that Bourke-White invited him to her hotel room, but he assumed responsibility for what happened afterwards. Whoever instigated the affair, its passion was mutual and intense. The liaison remained adulterous until Caldwell's wife secured a divorce two years later.[44]

From mid-July to mid-August of 1936 and again in March of the next year, Caldwell and Bourke-White traveled throughout the South, from South Carolina to Arkansas. Bourke-White was much impressed with Caldwell's ability to establish rapport with the people that she photographed. Describing the way in which he "became acquainted with some farmer and the farmer's problems," she wrote: "Erskine would be hanging over the back fence, and the farmer would be leaning on his rake, the two engaged in what I suppose could be called a conversation—that is, either Erskine or the farmer made one remark every fifteen minutes. Despite the frugal use of words, the process seemed productive of understanding on both sides."[45]

The photographer also came to appreciate the writer's insistence on authenticity. Before taking a picture of a black woman combing her hair, Bourke-White had rearranged the "little homemade things" on the top of the woman's makeshift chest of drawers. "After we left," Bourke-White recalled, "Erskine spoke to me about it. How neat her bureau had been. How she must have valued all her little possessions and how she had them tidily arranged *her* way, which was not my way. This was a new point of view to me." That photograph was discarded.[46]

Although she possessed great talent, Bourke-White, an outlander ignorant of the South, could not have taken so many striking photographs without the help of her collaborator, whose wide experience in the South enabled him to select telling subjects. In most instances, photographer and writer informed their subjects of their intentions. According to Bourke-White, she broke her self-imposed rule of not "stealing" pictures only once—when she and Caldwell slipped through an open window of a Holiness church so that she could snap shots of frenzied worshipers.[47]

In November 1937, Viking Press published *You Have Seen Their Faces.* The photographs were Bourke-White's; the text and the title were Caldwell's. The title confirms Caldwell's reason for engaging in the project.

The title implies that comfortable Americans, the kind of people who could afford to buy expensive picture books in the Great Depression, knew of the suffering on the land. What those affluent people needed was a goad that would spur them to support actions to alleviate the plight of the rural poor.[48]

The captions to the photographs, Caldwell said, were the product of collaboration. The language, however, suggests that he made the primary contribution. He admitted that the captions did not "pretend to reproduce the actual sentiments" of the people portrayed. By putting words into their subjects' mouths, he and Bourke-White were following the fashion of 1930s documentaries. If that technique impaired the volume's worth as documentary, it should be remembered that Caldwell considered himself to be the voice of poor, inarticulate southerners.[49]

Yet his sympathy for such people did not extend to what was, for some, the central aspect of their lives. The captions to the photographs "stolen" in a white Holiness church deny the worshipers any dignity. Under a picture of a woman dressed in her Sunday best with arms raised praising the Lord are these words: "Mildred has on a new pair of shoes today." Immediately following is a two-photo sequence in which another woman is dancing about the floor. The scene is described thus: "Mrs. Peterson is growing thinner." Perhaps the authors intended to avoid sentimentality and thereby render their subjects more fully human, but in these instances the humor offends.[50]

Occasionally, however, the captions employ humor to create an effect that is darkly comic and touching. A picture of a diminutive black girl, who appears to be of early school age, squatting in front of a hand-painted fish-bait sign with simple words misspelled bears the caption: "She's caught so many crickets she's got so now she sets like one." A young black person gazing forlornly through the bars of a jail cell says: "I've only been misbehaving." A white man sitting in front of a one-room shack with only three sides tells the reader, "I spent ten months catching planks drifting down the river to build this house, and then the flood came along and washed the side of it off. Doggone if I don't like it better the way it is now."[51]

Sometimes, photograph and caption come together to create an impression overwhelming in its poignancy. The representation of a white tenant couple, their faces hauntingly evocative of their suffering, bears the legend "A man learns not to expect much after he's farmed cotton most of his life." A black tenant standing in front of his shack that is surrounded by rows of cotton illustrates a pattern all too common in the South when he says: "No place to plant me a little garden when the white-boss says to plow the cotton in right up to my front door." A white woman, her steady gaze and erect bearing exuding dignity, her muscular arms and rough hands showing long acquaintance with hard work, says, as she rests from plowing, "We manage to get along." To a picture that highlights a little black girl with a reader in her lap in a roomful of school children sitting on benches without desks, the wood stove resting on a stack of books where a leg is missing, is appended the devastatingly pathetic caption "And so the fairy godmother in the storybook touched the little white girls with her wand and they were all turned into little princesses." A gray-haired white woman, her bronzed, leathery face corrugated with wrinkles, her haunting expression one of careworn resignation, says: "I've done the best I knew how all my life, but it didn't amount to much in the end." At their best, Caldwell and Bourke-White leave the reader with lasting impressions of the South's forgotten people—including the family upon whom the Lesters of *Tobacco Road* were based—the people Caldwell had been writing about for ten years. Now the camera testified to the truth of his portrait.[52]

Caldwell's text, divided into six sections interspersed among Bourke-White's seventy-five photographs, provides an overview of southern agriculture, describes conditions among black tenants in the fertile but plantation-ridden Arkansas delta, portrays the plight of white tenants in the barren ground of sandhills Georgia, chronicles the lifetime of a representative tenant farmer, scores demagogic politics and otherworldly religion for buttressing the status quo, and suggests ways whereby the lives of tenants might be improved. Throughout the narrative, it is clear that Caldwell writes out of love for the South, out of desire that it be made a better place, and out of hope that a decent life can be fashioned for the millions of rural poor who languish there. Several themes recur: hard work does not, of itself, bring success; year after year of failure destroys hope; racial mistrust diminishes the possibility of class action. Always, a thoroughgoing environmentalism informs his explanation of tenant conditions.[53]

Too often, however, Caldwell—as he had done in *Tenant Farmer* as well—extravagantly attributed the hellish environment that consumed tenants to the venality of landlords. Many of the South's landlords were hardly the prosperous and secure figures that he suggested. Even so, his contention that landowners as a class were the bulwark of a system that kept tenants impoverished was supported by the findings of social scientists. A 1934 study reported that 90 percent of eight hundred landlords that were surveyed opposed any change that would lessen tenant dependency. Nearly half disapproved of merely granting public relief to tenants "because of its demoralizing effect upon them." Although one is hard-pressed to find a decent landlord in Caldwell's writings—nonfiction and fiction—he realized that some fair-minded landlords existed. His proposal to initiate resolution of the tenant-farmer crisis included a role for the landlord.[54]

Near the end of *You Have Seen Their Faces,* Caldwell wrote that "there is an urgent need for a government commission . . . to make a study of tenant farming in the cotton country." Although several state and federal agencies and a presidential committee had conducted such studies by 1937, little had been done to improve tenant conditions. The commission that Caldwell envisioned would have "authoritative power" to act and would be "non-political in membership, and not subject to restrictions by individual senators and congressmen." It would consist of sociologists, economists, and agronomists familiar with the South, of "at least one sharecropper and one field hand," of a member of the Southern Tenant Farmers Union, and of a landlord. Unsure of "the final result of such a study," Caldwell was certain that the "first results . . . would be enough to show how little was previously known about the tenant farming system." In the words ascribed to a subject of one of Bourke-White's photographs, "there were plenty of people who couldn't get a living out of a farm long before the Government heard about it." Government planning, long overdue, was essential, Caldwell insisted, to liberate the South's economic slaves.[55]

In an eloquent, impassioned penult, Caldwell described elderly tenants, the kind of people who had often been portrayed in Bourke-White's photographs. "They are the wasted human beings whose blood made the cotton leaves green and the blossoms red. To the cost of raising cotton add the value of human lives." Hope lay in the young, as Caldwell made clear in the conclusion. By refusing to farm unless treated fairly, the young, still strong, still ambitious, could break the system that had broken their parents, could transform "a hell into a living paradise." In the great day when fear will have died and self-respect will have been gained, "America will wake up to find that it has a new region to take pride in."[56]

You Have Seen Their Faces was only one of many documentary books of the 1930s, most of which depicted the suffering of Americans trapped in hard times. Magazine editors and federal administrators sent writers and photographers to record throughout the country the catastrophe of the Great Depression. Caldwell and Bourke-White conducted their investigation on their own initiative, although their prospective publisher covered their expenses. Their book was among the first to portray the widespread destitution in the South. Unlike subsequent commentators, they ranged over a great part of the region, not confining their observations to a single area. Unlike later photo-documentaries of the 1930s South, *You Have Seen Their Faces* was not concerned to present the "health-giving elements in Southern rural life," as was, in part, Herman Clarence Nixon's *Forty Acres and Steel Mules.* Nor was it interested in philosophizing about "the true center of man's existence," as was James Agee and Walker Evans's *Let Us Now Praise Famous Men.* For Caldwell, the disinterestedness of Nixon and the introspection of Agee were puny responses to starvation.[57]

Caldwell's vision of a southern arcadia, so passionately articulated in *You Have Seen Their Faces,* was not to be realized. Hard times along with AAA policies, mechanization, and other factors reduced the number of tenant farmers by nearly four hundred thousand in the second half of the 1930s. Relatively few of the remaining tenants were able to benefit from the Farm Security Administration (FSA), a New Deal agency created in 1937 whose goals included providing low-interest, long-term loans to tenants so that they could buy their own farms. Over the course of its nine-year existence, the FSA, woefully underfunded for much of that period, supplied not quite thirty-one thousand loans for tenant purchases in the South among tenant farmers who, as of 1940, numbered nearly 1.5 million. Among those farmers displaced from tenancy, many were reduced to the status of day laborers. Others fled the land in search of opportunities elsewhere. Of those tenants that were left, many remained in grinding poverty. As late as 1950, in Caldwell's Georgia, black tenants averaged less than five hundred dollars in earnings, an annual income comparable to that of American industrial workers fifty years before.[58]

From Virginia to Louisiana, reviewers praised *You Have Seen Their Faces.* It was "a new kind of book . . . powerful and unsettling," a "new high" in Caldwell's career, "a strong book," "eloquent and vital," that presented "a fair picture." The author's "forceful and lucid style" made him "a powerful literary champion of ten million people." Coupled with Bourke-White's photographs, his "bold writing" called attention to the tenants' plight in a way that "statistics and the balance sheet" never could. His "persistent crusading" had done much to publicize the wretched condition of the South's rural poor, about which "something should be done, *must be done.*" [59]

Although some southerners lauded *You Have Seen Their Faces,* others damned it. Like the adverse criticism that had greeted Caldwell's fiction, hostile commentary on *You Have Seen Their Faces* seethed with self-righteous indignation. The book's most strident detractors were Georgians. "Why pick out the South," the *Atlanta Georgian* asked, "when you can find want and poverty rampant in the slums of big Northern, Eastern, and Western cities?" The book's "one-sided view" would create an impression among outsiders "that the South is a country of want and starvation." Caldwell was merely an exploiter who would "reap a profit . . . of poverty, misery and ignorance at the expense of the South." The source of the wretchedness of the rural poor, the *Atlanta Constitution* charged, was "the attitude of the sharecroppers and tenants, far too many of who [sic] do not care to improve their lot and will not cooperate." The effect of *You Have Seen Their Faces,* that paper predicted, would be "to cause another influx of Communists, labor agitators and theoretical sociologists." [60]

Also fearing "labor agitators," an editor in Alabama's black belt found particularly unsettling Caldwell's suggestion that tenant farmers unionize more extensively. Such action would "incite the farm hand against his all but bankrupt employer, force impossible wage and hour schedules, and play merry hell generally." If Caldwell wanted to engage in uplift, that editor opined, he should deal "in averages instead of seeking out the most pitiable and poverty-stricken families of a given community." [61]

You Have Seen Their Faces had the distinction of being damned not only by a Nashville conservative but also by a Chapel Hill liberal. Echoing his review of *Tenant Farmer,* W. T. Couch maintained that Caldwell's tenants were beyond help. Yet he also asserted that many of Bourke-White's photographs showed "people who seem to be healthy and happy in spite of poverty." Waxing defensive, Couch pointed out that economic misery was as entrenched in the urban North as in the rural South, although he did not offer that observation "as an excuse for Southern complacency." Couch was especially disturbed by Caldwell's stand on the race issue, one of many "aberrations" in *You Have Seen Their Faces*. "When Mr. Caldwell condemns the South for its 'refusal to assimilate the blood of an alien race of another color, or to tolerate its presence,' I cannot go along with him." The "intermingling of blood" would probably have dire consequences for the South. Moreover, Couch contended, "better relations exist between black and white in the Southern United States than between peoples of such widely different colors and heritages anywhere else in the civilized world." He doubted that any improvement could be made in "living conditions for the Negro" in the South "unless the advantages which he already enjoys are recognized." A "large indefinite sympathy" such as Caldwell's served little purpose because it had no "knowledge of conditions elsewhere" and therefore lacked "any definite idea of what improvement is."[62]

The issue of race illustrated two strikingly different sensibilities. Although Couch's suspicions were legitimate—Caldwell knew nothing about race relations in South Africa or in French West Africa, places that Couch had cited in his critique—Caldwell was right in a much more profound way. He identified injustice; he indicted it; he demanded that it be convicted.

The erudite Nashville conservative Donald Davidson had a great deal of fun reviewing what he perceptively yet derisively called "Erskine Caldwell's Picture Book." Correcting Caldwell's grammar here and there and using Latin phrases to demean his fiction, Davidson also replaced some of Caldwell and Bourke-White's captions with his own. In doing so, he sometimes mocked the seriousness of the subject. To a two-photo sequence that depicted a dispossessed family—husband, pregnant wife, and four children—who had walked across Georgia towing their meager belongings in a wagon, looking for work and shelter, Caldwell and Bourke-White appended this caption: "Those poor people walking all the way from Florida looking for a job, and hungry every step. It's a shame they have to walk so far, but they've got to go somewhere—they can't stay here." Davidson's rendition was "Poor Folks Near Ringgold, Georgia, Pulling Wagon." Caldwell's favorite picture, that of an aged couple with their grandson—the man blind, the woman hideously disfigured by a goiter, the little boy half-naked—that he and Bourke-White had captioned "Poor People Get Passed By," Davidson called "Old Woman with a Goiter." The representation of a haggard, grimacing woman, her mouth stained with snuff, holding her small child, which Caldwell and Bourke-White had captioned "Snuff is an almighty help when your teeth ache," became, in Davidson's version, "Snuffdipper and Infant." What Caldwell believed was the stuff of tragedy or pathos, Davidson considered banal.[63]

Not content to mock Caldwell's intentions, Davidson accused him of committing "gross . . . errors of fact," a charge that was grossly misleading. Citing census figures for 1935 that showed that only 716,356 sharecroppers resided in the South, Davidson denied Caldwell's claim that "*Ten million persons* [live] under the 'yoke' of the share-cropping system." As Davidson objected defensively to Caldwell's use of the word "yoke," he failed to note that Caldwell had specified that those ten million persons included not only sharecroppers but also other kinds of tenants and their families. Caldwell's number was much closer to reality than Davidson's. The census figures that the Agrarian cited showed that there were nearly two million tenant farmers in the South. Moreover, a careful study by a southern sociologist published in 1936 found that the average tenant household, excluding the head, contained seven people. Caldwell had read Arthur Raper's *Preface to Peasantry*. Moreover, he would assign it to students enrolled in a course that he taught early in 1938 at New York's New School for Social Research.[64] What is more important, he knew by experience what he did not have to read in books. Throughout the South, he had seen tenant houses bulging with occupants. And he had seen those people's faces.

Couch had properly scored Caldwell for failing to take sufficient account of the work southern social scientists had done on the problem of rural poverty. Davidson rightly criticized him for failing to emphasize the complexity of that problem. Davidson's fundamental objection to Caldwell's text, however, concerned the attribution of blame for the South's condition. Although Caldwell admitted that the South had been treated like "a country cousin," sitting at "second table" and being fed "short rations," he located the source of the region's poverty in class inequities within the South. To Davidson, the South's misery derived from sectional inequities within the nation. So, in his mind, *You Have Seen Their Faces* was "punily, sickeningly incomplete" because not only was the South the home of tenant farmers, it was also the abode of "tenant-bankers, tenant-merchants, tenant-manufacturers, tenant-teachers, [and] tenant-clergy." In the imperial North lay the provenance of the suffering of the colonial

South. Davidson found abhorrent Caldwell's insistence that the southern establishment bore primary responsibility for the suffering of the region's destitute.[65]

Caldwell's censure of the South paled beside Davidson's censure of Caldwell, who would, Davidson wrote, "make a splendid Curator of a Soviet Park of Recreation and Culture." Mean-spirited and occasionally misleading and inaccurate, Davidson's review concluded that the erstwhile Georgian was a traitor to the South. Moreover, like Couch, Davidson believed that Caldwell was much more interested in lining his pockets than in improving conditions in the South.[66]

Davidson's observation that *You Have Seen Their Faces* was addressed to an audience outside the South was equally applicable to the rest of Caldwell's nonfiction. Convinced that southern "haves" would not initiate change and that southern "have-nots" could not do so, Caldwell sought to focus national attention on conditions in his native region. Like his fictional portrayals of the South, the nonfiction pulls no punches. That Caldwell was not a dispassionate investigator but a propagandist does not detract from the worth of his accounts. The name recognition that the play *Tobacco Road* had provided insured a wide audience for his work. No other champion of the South's rural poor was as well known, and few were as impassioned, as Caldwell. If, as Davidson charged, he was telling " a very old story," it was still a story that could not be told too often.[67]

CHAPTER FIVE

Changing South, Unchanging Writer: Caldwell in Decline— and in Resurgence

In the course of a relationship that lasted for six years, three as illicit lovers and three as husband and wife, Caldwell and Bourke-White collaborated to produce four books, two of which dealt with people in the United States. Late in 1940, they set out on a cross-country journey that resulted in a book much different from *You Have Seen Their Faces. Say, Is This the U.S.A.* is a hodge-podge that lacks the unity of the earlier collaboration. Appearing when Americans were passionately engaged in debate over their country's response to war in Europe, the later book is by and large a celebration of America.[1]

From St. Johnsbury, Vermont, to San Diego, California, writer and photographer attempted to capture the strength and diversity of a great nation. Yet when they reached the South, whose treatment occupies one-fifth of the volume's contents, Caldwell's focus was racial injustice. In Soso, Mississippi, a black school principal complained about inequities in salaries paid to black teachers and to white ones. On the occasions that he mentioned the matter to whites, some suggested that "if half the Negro children dropped out of school, we would need only half as many teachers, and then the ones that were left could get twice as much salary." In Jacksonville, Florida, a young black coffin-maker lived underground because of his fear of white people. Daylight reminded him that "back up in Georgia they put me on the chain gang for three years because I owed a white man eleven dollars." In Saluda, South Carolina, two forlorn young black men sat in jail, the charges against them not specified, while "quite a few peeping-toms . . . and a lot more beer-drinkers driving cars" remained at large. Caldwell knew why: "it is much more trouble to bring in white boys." [2]

Following the trip that produced *Say, Is This the U.S.A.*, Caldwell traveled in February 1941 to the mid-South on assignment for *McCall's* magazine to report on farm conditions. After interviewing an influential planter in southeastern Missouri who was active in trying to improve tenant conditions, an official of the Farm Security Administration (FSA) in Little Rock, Arkansas, and impoverished tenants in the lower Mississippi Valley, Caldwell concluded that the South contained "more landless people than ever before." Their situation, he wrote, "is as critical as this nation has ever seen." Tenants not yet dispossessed suffered from malnutrition—their diets lacking milk, meat, and green vegetables—and lived in shacks that "look like pig pens." The destitute and the dispossessed, many of whom wanted to remain on the land because "farming is in their blood," were the victims of agricultural mechanization and of misguided federal policy that valued staple crops over food products. Land of their own, crop diversification, and scientific cultivation would enable those still farming to continue to practice their craft. Although the FSA was doing as much as it could to help the landless, its resources, Caldwell suggested, were inadequate. He realized, too, that the abandonment of staple-crop agriculture was a difficult task; tenants planted on orders from landlords, who grew the cash crops that satisfied creditors. Implicit in his essay was the suggestion that the government find a better way to provide land "and marketing facilities" to those threatened with dispossession. Already, he asserted, the farm problem had become "a national emergency," not just a regional one. If war came, how could the United States "have an all-out national effort" when millions of its people were malnourished? [3]

A week after his trip to the lower Mississippi Valley to gather material for the *McCall's* article, "Flight from the Land," Caldwell was in Birmingham, Alabama, to participate in a radio program. "Town Meeting of the Air," a weekly production of the National Broadcasting Company devoted to the study of current events and pledged to the promotion of "unity through understanding," dealt in its Birmingham segment with the topic, "Are We a United People?" The purpose of that program was to examine southern backwardness as a source of national disunity and to assay the reasons for the South's deficiencies. [4]

In addition to Caldwell, the participants were John Temple Graves II of the *Birmingham Age-Herald* and Mark Ethridge of the *Louisville Courier-Journal*. Speaking first, Ethridge, whom Caldwell had met as an adolescent when the journalist worked for the *Macon Telegraph*, focused on the colonial nature of the South's economy. He maintained that unfair trade practices—in particular, discriminatory freight rates imposed by northeastern industry and sanctioned by the federal government—did much to insure that the South remained a dependency of the imperial North.[5]

Caldwell followed Ethridge at the microphone. Ever a poor public speaker, Caldwell, his six-foot frame hunched over a table that was too low, read rapidly from his script, never looking up. Ever concerned with the plight of the southern poor, he placed the blame for the region's problems elsewhere than had Ethridge, "No longer," he said, could southerners "shift the blame for our shortcomings to the shoulders of the North." For seventy-five years the South had failed to deal adequately with its problems. Southerners must elect to office leaders who would express "the will of the people." The passage in 1938 of the Fair Labor Standards Act, a federal wages-and-hours law that had been opposed by many of the region's industrialists engaged in "the exploitation of Southern labor," showed that the people's wishes could receive political expression. Even so, two great obstacles to regional prosperity remained: one-crop agriculture and racism. Afraid that the agrarian way of life was dying, he called for crop diversification to insure its existence because in the future of "agricultural America . . . lies our survival as a democratic state or our decline as a people." Proclaiming himself "a Georgia-born Southerner," Caldwell, on stage in the heart of Dixie before an audience of more than a thousand people, forthrightly denounced the region's treatment of blacks. "The Negro for too long has been a slave. . . . America cannot afford to have a portion of its people enslaved socially and economically. In the South today there are Negroes who are being denied adequate education. There are some in agriculture bound to child labor. Some are subjected to substandards of living." Southerners, he concluded, should cease following the lead of politicians and newspaper editors who promoted sectional acrimony and instead come to grips with the region's internal problems.[6]

Speaking last, Graves, an accomplished lecturer, was charged with responding to Ethridge and Caldwell. Stating that the South suffered from "comparative poverty, the worst poverty to be found this side of the slums

of New York City," he repudiated the "would-be saviors who think all
our Southern roads are named 'Tobacco.'" Uneasy over Caldwell's focus
on the race issue, "the most difficult and delicate . . . problem with which
any people anywhere ever had to deal," Graves contended that only well-
intentioned white southerners should be trusted to handle the matter. The
ideas of both men, he averred, impeded the quest for the national unity
needed to face Adolf Hitler. To call for domestic reform in the "present
international situation" was unwise. Instead, there should be "a morato-
rium on every crusade, on every political, class, group, regional, or economic ambition in this country."[7]

Such a suggestion, Caldwell responded, was "absolutely wrong 100
percent." In the United States, he continued, "we have something we
should work on before we tackle something outside of America." For
whatever reasons, Graves's remarks were "the most roundly applauded";
Caldwell's, the most loudly rejected.[8]

If Caldwell was unpopular with the students, professors, and relatively
affluent urbanites who composed the audience at Birmingham-Southern
College, such people likewise ranked low among his interests. For more
than ten years, he had been writing about forgotten people in out-of-the-
way places. Throughout the 1940s, he would encourage other writers to
do so as well.

Building upon his interest in the lives of the folk throughout the United
States shown in *Some American People*, Caldwell, by the late 1930s, had
conceived the idea of a series of books that would examine American
folkways. The volumes would be broader in scope than were those of the
Rivers of America series and would deal more with the people themselves
than did the American Guide series of the Federal Writers Project. Caldwell envisioned American Folkways as a major endeavor, perhaps twelve
or fourteen books. His publisher, Viking Press, refused to undertake such
a sweeping project that might lose money. Along with other issues, that
refusal led Caldwell to make the fateful decision to seek another publisher. Duell, Sloan and Pearce, a new house eager to have an author as
established as Caldwell on its list, agreed to publish American Folkways.[9]

So insured, Caldwell, late in 1939, left New York on a cross-country
trip to enlist authors for the series. Bourke-White, his wife of nine
months, could not accompany him because she was on assignment in war-
torn Europe for *Life,* whose staff she had joined at the magazine's incep-
tion late in 1936. "I have been on the move for the past eighteen days,"

Caldwell wrote to friends, "and yet I'm only 3/4 across the country. My car shows that I've traveled 4,000 miles . . . and it'll undoubtedly show 10,000 by the time I get back." On the trip, which covered fifteen thousand miles, he caught chicken pox, which gave him, he wrote his parents, "a good excuse to rest for a week." [10]

By the end of the year, five writers had consented to contribute to American Folkways. Caldwell, however, had not found a writer to cover Tobacco Road country—and he never would. That he should write the volume on the sandhills South does not seem to have entered his thinking. In the spring of 1941, the first two books in the series appeared, both of which dealt with the Southwest. [11]

Throughout the forties, Caldwell devoted considerable time to American Folkways, which he described as having "no kinship whatsoever to the school of glorified road maps and quaint lore." Instead, the series intended to examine "the habits of thought and behavior of Americans from the point of view of the very men and women who propagated the national culture." That culture was the product of the rich diversity of American regions, whose molding influences showed "like a shining badge" on their inhabitants. Under Caldwell's editorship, which lasted for fifteen years, the series covered more than twenty cultural regions that spanned the length and breadth of the country. [12]

Of the twenty-five volumes published while Caldwell was editor, six dealt with southern regions from Kentucky to Florida. Some of the southern authors were established figures: Hodding Carter, Mississippi journalist; Harnett T. Kane, New Orleans writer; and Herman Clarence Nixon, political scientist, social historian, and whilom Nashville Agrarian. The others were relatively unknown: Jean Thomas, the "traipsin' woman" of the Kentucky mountains; Otto Ernest Rayburn, a close student of Ozark culture; and Stetson Kennedy, a young Floridian. [13]

Some idea of Caldwell's role as editor can be gained from his extensive correspondence with Kennedy from the summer of 1940 to the summer of 1942. Kennedy, who had served as chairman of a committee on folk arts of the New Deal's Florida Writers Project, had first commanded Caldwell's notice when Caldwell helped to judge a contest in documentary writing. The editor was happy to learn that the author he desired was interested in writing the proposed volume. Caldwell believed that Kennedy understood his wish "to throw the word 'folklore' out the window, for our purposes, and to create the usage of the term 'folkways,'" which meant "the study of contemporary life in terms of its social and economic implications." With such understanding established, Caldwell asked only that Kennedy supply "a readable, interesting history." Anything else, he wrote, "is up to you. There is no working plan to impose upon an author. The author creates his own method out of his own material." [14]

Caldwell insisted, however, that the volume, as had others in the series, cover a cultural region, not a political division. Kennedy should expand his subject to include not only Florida but also the southern parts of Georgia and Alabama. Caldwell insisted, too, that the title not mislead the book's readers. Kennedy wanted the title to be "Cracker Country." Caldwell objected: " 'cracker,' " he reminded Kennedy, "is associated universally with the state of Georgia, and there is no way in the world of getting away from that fact." He much preferred another title, "Palmetto Country," because he considered it more descriptive and less confusing. He did not realize that readers unmindful of the difference between cultural region and political division would expect the book to be about South Carolina, the "Palmetto State." After reading some of Kennedy's chapters in draft, Caldwell cautioned him against quoting excessively. The volumes in the series, he reminded the young writer, were supposed to reflect "the individuality of the authors." [15]

After six months' work, Kennedy was convinced that the instructions to authors needed to be more specific. Therefore, he drew up a prospectus that was much more detailed than the one the editor had composed at the outset of the series. Admitting that the idea of such guidelines had never occurred to him "in quite so absolute a form," Caldwell embraced Kennedy's proposal, secured the publisher's endorsement, and supplied the instructions to other writers in the series. The new prospectus gave a greater sense of direction to the authors, and at the same time it reiterated Caldwell's concern that each "give his book a maximum of individuality, a distinctive flavor typical of his region's folkways." [16]

As Kennedy pushed ahead with his manuscript, he sought Caldwell's advice regarding subjects to be treated. The editor suggested that the author consider covering Florida's tourists—the rich ones in Palm Beach and the poorer ones in trailer camps throughout the state. "By all means include lynching," Caldwell wrote. "The institution of the chain-gang should not be overlooked either." Although Kennedy's book failed to mention the wealthy of Palm Beach and the trailer-camp tourists and in-

cluded only a few references to lynching—omitting the notorious Claude
Neal case of 1934—it contained a chapter on penal conditions. "Waitin
on Time" was a strong indictment of chain-gang abuses and of racism in
the administration of justice.[17]

The editor was especially impressed with the chapter entitled "Jook
Tour." Wild and woolly roadhouses, jook joints, Kennedy wrote, were as
"Southern as jazz, fried chicken, corn bread, channel cats, chewing tobacco, and lynching." Popular among poor, working people who led hard
lives, the jooks were "rank weeds springing from a corroded culture."
Filled with anecdotal humor, "Jook Tour" nonetheless revealed Kennedy's anger over conditions that produced places where young women
could be brained with beer bottles.[18]

Caldwell liked "Jook Tour" so much that he suggested Kennedy
double its length. He also particularly admired another chapter, "Red
Lights Glowing." But he advised Kennedy that his description of prostitution "might be troublesome." If the chapter, wherein Kennedy cited specific instances of prostitution in his hometown of Jacksonville, was "to
beat the censor's heavy pencil," then the discussion of the subject must
have "a more folkway treatment." Caldwell advised the author to "bring
out the human elements in . . . [prostitution] by showing what position it
assumes in everyday life in the region." Moreover, Caldwell suggested,
"try to make [the chapter] . . . parlor reading for the housewives of Des
Moines."[19]

Kennedy incorporated Caldwell's suggestions. Without diminishing
the force of his indictment, he expanded his description of prostitution to
include other parts of palmetto country beyond Jacksonville. He also
sought to portray "the human elements." Prostitutes "are made, not
born," he pointed out, and poverty, more than anything else, was what
made them. Whether the chapter was palatable to the housewives of Des
Moines, or, what is more to the point, to the housewives of palmetto
country, can only be conjectured. Even as published, it must have been
strong meat for many readers. Because black brothels charged lower rates
than white ones, they enjoyed, Kennedy wrote, "a considerable amount
of white trade." Moreover, he reported the comments of a Jacksonville
taxi driver who had taken "white prostitutes (personally known to him)
to the homes of well-to-do Negro men."[20]

As Kennedy neared completion of his manuscript, Caldwell offered
suggestions on the placement of chapters and on the extent to which the

history of the region should be covered. Believing that "historical matter
. . . is . . . ordinarily . . . rather dull," Caldwell advised Kennedy to com-
press that material "as much as possible without losing the important
facts necessary to understand 'Palmetto Country.'" Only one-fifth of the
volume's 340 pages comprises historical narrative, and much of that is
based on folk sources. Most of the history deals with slavery and with
Reconstruction, and it examines those subjects from a perspective sympathetic to blacks.[21]

Meeting the publisher's deadline, Kennedy completed his manuscript
by mid-May 1942. An enthusiastic Caldwell wrote him a few days later.
He had done "a fine job. *Palmetto Country* is a book to be proud of." It
would be "an outstanding addition to American Folkways." When *Palmetto Country* came out late in the fall, the author of a syndicated book-
review column agreed. Kennedy's volume, John Selby wrote, "is the best
of the 'country' books so far." So impressive was the author's command
of his material that Selby accorded the book even higher praise. *Palmetto
Country,* he contended, "ranks in usefulness with the Federal Guides, still
the most valuable contribution to American life of any recent books."[22]

Many of the volumes in American Folkways failed to approach Kennedy's achievement. Years later, Caldwell opined that only half of the books
should have been published, that there had been too many too fast. The
twenty-five that he edited doubled the number that he had initially envisioned. Moreover, even though he had traveled through much of America,
what he knew best was the South. He lacked the experience to make informed judgments on works dealing with other regions, although some
of those books were well received by reviewers.[23]

Even so, for much of his fifteen-year tenure, Caldwell was an indefati-
gable editor with a boundless enthusiasm for the project. His interest was
so great that, shortly after embarking on a photojournalistic trip to the
Soviet Union with Bourke-White, he wrote to his secretary to remind her
to correspond occasionally with the Folkways authors "so that you will
be familiar with the situation regarding each individual writer." He also
asked his secretary to send copies of reviews of the first volume, scheduled
to appear soon. From Moscow, in mid-June 1941, as he, his wife Margaret, and millions of Russians worriedly awaited an imminent German in-
vasion, he wrote to Kennedy regarding his suggestions for a more thor-
ough prospectus for the series.[24]

Kennedy appreciated Caldwell's work. Shortly before Doubleday published his *Southern Exposure* late in 1946, he wrote to his former editor, "Had it not been for your kind invitation to write 'Palmetto Country,' I would probably still be struggling with the little magazines. Your editorial guidance on that job has also stood me in good stead on this one." Another contributor wrote to the publisher to express his appreciation of the editor's efforts. "Caldwell is a wonderful editor to work for," said George Milburn. "I haven't had anyone spur me on to my best effort in the way he does since H. L. Mencken was editing the *American Mercury*." Perhaps the highest praise came from the American Folklore Society, which, early in 1945, invited Caldwell to become a member.[25]

The commendations of folklorists and of the series' authors were balanced by the ongoing coolness of the publisher toward the project. Throughout the life of the series, Duell, Sloan and Pearce complained of the costs involved, even though Caldwell was paid very little for his editing responsibilities and the series during the 1940s earned a profit. In 1954, still convinced that some of the volumes had made important contributions to the understanding of American character but tired of wrangling with the publisher, he resigned the editorship.[26]

By Caldwell's account, his motive for initiating American Folkways was "to promote the regionalism of the country. I've always been a regional writer, and I think the best writing is regional." In the early 1940s, however, he was not able to devote much time to writing about the South. During his extended trip to the Soviet Union in 1941 with Bourke-White, he placed himself in danger in order to witness fighting between German soldiers and Russian partisans, and he covered, again at great risk, the German aerial bombardment of Moscow for CBS radio. His experiences resulted in four books: one, a collaboration with Bourke-White; two others, accounts of the air raids and the partisan fighting, respectively; the last, a novel dealing with guerrilla warfare.[27]

Amid all his activities in Russia, which also included filing reports to the North American Newspaper Alliance, Caldwell made time—to the consternation of his wife—to work on a cycle of short stories set in the South that he had begun in 1937. After returning to the United States late in 1941, he continued to work on the story cycle during the next year, finishing the last story on his birthday.[28]

He completed the book amid domestic turmoil. The passion that he and Bourke-White shared was not enough to save their union. His stony silences, which indicated his disapproval of something that she had done, unnerved her. That they had not had a child saddened him. Dejected when she was away on assignment, he resented her long absences. She resented his resentment. Each was self-centered and each tried to dominate the other. Both were more committed to their work than to their marriage.[29]

In the spring of 1942, not long after their third anniversary and not long after they lost their unborn child, Bourke-White asked *Life* to give her another assignment to cover the war. After her departure for Europe in August, Caldwell left their home in Connecticut and journeyed west, eventually arriving in California, where he wrote a script about the war for Hollywood's moviemakers. By early autumn, he had settled in Tucson, Arizona. There, he soon met a pretty, twenty-year-old coed named June Johnson. Five days before Christmas, he secured a divorce from Bourke-White in Mexico. Never a man to be without a woman for very long, he married June the next day.[30]

The story cycle was published in the spring of 1943. Different from his previous fiction, although not as dissimilar as the publisher and many reviewers proclaimed, the fourteen stories in *Georgia Boy* chronicle the doings in sandhills Georgia of the Stroup family—father Morris, mother Martha, and son William—and their black yard boy, the orphaned Handsome Brown. The stories are a tour de force in terms of narrative, told from the viewpoint of twelve-year-old William, who reports matter-of-factly the antics of a ne'er-do-well father whom the boy nonetheless respects.[31]

Morris, who occupies center stage in most of the stories, lies, cheats, steals, runs after women, and abuses the yard boy. As in much of Caldwell's earlier fiction, the humor that is employed to describe Morris's escapades heightens the horror of his actions. What kind of man would bring another woman to his house with his wife present? What kind of man would enjoy loafing while his wife takes in laundry to support the family? What kind of man would take his son's quarter to attend a carnival girly-show? What kind of man would suggest a fishing trip with his son and then cavalierly cancel it to engage in a get-rich-quick scheme that involves theft? What kind of man would steal from an orphan who works for him without pay and would also humiliate the boy publicly?[32]

Handsome Brown, being black, can do little about the sorry treatment Morris affords. William, being twelve years old, only wants the company of a father who is gone much too often. Martha, being white and grown, wreaks a satisfying revenge on a poor excuse for a human being. In a story that was the third one written in the cycle but that, significantly, was placed last in *Georgia Boy*, Martha cooks Morris's prize gamecock for supper. After the family has eaten, she tells him that College Boy was the staple of the chicken pie. Her motive, to avenge her mortification over her husband's cock-fighting, does not diminish the audacity of her act. That William is as outraged as Morris by Martha's act highlights a major theme of *Georgia Boy:* a boy's love for his father. Although Morris provides most of the humor in the stories, the author's sympathies lie with a neglected boy, with a dependent young black man, and, most of all, with a strong, long-suffering woman. Martha, Caldwell wrote to his publisher, "bears the cultural load of her community as well as that of raising her family with the grace of any woman who has been supporting herself and [her] household by washing and ironing for as long as she can re-member."[33]

Contrary to the publisher's description, which Caldwell considered simplistic, the book is much more than "an invitation to laughter." The author attempts to undertake a serious examination of the plight of women and blacks. Yet the narrative point of view, although skillfully executed, prevents him from doing what he did best: constructing a story that was both artistically satisfying and socially significant. He was not able fully to employ the focus of narration to exhibit his anger over the treatment of outcasts. He could not make William Stroup a Huckleberry Finn. Moreover, he failed to provide an environmental explanation for the shiftlessness of the central character, Morris Stroup.[34]

It is difficult to ascertain the socioeconomic status of the Stroups. The reader can only assume that the reason they do not live on the farm they own is that Morris refuses to work it. In the town of Sycamore, where the family lives and where Morris has more opportunity to philander and to engage in scams, Martha is the provider. Whatever else they are, the Stroups are not poor-whites, although the publisher presented them as such and some reviewers, including southerners, perceived them as such, even comparing them to the Lesters of *Tobacco Road*. As Caldwell knew, poor-whites would not be landowners, as the Stroups are; a poor-white would not be a member of a social club, as Martha is; a poor-white would not receive a political appointment, as Morris does.[35]

Here and there across the South, reviewers expressed relief over the work of a new Caldwell. An "eminently satisfying story," *Georgia Boy* was, according to one wild misreading, "good, clean fun." Southerners, wrote a Georgian, "can rest easy, as Mr. Caldwell has decided to quit advertising the unfortunate conditions of 'Tobacco Road.'" The following year, Caldwell would prove that reviewer dead wrong.[36]

Tragic Ground, a novel often compared to *Tobacco Road*, reaffirmed Caldwell's everlasting concern for the southern poor. A far cry, however, from *Tobacco Road* in locale and in execution, *Tragic Ground* signaled a serious decline in his art. Morris Stroup is no Jeeter Lester, and neither is Spence Douthit, the protagonist of *Tragic Ground*. A year's unemployment, the result of the shutdown of a war plant in an unnamed Gulf Coast city, fails to explain Spence's shiftlessness. Although he is not mean, only twice do his actions evoke the reader's sympathy. When he hears the story of his teenage daughter's friend, who has become a prostitute since her widowed mother abandoned her, he "brushed the back of his hand over his eyes." Later, after he learns that his thirteen-year-old daughter, who has also turned to prostitution, has been sent to reform school for five years, he "brushed away tears that had begun to blind him." His sympathy for an abandoned girl and his belated concern for his daughter's welfare are hardly sufficient to balance his otherwise reprehensible behavior.[37]

Spence peppers his talk, especially in conversations with women, with expressions that would have made Jeeter blush—"dogbite my pecker" and "I was feeling like a rabbit with his balls caught in a sewing machine"—and relishes the prospect of living on welfare. Jeeter, facing greater obstacles, always hoped to plant a crop. If Caldwell intended to show that merely moving from the country to the city could make a Spence of a Jeeter, he failed. Historical forces go far toward explaining Jeeter's plight; there is no such explanation of Spence's condition. Although shiftless in the country, Spence, upon moving to the city, falls too far too fast to be credible. If Caldwell did not believe that the Jeeter Lesters of the South were beyond redemption, he suggests that the Spence Douthits are incorrigible. At the novel's conclusion, after social workers have arranged to take the family back to its home in the country, Spence confides to his wife, Maud, that he intends to return to the urban slum of Poor Boy. "You just can't keep digging a man up by the roots and setting him down in different parts of the country and expect him to be satisfied for the rest of his life." Three years of experiencing the city's attractions—dives, gambling dens, and whorehouses—have had an irreversible impact on a weak man like Spence.[38]

The characterization of Spence demonstrates Caldwell's belief in individual accountability. After listening to Spence deny any responsibility for his condition, Jim Howard Vance, a wounded soldier and the author's spokesman, who is sympathetic to the plight of his prospective father-in-law, tells him flatly: "You can get out" of Poor Boy. Spence believes, however, that fate has determined his condition and that to struggle is pointless. He is resigned "to living out the remainder of his years . . . on bounty or luck."[39]

Floyd Sharp, Spence's neighbor who had also worked at the defunct war plant, is not so resigned. Unlike Spence, who does not mind being supported by his hardworking twenty-year-old daughter, Floyd attempts to be self-reliant. Desperately trying to provide for his wife and their eight young daughters and to maintain his dignity, the forty-five-year-old Floyd operates a small store in Poor Boy because he cannot find a job elsewhere. Earning barely enough to keep his family from starving and far from enough to enable them to return to the country, he nonetheless resists the temptation to sell marijuana, although other men in the shantytown do. Agonizingly, he watches his oldest daughter, who is only twelve, turn to the streets. When he discovers her having sex with a pimp—who, begging for his life, claims that she, hoping to earn fifty cents, was the instigator—he kills him. "I ain't sorry," he tells Spence. "I'd do it all over again if I had to. . . . I've done my duty." Later, after he decides not to burn Poor Boy to the ground because, with all of its vice and squalor, it provides the only shelter its poverty-ridden inhabitants have, Floyd plans to confess his crime to the authorities. He reasons that confessing will enable him to expose the desperation that Poor Boy breeds. Moreover, to confess will furnish a way to provide for his children. The authorities, he tells Spence, will "send me away for a while, but they'll put my girls in a home and take care of them." When Jim Howard, the most perceptive of the characters, learns that Floyd has confessed, he predicts that the court will probably "send him to the chair."[40]

Although Caldwell agreed with Spence's conclusion that the murder Floyd committed was a "futile rebellion against his poverty," he rejected Spence's contention that poverty was inevitable. His position was the same as Jim Howard's. As the novel ends, an exasperated social worker says to some Poor Boy residents, "You'd wither the soul of a saint!" Jim Howard passionately responds: "I don't think that's being fair. . . . It's not our fault that everything got into a mess down here. Back home people like us are just as good as people anywhere else in the world. If you want to do the right thing, you ought to put all the blame on Poor Boy, because it's Poor Boy that causes all the trouble. The finest folks in the world would get mean and bad if they had to live in a place like this." If Caldwell found it difficult to believe that Poor Boy should bear all the blame for Spence's behavior, he contended forcefully that environment dictates Floyd's actions. Some of the poor might be irretrievably lost, he argues, but others could be saved.[41]

For a number of reasons, *Tragic Ground* is a disappointing novel. The situation upon which the story depends is implausible. In 1943, when factories across the South were running around the clock, seven days a week, and when workers were toiling double shifts, the plant near Poor Boy shuts down. Had Caldwell made the novel a story about black southerners, he could have expressed more credibly his concern for people who had been left out of the wartime boom. For countless thousands of white southerners the war brought rolls of folding money that they could not have envisioned earlier.[42]

Tragic Ground suffers also because of its setting. The agrarian Caldwell was out of his element in the city. Yet he had no choice but to move his fiction to town if he was to continue to infuse it with social commentary as demographic change swept over the South. The flush times of the Second World War lured to the factories many of the poor white southerners who had not already been forced off the land by hard times or by New Deal policies.[43]

Although the novel's title indicates Caldwell's seriousness of purpose, *Tragic Ground* lacks the power of *Tobacco Road* and *God's Little Acre*. In the earlier novels, his use of humor and his treatment of sex heightened the impact of his social message. In *Tragic Ground*, where there is little humor and much sex, they diminish that message. Unlike *Tobacco Road* and *God's Little Acre*, *Tragic Ground* fails to lodge in the reader's memory.

Among southern reviewers, opinion was divided over the matter of Caldwell's intent in the novel. To the *Charlotte News*, he was not "bitterly angry that such deplorable conditions exist" but instead had told "his lurid tale with all the energy and enthusiasm of a small child attacking a dish of ice cream." The *Louisville Courier-Journal*, however, after praising Caldwell for avoiding "the naive sentimentality of many social writers," concluded: "If the novelist can contribute in part to the great task of social betterment, one must rank among the most sincere and powerful advocates of true democracy the name of Erskine Caldwell." Although the bulk of his work confirmed that contention, the case of *Tragic Ground* is problematic. Jonathan Daniels perceived the ambiguity. "It is doubtful," he wrote in the *Saturday Review of Literature*, "whether 'Tragic Ground' will stir thoughtful readers as much as it pleases those who love a loud and bawdy tale."[44]

Criticism such as Daniels's perplexed Caldwell. "Sure," he wrote to a friend, the book "is dirty in the sense that people are dirty—but to me there is no such thing. People are what they are, and if you write about what they are, you are a fraud if you try to make them appear different. . . . They grunt and they groan in an effort to win an existence, and it is not always pleasant to watch or to hear about. . . . [The novel] is not dirt for dirt's sake any more than it is art for art's sake. I am merely trying, in this work and in others, to reveal life." Yet the life revealed in *Tragic Ground* is incredible and clumsily portrayed, as Caldwell himself suspected. "I don't know," he confided to the same friend, "if the novel is any good or not. . . . I know it could be a lot better." He was right; it could have been a lot better.[45]

Having returned to the novel with *Tragic Ground*, Caldwell would devote almost all of his writing to that form for the remainder of the 1940s. In the novels of the late forties, he was attempting to complete what he described as "a cyclorama of Southern life." Although he acknowledged that he had "had no such plan in mind in the beginning," by the end of the 1930s he professed to have discovered an organic pattern in his novels. Near the end of the 1940s, he wrote to a sympathetic critic that "eight or ten volumes" would be required to depict "the most important phases of community life . . . of a particular region in the South." By that time, he had completed eight of the novels. Within the next two years, he would finish the cycle by writing two more.[46]

From *Tobacco Road* to *Tragic Ground*, the first five novels of the cyclorama had appeared over the course of twelve years. The other five were published in a span of only five years. The decline of art so noticeable in *Tragic Ground* is equally apparent in most of the novels of the late 1940s. If writing about urban life was not Caldwell's forte, neither was portraying the upper class, as he attempted to do in *A House in the Uplands*, the first of the postwar novels. Featuring the dissolute, sadistic Grady Dunbar, a representative of fallen gentry, *A House in the Uplands* is more a domestic tragedy than social commentary. The master of a run-down plantation whose two hundred acres are a mere shred of its original two thousand, Grady beats his wife, refuses to make love to her, cheats with black women, drinks excessively, gambles obsessively, believes that working is beneath one of his station, and keeps his tenants, white and black, in a state of peonage. Like his forebears, he dies violently, killed in a shoot-out with the owner of a dive to whom he owed twenty-five hundred dollars in gambling debts.[47]

Unlike the portrayal of Spence Douthit, the depiction of Grady Dunbar takes pains to account for the sources of his behavior. Unaccustomed to having "to count the cost of anything," Grady's ancestors lived profligately. He expects to do so as well, even though the sterile remnant of the Dunbar plantation cannot sustain his extravagance. His arrogance and willfulness, the products of generations of such behavior, are reinforced by an indulgent mother who tells her daughter-in-law that "Grady is entitled to certain privileges." Unknown to his mother, those privileges include the run of the quarters, where Grady, like his father and grandfather before, finds sexual gratification. It was Grady's father who introduced him to what the Dunbar men believe are the superior allurements of black women.[48]

Caldwell's attempt to invest Grady's actions with an environmental explanation fails. The obstacles Grady faces are slight when compared to those confronting a character like Jeeter Lester, and the reader cannot view him sympathetically. Although Caldwell had returned to a rural setting, he peopled it with characters that could not adequately engage his imagination.

Just as the urban setting of *Tragic Ground* and the aristocratic protagonist of *A House in the Uplands* added new dimensions to Caldwell's southern fiction, so did *The Sure Hand of God*. In that 1947 novel, for the first time in an extended work, the author fashioned a woman protagonist. The recently widowed Molly Bowser—thirty-four, fat, and losing her looks—cannot find a man to provide for her and her sixteen-year-old illegitimate daughter Lily. Therefore, she tries to insure that Lily marries well. She fails, and as the story ends, having been evicted from a middle-class neighborhood, she takes up residence in the red-light district of the Georgia town in which she lives.[49]

Hardly Caldwell at his best, *The Sure Hand of God* is nonetheless a strong novel because of the deft characterization of the protagonist.

Molly—significantly, she is not given a surname until she marries at age thirty-two—knows full well that she must be agreeable to men if she is to have any chance of fashioning a decent life for herself and Lily. Her past has been hideous. She was the daughter of a tenant farmer; an orphan at twelve; the sexual object of the men in the family of the landlord who took her in and forced her to work sixteen-hour days; a mother at eighteen, unsure which of the three men in the landlord's household fathered her child; a kept woman at twenty-five. Because of her manifold misfortunes, Molly never loses sight of her goal: to prevent a similar fate befalling Lily. Yet Molly's experiences have made her a wine-bibbing, dope-shooting hedonist whose reputation, made even more unsavory by sanctimonious churchgoers, renders unattainable her desire to fashion a better life for her daughter. The comic dimension of her character makes her, like her country cousin Jeeter Lester, more fully human, and the black humor of the story makes bearable its tragedy.[50]

Not since *Tobacco Road* had Caldwell provided a stronger environmental explanation of a character's behavior. As though to emphasize the early authorial exposition of Molly's actions, later he uses a character to explain them. The worldly-wise banker, Frank Stevens, who succeeds in dissuading his nephew Claude from marrying Lily, acknowledges that Molly "could become a respectable woman in different surroundings." But, he asks Claude, "who's going to take the trouble" to rehabilitate her? "The time to have done that was twenty years ago." Just as the narrative voice and a character's observations underscore Caldwell's intent, so, too, does the irony of the novel's title. It is not "the sure hand of God" that bruises Molly but the hostility of callous human beings.[51]

Like *God's Little Acre,* the novel that followed *The Sure Hand of God* focused upon the disintegration of a family. Unlike *God's Little Acre,* however, *This Very Earth* has an urban setting. Moving from country to town has a disastrous effect on the Crockett family. The eighty-five-year-old grandfather, born and bred on the land, tries to supply the steadying influence that his recently deceased daughter-in-law provided. His efforts to keep the family together are to no avail. He dies trying to defend a granddaughter who is the victim of a deadly assault by her husband. Another granddaughter becomes the kept woman of a congressman. Yet another leaves town to avoid the attentions of a married man. His eleven-year-old grandson, introduced to booze and black girls by his father, is sent to live with an older brother, a reputable lawyer who was raised in the country. At story's end, grandpa's son Chism, who has left the family-owned farm because he does not want to sweat "like a cussed farmer," is alone except for his hunting dogs. The very earth that the Crocketts abandoned might have sustained them as a family.[52]

Notwithstanding the implications of its title, *This Very Earth* is narrowly domestic rather than broadly social in focus. Therein lies its fundamental weakness. Despite Caldwell's concern for the plight of women, he was not able to portray Chism's grown daughters as believable characters. Molly Bowser's search for a husband is born of economic necessity. Vickie Crockett's infatuation with a sleazy politician and her sister Dorisse's thralldom to a brutish husband are insufficiently motivated, and their emotional dependency rings false. The novel suffers also from Caldwell's inability to render credibly the dialogue of romantic love, from a structure that is overly episodic, and from humor that, although appropriately rare, is flat and forced.

The pervasive poverty of the 1930s that had called forth much of Caldwell's strongest writing had abated, among white southerners at least, after the Second World War. Yet racism, the other great social evil that had evoked his best work, continued to exhibit much vitality. Because *Place Called Estherville,* the next novel in the cyclorama, denounces racism with great ardor, it ranks among the most socially significant of all of Caldwell's novels.

Unlike most of his previous novels, whose action occurs within a few days, *Place Called Estherville* covers nine months in the lives of its protagonists. Late adolescent siblings who have moved to town from the country to care for their aged, invalid aunt, Ganus and Kathyanne Bazemore are light-skinned, handsome blacks who prove to be irresistible to Estherville's whites. Ganus's innocence and good looks get him killed by the husband of a teenage slattern. Kathyanne's beauty gets her pregnant by the husband of her white employer.[53]

The strength of the novel rests largely upon the characterization of Kathyanne. With stoic dignity she endures the advances of a respectable banker, the envy and ridicule of an employer, abduction by teenage boys bent on rape, violence at the hands of a policeman whose overtures she rejects, and an unwanted pregnancy. Despite the twin burdens of being black and female, she refuses to allow her spirit to be broken. Having suffered much, she looks forward, as the story ends, to a measure of happiness as the wife of a young black man who will help her raise her daughter.[54] In the characterization of Kathyanne, Caldwell added another new dimension to his fiction, a fully drawn black woman. Moreover, in a novel peopled by an assortment of moral dwarfs, she possesses integrity of gigantic dimensions.

So does Horatio Plowden, a minor yet significant character. Likely patterned after a physician Caldwell had known in Wrens thirty years earlier, Dr. Plowden, introduced in the final chapter, voices the author's views on the matter of race. On his way to attend Kathyanne in childbirth, the doctor meets the town's night policeman, who asks, "Who're you going to see at this time of night, Doc? Some nigger who ought be dead anyway?" Eloquently and prophetically, Plowden responds: "We're all human beings. . . . You're going to have to learn to treat all people alike, white and colored, or else there won't be any place for you one of these days. I know that you and a lot more like you think you can keep this a white man's town, but you're wrong. The world has changed a great deal in the last generation, and it's going to change a lot more in the next generation. I may not live to see the whole change come, but I hope you do."[55]

Within an hour the doctor lies dead, the victim of a worn-out heart exhausted by forty years of overwork. Yet he dies with the joy of having earned the gratitude of a young black woman who never before had been given reason to trust a white person. Although the conclusion of the novel approaches sentimentality, it nonetheless reflects the compassion of two decent men, character and author.[56]

The high achievement of *Place Called Estherville* would not soon be repeated. The year after its publication, the final novel of the cyclorama appeared. *Episode in Palmetto* is the weakest of those novels because Caldwell failed more obviously than before at something that he could not do effectively: write a purely domestic story. Chronicling the escapades of a pretty young schoolteacher who beds not only a married man but also a sixteen-year-old boy, the novel is the stuff of soap opera, the kind of drugstore trash that critics had begun to accuse Caldwell of writing.[57]

With only a few exceptions, reviewers across the South panned the novels of the late 1940s, frequently scoring Caldwell for continuing to cultivate themes whose vitality he had already depleted. If his earlier work had served a worthy purpose, the later novels were, said one critic, "a vitiated crusade against the Southern backwoods social structure." Many charged that he seemed to be unaware of, or unwilling to record, the changes that were sweeping the South. The detractors seemed unwilling to acknowledge Caldwell's reluctance to be a chronicler of progress when many southerners had not yet enjoyed its blessings. The repetition so denounced by critics resulted in great measure from his insistence on imagining the lives of people who were being left out of the postwar boom.[58]

Conspicuous among such southerners were poor women such as Molly Bowser and Kathyanne Bazemore. It is surely no accident that the most reviled of the late-1940s novels was *Place Called Estherville,* which features a poor black woman. The story was "dreamed-up racial tripe" that "bears for the single- or simple-minded a sermon on Southern exploitation of the black." Caldwell seemed not to realize that among white southerners "the Negro question is not to be trifled with." Despite renewed criticism that Caldwell was repeating himself, what frightened reviewers was the author's prophecy of changes to come in a dimension of southern life that they hoped would remain immutable.[59]

Initially concerned with the plight of marginal people in hard times, Caldwell continued to create such characters as economic conditions improved. If the art of most of the postwar novels is vitiated—the result of their domestic nature and of the author's waning powers—and if the pattern the author posited for the cyclorama is difficult to discern, the compassion for the unfortunate, for those who remained on the margins of society after 1945, was nevertheless as strong as ever.

Aware that the completion of the cyclorama marked a watershed in his career, Caldwell proceeded to write his autobiography, which was published in 1951. His purpose in *Call It Experience,* he wrote in the book's preface, was "to set forth some of the experiences of an author which may be of interest to curious readers and would-be writers who seek visions of the wonderland in which all authors are believed to exist. . . . What is to be found here is less a personal history than it is an informal recollection of authorship." True to his intent, he omitted much of his personal history, failing even to mention his ex-wife Helen and their children and his wife June and their son. Moreover, he distorted to his advantage some of the personal history that he did include. His recollection of authorship was informal with a vengeance. *Call It Experience* sags under a heavy load of trivia: the names of hotels where he stayed while working; the food that he ate when he visited Czechoslovakia to gather material for a book; the inconsequential, albeit humorous, anecdotes of his career as a writer. Never does he acknowledge any other author whose work might have affected him, and never does he engage in a serious discussion of the matter of literature. No doubt curious readers and would-be writers found *Call It Experience* entertaining. Had they known, however, how little it revealed of the self-defining experience of its author, they probably would have been deeply disappointed.[60]

After completing his autobiography, Caldwell returned to writing fiction primarily. Between 1954 and 1973, he published eleven novels and thirty-two new stories. Very few of the stories, all of which appeared in the 1950s, including those published in a collection entitled *Gulf Coast Stories,* are distinctively southern. Although some that are southern showcase the rollicking humor that was a Caldwell trademark, hardly any convey the broad social concern of his great stories of the 1930s. One, however, provides further evidence of his enduring agrarianism. Devoid of his patented humor and sex and hardly a short story at all but rather a meditation, biblical in tone, on what constitutes the good life, "The Story of Mahlon," in just fifteen hundred words, touchingly depicts a farmer's passion for the land. The bachelor Mahlon, his name an elision of "male alone," resists, as Jeeter Lester does, the urgings of others to move to town and get a factory job. Uninterested also in the "pretty girls" that neighbors say he would meet in the city, Mahlon nonetheless realizes that the soil upon which he often lies prone, like a man making love, is not enough to fulfill his agrarian idyll. Lying "silently through the night with his face pressed upon the ground," he comes to know at story's end that he needs a wife.[61]

Although few of the short stories possess regional characteristics, virtually all of the novels, more than half of which appeared in the 1960s, are distinctively southern. And nearly all of the southern novels demonstrate further the decline of Caldwell's art after the early 1940s. Plots clumsily constructed, characters whose actions are insufficiently motivated, humor grafted onto inappropriate situations—all, to greater or lesser degree, mar the late novels. Even the sex, by turns sleazy or quaint, grows tiresome.[62]

Yet for all of the weakened art, the social concern continues unabated. Collectively, the novels focus on the effects of sexism and racism. Although Caldwell was usually unable in the late works to turn noble intentions into strong fiction, occasionally he fused argument and art to create a work of considerable power. Despite many flaws—misplaced humor, poor plotting, and occasionally leaden writing—*Claudelle Inglish* is a strong indictment of a masculine culture that forces a young woman, on the advice of her mother, to use sex to get what she wants. Roughly ten years later, *The Weather Shelter*, like *Claudelle Inglish* a work strengthened by its rural setting, offered a powerful condemnation of racism, white and black, as it also presented a poignant story of a white father's love for his mulatto son. What shines through many of the late novels, whether they are strong or weak, is Caldwell's sympathy for the social outcast, whether a retired prostitute turned boardinghouse keeper, the mulatto mistress of a morally obtuse good old boy, a black teacher whose defiance of his white tormentor brings serious injury, an adolescent mulatto pursued by a lynch mob, or a white sharecropper who loses everything dear to him.[63]

The characterization of the sharecropper is, in fact, the finest in any of the post-cyclorama novels. Clyde Inglish, Claudelle's father, suffers the desertion of a wife who is tired of being poor, strives unsuccessfully to stop his daughter's wanton behavior, and cannot prevent her murder by a jealous suitor. His diligence, integrity, and sensitivity avail him nothing, and he is bereft of wife, daughter, and the land he loves to farm. In the agrarian Clyde, the agrarian Caldwell created the kind of character that distinguished his great work of the 1930s. Clyde Inglish is as surely the victim of forces beyond his control as are Jeeter Lester, Jesse English, Clem Henry, and other Depression-era characters.[64]

Whatever were the strengths and weaknesses of Caldwell's postwar fiction, millions of readers in the late 1940s and in the 1950s were far more interested in his writing of the 1930s and early 1940s, although for reasons that often had little to do with its literary quality. Caldwell did everything in his power to fan that interest. The appearance of cheap paperbacks—many of them selling for only twenty-five cents—that swept commercial publishing after the Second World War fattened Caldwell's pocketbook. From the end of 1945 to the middle of 1951, his paperback publishers—first, Penguin Books, and, after 1947, New American Library (NAL)—issued eleven reprints of his works. Led by *God's Little Acre*, the paperbacks sold more than 25 million copies. Without writing a word, Caldwell became richer by nearly one hundred thousand dollars.[65]

Always interested in making money, and understanding the dynamics of paperback publishing, Caldwell avidly cooperated with NAL's efforts to promote his works. Believing that a "storyteller's purpose is to reach as large a market as possible," he tried mightily to expand that market.

He lunched with the distributor's wholesalers. He posed—with his dog, Crackerjack—as a whiskey company's "man of distinction." He tolerated the lurid covers of his paperback editions. Declaring that he would "rather move in a crowd than read," he appeared at drugstore newsstands to autograph copies of his books for admiring throngs that were described as "Sinatra-like" in size and behavior.[66]

Such shenanigans, which outraged the literary establishment, further undermined his waning reputation among critics and other writers. One incident provides telling evidence of this development. In the summer of 1948, on his way to speak to a group of aspiring writers convening at the University of Kansas, Caldwell stopped in Kansas City, Missouri, at the request of his distributor. There, as the star of the grand opening of the twenty-fifth super drugstore in the Katz chain, he spent three hours autographing copies of his books, posing for photographs with employees and customers, and chatting with anyone who wanted to make his acquaintance. When the other authors participating in the conference—among whom were the southerners Allen Tate, Caroline Gordon, and Katherine Anne Porter—learned of the incident, they shunned him. In their view, he was a writer who brazenly courted popular favor. Although Caldwell sat politely through sessions led by other participants, when it was his turn to lecture, "the entire staff," according to a journalist present, withdrew "for a private dinner in the ivory tower."[67]

Thirty years after the episode in Lawrence, Kansas, Caldwell's paperback publisher apologized to him in print. "If, even indirectly," Victor Weybright of NAL wrote, "my promotion of Erskine Caldwell in the paperbound mass market has contributed to the omission of supreme critical acclaim, it is my only regret as a publisher."[68] The damage, however, was irreparable.

As some southern writers were spurning Caldwell, many southern readers, who became familiar with his works only when they appeared in paperback, went further and damned him. With the publication of his paperbacks came an avalanche of mail. Many of the detractors who wrote to him objected to his writing trash. An outraged Louisiana minister who had purchased God's Little Acre because the title suggested "something that would be of a religious nature" charged Caldwell with trying "to ruin our young people for the sake of a few dollars." "Man, if you know anything about praying," the preacher continued, "you better get started to asking God to forgive you for all the harm that you have already done."

The wife of a Tennessee sharecropper, the kind of person that Caldwell had been trying to help, believed that he was beyond forgiveness, that he "should be able to sit for a picture of the Devil." His books—she had burned the four that she owned—were not only unbelievable but were also "dirty, just plain dirty" and were "opening minds—in many cases young minds—to sin and hell." Twenty-two high-school students in Richmond, Virginia, members of a youth crusade to clean up literature in the city, agreed that Caldwell was ruining the morals of the young. "Would you like to think that people are going to hell every day because of your works?" asked one. Another charged that his books were producing "a generation of sexual maniacs." Yet another wondered why Caldwell wanted to "bring out the wild passionate emotions of the Southern people." All of the adolescent correspondents believed that literature could influence thought and action. One conferred great praise when she opined, "With your power it is evident that you can change the world." All implored Caldwell to use his talent for good and to write only wholesome, decent books.[69]

At the crest of Caldwell's popularity from the late 1940s to the mid-1950s, the many southerners who condemned him as a writer of trash usually based their judgment on the superior books first published in the 1930s, not on the inferior ones that he wrote subsequently. It was not, for example, the trashy *Episode in Palmetto* that provoked their wrath but the artistic *Tobacco Road* and *God's Little Acre*.[70]

If many readers were offended by what they considered obscene in Caldwell's works, others objected particularly to his treatment of race. From New Orleans came a letter calling him a "Negro loving Bas[tard]." A Georgian accused him of "traducing" his native state by supporting integration and amalgamation. His treatment of interracial sex was scathingly denounced by both a Carolina white woman and a Georgian who identified himself as "a full blooded Negro." The white woman denied that "any decent or even bad white girls mix with Negro men." The black man, after branding Caldwell "a dirty, lying son-of-a-bitch," pronounced his depiction of miscegenation "a profound lie." All of the correspondents, including the black Georgian, shared the sentiment of one who asked, "Where is your So[uthern] patriotism?" Speaking in 1948 to a civic club in a small south-Georgia city that fourteen years later would be the scene of large civil-rights demonstrations, an industrialist bluntly answered that query. "As a traitor," he said, "Benedict Arnold was a piker compared to our Erskine Caldwell." That Georgia worthy claimed to perceive the ultimate goal of "rabble rousers" like Caldwell: to plant "the seeds of racial hatreds to grow into the oaks of Communism."[71]

The vilification continued into the 1950s. A Florida editor agreed with the sentiments of the Georgia industrialist. Decrying Caldwell's "planned calumniation of the South," the journalist branded him a tool of race-mixing Communists. Twice in the 1950s, the state of Georgia threatened to censor certain of the miscreant's works. When a political leader in Augusta learned of plans to film *God's Little Acre* nearby, he exploded: "That man has done more to hurt this area and the South than any man alive." Other Augustans agreed. The movie, which was, like the film *Tobacco Road*, a travesty of the novel that inspired it, was made in Stockton, California.[72]

The calumny directed at Caldwell by southerners, however, was equaled by praise. For every letter that he received that condemned his work, there was another that extolled it. Some of the fan mail came from people desiring autographs, seeking assistance with publishing their work, or wanting Caldwell to tell the stories of their lives, many of which made his fiction seem tame. Much of the correspondence, however, came from southerners who had no ulterior purpose, who merely wanted Caldwell to know that they admired his work. And some of the correspondence antedated the appearance of his work in paperback. The publication of *You Have Seen Their Faces* inspired a Tennesseean to thank him "for faces which I shall never forget to see," prompted the son of a tenant farmer to describe the work as "without a doubt the most true to life and interesting book I've ever read," and caused a native Georgian teaching in Texas to wish Caldwell "continued goodwill" because "we need liberal Georgians, God knows." *Trouble in July* brought praise from a white Georgian who said that she had long objected to the "abuse of the hapless Negro."[73]

As was the case with mail from detractors, letters from supporters greatly increased in number as Caldwell's books appeared in paperback after 1945. From housewives to college professors, correspondents applauded the narrative power, the realism, and the social concern of his writings. Young men—mostly college students and soldiers—were especially interested in his work. For some of those readers, the attraction came from the alluring covers of the paperbound editions and the sexual content of the fiction—Griselda Walden's "rising beauties" were particularly admired. But for many, including some who were initially drawn by the sex, the appeal of Caldwell's work was much broader. A soldier from Tennessee, who was "deeply impressed by the style" of certain short stories, estimated that Caldwell had "moved realism & Southern literature ahead a century at least," which was an "accomplishment [that] will echo for a long time down south." A student at the archly conservative University of the South, who had chosen Caldwell's work as the subject of a term paper because he wanted "to drag . . . [Caldwell] . . . over the coals" for maligning his hometown of Augusta, had undergone a change of heart after rereading *Tobacco Road* and *God's Little Acre.* Those novels, the student claimed, were "good books" that were not "overly realistic, but on the contrary . . . are not realistic enough." He averred that a tour of the settings of the novels would convince critics that the speech of Caldwell's characters "is whiter than the proverbial snow compared to the real McCoy." His fellow Georgian's short stories, the student continued, were "splendid little clippings from the great newspaper of human nature." The young man's instructor did not share his enthusiasm for Caldwell's work. When informed of the student's topic, the professor—whose "face assumed the expression of one who has just made a meal of dill pickles dunked in the juice of green persimmons"—warned him not to expect a good grade. Another student—this one at the University of Louisville— whose father had served as an itinerant Presbyterian minister in North Carolina among Caldwellian people that the student had "learned to like and understand" labeled Caldwell "my favorite author."[74]

What was probably the first official recognition of Caldwell's work by a new generation of college students came from an unlikely place, a Baptist school in Mississippi. In 1947, the student magazine at Mississippi College ran a feature in its November number entitled "The Erskine Caldwell Crusade." According to the editor, the article was prompted by "a long interest" among some students in Caldwell's works, especially *You Have Seen Their Faces.* The authors of the piece, both of whom were literary editors for the magazine, argued, as one of them recalled later, that "far from being a mere titillator and commercial-minded writer who was after the sleaze market, Caldwell was like a sociologist, writing serious studies of life as it truly was in much of the South." Having discovered Caldwell's fiction on drugstore racks, that student, who remembered seeing unemployed Mississippians standing in bread lines years before, resented "the standard Southern Baptist view that anything Caldwell wrote was Nasty and certainly not Literature." He believed that the sex in the fiction, while describing "a moving force" in people's lives, allowed Caldwell "to reach an audience who might be able to see the [other] facts of life he portrayed." The magazine's editor, who claimed to speak for the student body, saluted Caldwell. "We look forward," he concluded, "to the day when America truly means brotherhood and when the people turn in quiet dignity to pay tribute to those of vision to whom so much is due."[75]

Like these college students, other Caldwell readers who were sensitive to the South's failings would have found absurd the claim by a weekly newsmagazine in 1957 that he was a "cracker-barrel pornographer." *Time*, however, influenced the opinions of millions of people; the Mississippi College *Arrowhead* influenced the views of virtually no one.[76]

Time's savage indictment signaled the nadir of Caldwell's career. Moreover, the first five years of the 1950s had been among the worst of his life. Troubles, professional and personal, plagued him. Maxim Lieber, the literary agent who for nearly twenty years had represented him vigorously, if not always wisely, fled the country, a victim of hysterical anticommunism. Caldwell's own association with Communist fronts in the 1930s made him a target of the same hysteria. Difficulties with publishers and the waning popularity of his paperbacks among American readers added to his woes.[77]

Yet professional problems paled beside personal troubles. Symptoms that suggested cancer sent Caldwell to the Mayo Clinic in Rochester, Minnesota, for extensive examinations. After seventeen days in the hospital, he was relieved to learn that his colon was not cancerous.[78]

There was no relief, however, from the domestic turmoil that worried Caldwell most. His relationship with his third wife, June, who was nearly twenty years younger than he, had become strained fairly early in their marriage. He resented her many social activities because they interrupted his work. He subjected her to the same angry silences that he had inflicted on Bourke-White. For her part, June abhorred her husband's addiction to his work. She began to see herself as only an ornament, a famous writer's wife who had no identity of her own. To Caldwell's dismay, she began to visit a psychoanalyst. After many sessions over many years, the analyst, who charged fees of four hundred dollars a month, advised her not to sleep with her husband. Caldwell loathed June's addiction to her doctor. Early in 1953, June having requested separation, he left their Tucson home and moved to Phoenix. Separated from his wife, he refused to seek divorce because of his love for Jay, their eight-year-old son. Late in November 1954, June filed suit to end the marriage. After much haggling and many delays, the suit was settled twelve months later.

A little over a year after the divorce, on New Year's Day 1957, Caldwell wed for the last time. That wife, Virginia Moffett Fletcher, a woman he had seen from time to time during his troubles with June, would remain his helpmate until he died. Their happy union of thirty years equaled the span of his three previous marriages.[79]

By 1960, Caldwell had abandoned his forte, the writing of short stories. Although he would publish six novels in the course of the 1960s, the nonfiction of those years is his best work of the decade. As always, his most accomplished nonfiction was travel writing, and, as in the 1930s, his best nonfiction dealt with what he knew best—the South.[80]

In the travel accounts of the 1960s, Caldwell employed the method he had developed thirty years before, which combined the techniques of reporter and fiction writer. In gathering information he would make sketchy notes that usually included places, names, and other significant data. Soon thereafter, he would, as he described the process, "reconstitute—not recreate but reconstitute—the atmosphere, the tenor" of a scene or an incident. The sexagenarian Caldwell worked vigorously on the travel books. He and Virginia would rise each morning at six, spend the day in search of material, and check into a motel around four in the afternoon, when he would begin to write. During one project, he pecked at his typewriter with only one hand because his ailing one was hoisted to the ceiling to relieve pain.[81]

The ideas for the nonfictional works were those of his new publisher, his fourth since Scribner's thirty years before. Farrar, Straus and Cudahy wanted three books: a travel account of American life, a study of race relations in the South, and an examination of the cultural impact of evangelical Protestantism on the contemporary South. Roger Straus, more sensitive to Caldwell's talents than any editor since Perkins of Scribner's, knew his strengths: his interest in the folk, his lifelong opposition to racism, and his fascination with religious expression. Caldwell would fulfill his publisher's expectations in the first two volumes but not in the last, where his devotion to his father's memory got in the way.[82]

A cross-country trip of 1963 resulted the next year in a book very much like *Some American People,* which had been published nearly thirty

years earlier. In *Around About America,* Caldwell related his observations of many things: New England character, suburban sprawl, a poolroom in Colorado, Basques in Nevada, and Indians in Oregon, to name
a few. His comments on the South, which occupy one-fourth of the book,
doubtless had an effect on professional southerners not unlike that of his
devastating critiques of rural poverty and racism thirty years before. In
the coal fields of southern West Virginia, he reported "hard-core unemployment, widespread and chronic." Amid majestic terrain that provided
breathtaking scenery but that lacked "standing room for a cow or chick-
ens," miners and their families lived in "shacks and hovels." Stopgap measures such as the distribution of food stamps and the creation of make-
work projects hardly provided adequate solutions to a problem of such
magnitude. What was needed was a "national service corps," modeled on
the recently established Peace Corps, through which displaced miners
could receive training for other kinds of work and become "self-
supporting and self-respecting." Without sweeping federal action, the
"waste of human resources" in this part of Appalachia would continue
to present "a tragic and depressing condition in what is called dynamic,
prosperous, and plentiful America."[83]

Just as the persistence of poverty continued to haunt Caldwell, so did
the perpetuation of racism. "The segregationist," he told a newspaper interviewer early in 1961, "is morally, sociologically and democratically
wrong." Incidents in Alabama and Georgia described in *Around About
America* showed him the frenzy that beset white southerners over what
should have been inconsequential matters. A white employee of a rental
car agency at the Birmingham airport flew into a rage when a black co-
worker, attempting to perform his assigned task, tried to record the mile-
age on a car leaving the lot. "Get your goddam nigger face out of here,"
the white driver shouted. "No black nigger's going to get that close to
me." Enraged by "goddam stinking niggers these days [who] act like they
think they're just as good as a white man," that worker hoped to get the
black man fired. A black New Englander driving with his family to Florida also felt the sting of white prejudice. Stopping at a restaurant in south
Georgia whose owner had posted signs boasting its fine food and southern hospitality for many miles along the highway, the black man was
hardly surprised when the proprietor refused to seat him. Yet the owner
also refused to sell him not only box lunches but even a bottle of milk for
his family, which included three children, waiting in the car. "Go on down

the road until you come to one of those Yankee-kind chain stores," the proprietor yelled. "Nobody else around here is going to sell nothing to niggers."[84]

Despite such episodes and despite the ubiquity of Confederate flags— emblems that, Caldwell believed, should be displayed in museums and not atop government buildings because they insulted black southerners and symbolized rebellion against the country—in the heady atmosphere of the civil rights movement, Caldwell was sanguine about the future of race relations. His optimism derived largely from the growing awareness among blacks that they were "entitled to full citizenship." Because of their efforts, he predicted that "equal rights and racial freedom" would be achieved within fifteen years. Moreover, he believed that "after many generations" racial assimilation "will create brotherhood."[85]

The optimism was short-lived. Subsequent to a trip taken a year after the cross-country journey described in *Around About America*, Caldwell engaged in little discussion of brotherhood. The organizing principle of *In Search of Bisco* was his attempt to locate a black man who had been his playmate in early childhood. Yet in most of the book the search for Bisco is secondary to a description of Bisco Country, the region from South Carolina to Louisiana. What Caldwell found in his first extensive nonfictional examination of the South since 1937 was hardly edifying. Just as he had delivered a two-fisted assault on poverty in *You Have Seen Their Faces*, he dealt a hard-hitting attack on racism in *In Search of Bisco*.[86]

There are a few bright moments in the book, such as the account of a retired white farmer in Georgia who, having worked closely with blacks all his life, believes that support for civil rights is a moral imperative, and the portrait of a fiercely independent white man in the hills of north Alabama who angrily resents race-baiting politicians that tell him how to vote. By and large, however, the whites that Caldwell encountered were die-hard segregationists who contended that most blacks were happy with the South's racial arrangement and that unrest was created by the federal government, outside agitators, and a few local troublemakers. Occasionally, the arguments of the die-hards were merely ludicrous. An Alabama realtor and civic leader contended that black equality would be a long time coming because only with the passing of many generations would the brains of black people grow large enough to qualify them for equal treatment. More often, the arguments of the die-hards were vicious and obscene. In Mississippi, a member of the White Citizens' Council, an organization that Caldwell described as an uptown version of the Ku Klux Klan, betrayed the underlying fear of change in race relations harbored by many whites.

> You go ahead and give the niggers just one little foothold and there'd be no end to what they'd want next. . . .
> Given a chance, they'd make whores out of all white women. . . . You let a crowd of niggers stand around on the street corner and watch a white woman walk by and you don't have to guess a second time what they've got in mind. You'd be right the first time when you said what they were thinking about was getting their hands on her titties and their balls between her legs.[87]

An Arkansas rice planter agreed. Any gains made by the civil rights movement encouraged "the niggers" to seek more. "You give them an inch . . . and they'll stop at nothing. They'll claim it's discrimination unless they can get white women next." Happily, machines had replaced black men in the rice fields of the Grand Prairie, which allowed "a white woman without her titty-bags on . . . to go where she pleases day or night . . . and not get stripped naked and thrown down and nigger-raped."[88]

The fears of white racists were hardly justified. Among the eight blacks—seven men and a woman—featured in the book, none displayed an interest in interracial sex. The old ones wanted economic security. The young ones wanted economic opportunity, the chance to get a good education and to find a decent job. None evinced the racist sentiments expressed by most of the whites that Caldwell encountered, although some had compelling reasons to do so. An old Arkansas sharecropper, whose situation was reminiscent of that of Caldwell's character Abe Lathan twenty-five years before, had been forced off the land he had worked all his life. A young Mississippi sharecropper, whose landlord refused to allow him to bury his father on his land, had no choice but to inter him by the side of a road and mark his grave with a rusted bread sign.[89]

The degradation of black southerners, Caldwell contended, was largely the result of the efforts of affluent whites, whose wealth usually derived from the labor of blacks. Instead of leading their fellow southerners down the right path, well-to-do whites too often failed to act ethically, took the wrong course, and encouraged poorer whites to follow them.[90]

In Search of Bisco brought a reawakening of interest in Caldwell's work among southerners. Newspapers from Norfolk to Austin ran reviews of the book. Some were defensive and hostile. The *Austin American-Statesman* lamented that in Caldwell's rendering "there is no news but bad news and no South but a bad South." The *Pensacola News Journal* found "nothing new in this one-sided slap at dear old Dixie." Branding Caldwell a "fire-breathing liberal," the *Charleston News and Courier* asked "why is it the Negroes are all sinned against and the whites all sinning?"[91]

In contrast to the antagonistic responses of some commentators, other reviewers across the South applauded Caldwell's portrayal of race relations in the region. *In Search of Bisco* was "thoughtful and thought-provoking," "enlightening," "eloquent and painful," "stark [and] eloquent," "strong . . . [and] moving," "serious [and] earnest," "biting commentary . . . well worth reading and studying." Two Atlantans offered the most fervent praise. In the *Daily World*, Atlanta's black newspaper, Ray McIver, Caldwell's new black friend, called *In Search of Bisco* "a helluva good book, . . . possibly Mr. Caldwell's finest book." In the *Journal*, Frank Daniel, Caldwell's old white friend, reminded readers that Caldwell had been exposing racial injustice for more than thirty years. "Few writers," Daniel wrote, "have the authority and the power to speak now as he can here."[92]

In a letter to Caldwell written shortly before publication of the review, Daniel said: "You are writing better today than ever. *Bisco* says more and says it with more power than anything I've read on the subject. Its implications and reverberations are limitless."[93] Daniel's admiration of his friend and his hope for the success of the civil rights movement caused him to overrate *In Search of Bisco*. The book lacks the power of Caldwell's great work of the 1930s. Even so, as Daniel rightly suggested, *Bisco* provides strong testimony of Caldwell's untiring quest to promote social justice.

Hard upon the publication of his treatment of race in the 1960s South, Caldwell undertook his publisher's third assignment, which entailed an examination of another subject that had long held his interest. *Deep South: Memory and Observation* assays the twentieth-century evolution of evangelical Protestantism in the region identified in the book's title. The author's method of juxtaposing memory and observation, of interlarding reminiscences of his father's ministry early in the century with assessments of religion in the 1960s, was rejected by the publisher, who insisted that he rewrite the manuscript to provide an expanded account of the 1960s only. His refusal to do so required that he seek another publisher.[94]

Had Caldwell heeded the advice of Farrar, Straus and Giroux, *Deep South* would have been a tighter—and weaker—book. The "memory" portions feature some of the most poignant writing that he ever produced, and they supply fitting touchstones for the "observation" segments. Comparing his memory of his father's experience with his own observation of southern religion in the 1960s, Caldwell concluded that within white Protestantism the social gospel had made little progress.[95]

In less affluent churches, which were often located in small towns and rural areas, religion continued to be, as it had been in his father's time, narcotic, escapist, and sometimes salacious. Churches whose worship services resembled "night clubs and other places of theatrical entertainment" could hardly be expected to be seedbeds of social reform. Too often they were hothouses of reaction. The minister of one such church was an active supporter of the Ku Klux Klan. A member of a similar church, a storekeeper who described himself as "a good Christian" for "nearly forty-five years," gave vent to repulsion sparked by a Jewish competitor who allowed black customers to try on clothes and who even helped them find shoes that fit. Such practices were outrageous to that good Christian. "I'll go bankrupt and get put out of business before you see me squatting down in front of a black nigger, lacing and unlacing shoes for him like he was a white man." [96]

Notwithstanding all of the fanaticism, religious and secular, displayed by members of fundamentalist churches in the countryside, Caldwell delivered his harshest judgment upon the affluent members of fashionable churches in the big cities of the South. Headed by slick preachers and slick officers, such congregations contained "the beautiful people of religion," the upwardly mobile who embraced the church for the wrong reasons: getting ahead, meeting women, and going to their destination in eternity—be it heaven or hell—"de luxe" rather than "second class." The "First Baptist" disease—a condition wherein boosterism triumphed over social conscience—was all too contagious.[97]

To Caldwell, both sides, the complacently conservative and the fanatically fundamentalist, were badly flawed primarily because both opposed the cause of civil rights. The spokesmen of contemporary white Protestantism featured in *Deep South* stand in sorry contrast to his father, who had always advocated fair treatment of blacks and who had consistently denounced both the conspicuous display of wealthy urban churches and the wild emotionalism of poor rural ones.

If too many white churches were "devoted exclusively to the incestuous practice of religion for religion's sake," hope lay in the fundamentalist yet socially conscious black churches that were the vanguard of the civil rights movement. In his truncated account of black Protestantism, added at the suggestion of his new publisher, Caldwell displayed only a sketchy knowledge of its historical development. Yet he understood well the importance of clergymen in the black community. Many black ministers reaching their prime in the 1950s and 1960s were educated men, "calm and capable in judgment," who had the ability "to persuade the older generation to put aside its fear of the white man and at the same time restrain the younger generation from engaging in impetuous retaliatory acts." To the greatest of these men, he had written earlier: "Of all contemporary Americans, you are the most deserving of . . . [the Nobel Peace Prize.] I am proud to be one of your fellow citizens." Although he did not so stipulate in *Deep South,* it is apparent that Caldwell believed that black men such as Martin Luther King Jr.—enlightened, reasonable, committed to social Christianity—upheld the principles that his father had championed to a far greater degree than did most white ministers.[98]

Because religion was not as timely a topic as race in the 1960s, *Deep South* received much less attention from southern reviewers than had *In Search of Bisco.* Among the southerners who noticed *Deep South,* one described it as "lackluster . . . dull and repetitious." Another claimed that Caldwell intended "to downgrade the Christian faith and to group all Protestants as frenzied, foot-stomping zealots." Much more perceptive was the review by Edwin M. Yoder Jr. of the *Greensboro Daily News.* Although Yoder ignored Caldwell's savage indictment of the social irresponsibility of fashionable urban churches, he praised his treatment of "backwoods religion," whose practitioners "are poor people who find refuge from the world's woes and threats in a vicious old God, white and Anglo-Saxon, who vouchsafes His hate of Negroes, Jews, and Catholics." Further echoing Caldwell, Yoder noted that as white fundamentalism opposed change—"the sawdust aisle is the focus of Ku Klux orthodoxy," he wrote—"black fundamentalism is far more interested . . . in questions of social justice." Caldwell's insights, Yoder concluded, "are shrewd and ring of truth."[99]

Just as Caldwell had not divulged the danger that he occasionally faced in his trips across the South in the 1930s, so he refused to disclose his apprehension about the journeys of the 1960s. Fearing for his safety, his nonagenarian mother advised him not to undertake the investigations. Her son and his wife usually took the precaution of flying to a city near their destination and then renting an automobile for further travel. It was important, Erskine told Virginia, not to drive a car bearing license tags from outside the South. Once, when they drove their own car, a restaurant owner in Louisiana told them: "If you people from other places would stay out of the South, we wouldn't have any trouble." On another occasion, when not in her husband's presence, Caldwell's wife, whose speech indicated that she was an outsider, was intimidated by lawmen in a Deep South town.[100]

For all of his unease over his and Virginia's safety, Caldwell was gratified by the attention that his 1960s nonfiction, especially *In Search of Bisco*, received from southern reviewers, some of whom were sympathetic to his goals. Moreover, he knew that some of the South's educators had begun to notice and to applaud his work of the 1930s. The writer who had stood his ground for thirty years found that an articulate minority of southerners was ready to honor him. At long last, the changing South was trying to catch up to the unchanging writer.

Late in the 1950s and with increasing frequency throughout the following decade, colleges and universities, now aware in a socially conscious climate of Caldwell's lifelong interest in beneficent social change, led the way in bestowing accolades. Unknowingly following the lead of black Fisk University, which had invited Caldwell to attend special events in the 1940s, white institutions from Virginia to Texas solicited his presence, sometimes over the objections of alumni and other people. Despite his aversion to making speeches, he came, and he was always received graciously, sometimes enthusiastically. At the University of Georgia in 1958, he was lionized. At Erskine College the following year, a literary society that had existed for more than a century inducted him as its second honorary member—after Robert E. Lee. At the University of Virginia the next year, the prestigious Raven Society made him a member. That alma mater would honor him on a number of occasions later as well.[101]

Moved by the recognition accorded by academicians—and by journalists such as the influential Ralph McGill of the *Atlanta Constitution*—

Caldwell, while still harshly critical of the South's shortcomings, often expressed pride in his Georgia roots. "I . . . will always be a Georgian," he told an Associated Press writer. "Nobody can take that away from me and I'm glad." "I like to think," he wrote to Georgia's governor, "that I am as much a Georgian as Brer Rabbit." "Wherever I am," he disclosed to a Miami editor, "I'm a Cracker and glad of it. I wouldn't want to have to live another life and be something else." [102]

In 1968, after ten years of growing approbation from some of his fellow southerners, the nomadic Caldwell, having lived in Maine, Connecticut, Arizona, and California, settled in the South—albeit on its periphery—for the first time in more than forty years. His new home on the Gulf Coast of central Florida, he said without irony, "is close enough to the old home of Georgia." [103]

The recognition by southerners would continue for the rest of Caldwell's life, prompting the *New York Times* to observe in 1978 that he had been "rehabilitated as a regional literary lion." Colleges and universities continued to invite him to lecture and sought to obtain manuscripts and first editions. The University of Virginia honored him with a dinner on his seventy-fifth birthday. The University of Georgia and the Georgia Endowment for the Humanities produced films about his life and works. A southern publisher reissued some of the significant works of the 1930s. A fellow Georgian, President Jimmy Carter, whose candidacy Caldwell had warmly endorsed, wrote him a complimentary personal letter and also invited him to a White House reception. Towns in which he had lived as a boy sought his presence at centennial celebrations. Almost always, Caldwell accepted invitations and fulfilled requests. And he continued to write, producing two lackluster novels and an interesting travel book in the first half of the 1970s. [104]

The social concern also continued unabated. His penultimate novel scores southern racism, and the portions of the travel account devoted to the South highlight the limits of material progress and the constricting nature of evangelical Protestantism. Soon after the publication of the travel book, *Afternoons in Mid-America,* Caldwell envisioned a photo-journalistic portrayal of the Deep South, perhaps along the lines of *You Have Seen Their Faces.* He asked his old friend Frank Daniel to recommend a photographer "who is earnest and *social-minded* and ambitious and fairly young who would want to take pictures of people for fame & glory and not much money." The project fell through, but the fact that

Caldwell, pushing seventy-five, wanted to conduct it provides yet further evidence of his undying concern for the South's downtrodden.[105]

Nine years after his return to the South, ill health forced Caldwell to move back to the West, to the dry climate of Arizona. Living quietly with Virginia in Scottsdale, he worked on his final book. In 1983, after almost four years' labor, he completed the manuscript, an autobiography entitled "With All My Might." Then, for the next two years, he and Virginia traveled occasionally—to France, to Italy, to Switzerland, to Bulgaria, and to various places in the United States. They took many of the trips to receive awards that had been bestowed on him. Despite the honors, he found that major American publishers were reluctant to issue his autobiography. Finally, in October 1986, a French house published the book.[106]

By that time, Caldwell was seriously ill. Back in August, doctors had discovered that he suffered again from lung cancer. This strain was much more virulent than the kind that years before had forced surgeons to remove half of each of his lungs. For eight months, he fought the devastating disease. An oxygen tank with a fifty-foot line attached to it allowed him to breath and to move about his house. He endured the ravages of chemotherapy for six months, until his body no longer could tolerate the treatments. He steadfastly refused medicine that would have eased his pain and would have helped him sleep. Throughout the ordeal, he never lost his sense of humor. Playfully, he suggested that his ashes be buried on a dead-end street. The night before he died, as his condition deteriorated rapidly, he asked a visiting neighbor, who was a physician, how much he charged for house calls. The end came on April 11, 1987.[107]

A month before Caldwell's death, an American publisher, at long last, issued *With All My Might*. It is supremely fitting that his farewell was published by a press in his native Georgia, a place that had supplied such rich material about the poor people whose lives he had strived to improve.[108]

CHAPTER SIX

Caldwell's Achievement

There were two Erskine Caldwells, and in a sense other than those that the critic Malcolm Cowley identified in 1944, the year of Ira's death and a turning point in Caldwell's career. Cowley's dichotomy—Caldwell as sociologist and as poet, the one at war with the other—seems contrived and foreign to Caldwell's comprehension of his own work. Another duality, which Caldwell understood, is strikingly apparent to the observer of his sixty-year career. In 1930, as he was struggling to establish himself, Caldwell asked Maxwell Perkins for advice. Should he focus his writing on New England or on the South? Perkins gave sound counsel: write about the South. Although he settled outside the South before he was twenty-five, the young Caldwell was able to create his strongest work by drawing on a wealth of experience and observation amassed while growing up. After his move to Maine, the frequent, extended visits that he made to his parents' home along with his extensive travel through the region enhanced his knowledge of the South.[1]

As Caldwell entered middle age, he began to lose touch with the South, the source of his strength. Although in the early years of his association with Margaret Bourke-White he wrote the powerful text of *You Have Seen Their Faces* and continued to create some excellent fiction, after their odysseys of 1936 and 1937 he came to the South less frequently. Margaret was not Helen. She would not accompany him home to Georgia for three-month visits. Instead, he often accompanied her on whatever globe-trotting junket her next job required.

As Caldwell settled into middle age, having divorced Bourke-White and married a woman barely half his age, he virtually lost contact with the source of his strength. Caught up in the social whirl of country-club

Arizona—which the country boy came to loathe—his father dead, his mother removed from the South, he thought he had no reason to go home. And the power of his work was diminished.

As Caldwell entered old age, with a new wife who understood his needs and with a new publisher who appreciated the source of his strength, he returned to the South to gather impressions that he transformed into the best work he had composed in twenty years. That those books, *In Search of Bisco* and *Deep South*, are nonfiction should hardly be surprising. According to Bourke-White, Caldwell often said that "the life of a writer is just ten years," by which he obviously meant the life of a fiction writer. In terms of his own fiction, his statement is well-nigh accurate. Although he never complained about sixty years of perspiration, he had no control over inspiration, which, he believed, came out of material so compelling that the writer had only to follow where it led. The creative writer, he told one interviewer, "doesn't even know what he's doing sometimes." To another he said, "I never had any control over the things I was writing about."[2]

The source of his strength, the material over which he had no control, the things that he could write about "like a damn fool"—all lay in the South. When the stream of imagination ran dry, he relied on memory and observation to create the strongest works of the latter part of his career. Throughout that career, despite much writing about other places, only the South could elicit both the best and the worst of his work: the worst when he severed ties to the region, the best when he maintained or reestablished them.[3]

The young Caldwell possessed greater first-hand knowledge of the South than any other writer of his generation. No other writer had grown up in as many southern states. No other writer had, in maturity, traveled as extensively through the South. Caldwell's experiences, together with the inestimable influence of his father, gave him a perspective unique among significant writers of the southern renaissance. Introspective protagonists like those in Thomas Wolfe's novels seldom appear in his work, a fact that may help explain why he abandoned writing a screenplay of *Look Homeward, Angel*. He had no interest in celebrating the past, as the Agrarians did, or in brooding over it, as William Faulkner did. Only when the past produced people like the Lesters was Caldwell concerned with presenting it. Yet his appreciation of the power of the past, of the agony and despair that history generated, distinguished his work from that of the sharecropper realists, whose concerns he shared. Though often defeated, the protagonists in novels by writers such as Edith Summers Kelley, Dorothy Scarborough, and Harry Harrison Kroll—who live like lords in comparison to the Lesters—at least strive to improve their condition. The force of history has so overwhelmed most of Caldwell's croppers that they are mere pawns of their environment.[4]

Because the Caldwells' many moves from town to town during Erskine's childhood and adolescence took place within the South, he did not lose the sense of place that figured prominently in the writing of the renaissance. The southern towns and villages in which he lived were very much alike, whether in Georgia, the Carolinas, Virginia, or Tennessee. It is not happenstance that much of his fiction is vague with the specifics of geography. To him, the South, particularly the Deep South, was one.

Caldwell's sense of place did not mean that he possessed a sense of community. Thus, paradoxically, he was spared a burden that oppressed many other writers of the renaissance. The frequent movement from one place to another prevented the development of lasting attachments that might have softened his attitude toward his material. In fact, he harbored a simmering resentment of the shabby treatment that many communities afforded his family. As an old man, he recalled that nearly everywhere the family settled—whether his father was there as supply preacher or as regular pastor—their housing was deplorable. At some stations, the Caldwells lived in manses that were cramped, dilapidated, highly flammable, and otherwise unsuitable. At other places, they did not enjoy the luxury of residing in a run-down manse and lived instead "in one large room . . . at a boardinghouse" or "in several rented rooms on the second floor of an unpainted farm house." In the Bible Belt, a region awash with poor Baptists, relatively affluent Presbyterians failed to take care of their own.[5]

Despite the absence of a sense of community in most of his work, Caldwell possessed a deep love of the land. Like the founder of the university that he admired greatly but attended haphazardly, Caldwell the skeptic believed with Thomas Jefferson the deist that "those who labour in the earth are the chosen people of God." By Caldwell's time, however, laboring in the earth brought only misery, heartache, and despair to millions of southerners.[6]

Caldwell's leftist political activity, which grew out of his social concern, added to his exceptionalism among major southern writers of his generation. In his great years, the 1930s, he brought together art and argument to create writing of a very high order. No other southern writer of comparable talent evinced an interest in the issue of class equal to his. What marks his best fiction dealing with that theme is his ability to avoid sentimentality. There is emotion in abundance, but seldom is it maudlin. If, for example, Jeeter Lester were only pitiable, then the reader, after feeling sorry for him, could forget him. But because his behavior is so outrageous, it is unforgettable, leaving the reader at once amused, angered, unsettled, and wondering how he or she would act in similar circumstances.[7]

What many scholars and critics have described as the grotesque behavior of Caldwell's characters, he considered realistic.[8] It is safe to assume that none of those commentators, from the 1930s to the 1990s, witnessed what Caldwell had seen. First in east Georgia, and later throughout the South, he came face to face with the kind of body-breaking and soul-numbing poverty that today is associated with countries of the Third World. That the victims of such poverty were not typical of the South did not make them any less real. In Caldwell, the poorest people in the poorest part of the country found a strong and sensitive champion who, in fiction and nonfiction, castigated politicians from courthouse to Capitol for failing to deal adequately with the problems of the South's dispossessed or for refusing even to admit that such problems existed.

Among the poorest people in the poorest part of the country, the most forlorn were women. Although gender is a minor theme in Caldwell's early work, his Depression stories that include women characters display a comprehension of the special problems facing them that is remarkable for a man who had so many difficulties with women in his own life. He understood the travail of Julia Craddock, a cotton farmer's wife; he understood the antics of Ellie May Lester, who had to rely on her sexual enticements to save herself from starvation; he understood the sacrifices made by other of his Depression women to try to preserve the dignity and self-respect of themselves, their families, or others close to them. Significantly, in his later work, when poverty no longer possessed the urgency that it had in the 1930s, the plight of women assumes greater importance. Trapped in a man's world, forced by circumstances that they cannot control to behave in a manner not of their choosing, Caldwell's women often act in ways that are shocking to conventional sensibilities. Yet seldom does their creator view them without sympathy.

As culpable as politics for the failure to address the South's woes was conservative Christianity. In Caldwell's view, religion, as commonly practiced in the South, was the opiate not only of the masses but also of the well-to-do. In the 1920s and 1930s, most churches, conservative in social expression yet radical in spiritual display, too often neglected the temporal well-being of the destitute and instead beguiled them with an otherworldliness that amounted to little more than shamanism. To their great shame, too many ministers preached only the sweet by-and-by as they ignored the bitter here and now. In the 1960s, white churches failed abysmally to promote the cause of civil rights and were sometimes in the vanguard of resistance. From the earlier period to the later, many self-styled "good Christians" exhibited undue concern with other people's behavior and far too little interest in their physical and social welfare.

That Caldwell failed to portray the salutary effects of conservative Christianity in the lives of its practitioners reflects his conviction that the principal purpose of religion should be to effect society's improvement. As the son of a minister who was often maligned for propagating the social gospel, he saw "good Christians" at their worst. Thus he could not see that the otherworldliness that he perceived as narcotic was for many southerners energizing. The promise of eternal life through the saving grace of Jesus Christ made bearable the earthly lives of countless southerners, white and black, rich and poor. To the poor, the people that Caldwell was most concerned with, religion was virtually everything. The people's writer failed to perceive the totality of the most important dimension in the lives of the people that he wrote about.

Yet his vision was valid within its limits. Should one doubt the reality of Caldwell's rogue preachers, he need only remember the recently deposed televangelists from Carolina and Louisiana who were revealed to be little more than concupiscent frauds. Should one question the reality of Caldwell's portrayal of socially irresponsible religion, she need only know that eleven o'clock on Sunday morning is the most racially segregated hour of the week and she need only hear sermons that describe AIDS sufferers as evidence of God's wrath. Should one deny the reality of Caldwell's depiction of booster Christianity, he need only observe highway billboards and television commercials that seem concerned more with increasing the membership of a given church than with creating the kingdom of God on earth. With religion, as with every other social theme that he treated, Caldwell spoke harsh truths. To the social gospeler's son, the church, of all institutions, should be striving to make the world a better place.

Nowhere is Caldwell's exceptionalism as a southern writer more evident than in his treatment of race. Although there were a few other white southern writers in the 1930s who dealt with the issue in an enlightened manner, none mounted as sustained an attack against the evil of racism as Caldwell. Moreover, his plain style, forthright and direct, insured that the reader would comprehend his message.[9] Notwithstanding the artistic power with which he invested his delineation of the effects of poverty, it is his anger and agony over the poison that racism injected into southern life that called forth his best work. A skeptical reader might argue that Jeeter Lester bore some responsibility for his condition. No rational person, not even a white southerner in the 1930s, could contend that Will Maxie, Candy-Man Beechum, Clem Henry, and Christy Tucker deserved their fate. They were not razor-toting "bad niggers" who loafed around Darktown spoiling for a fight and plotting to ravage white women. It was their self-respect, their good habits, and their skin color that got them killed.

Caldwell assaulted the citadel of racism throughout his career: from the 1930s, when he led the charge amid denunciation even from southern liberals, to the 1960s, when he was one of many warriors—one whose earlier battles went unacknowledged by other writers who were by then in the vanguard. A profoundly moral writer, Caldwell never blinked at the most vexing issue in all of the South's history. His proposed solution, advanced as early as the mid-1930s and offered throughout the rest of his life, was as radical as his criticism of the problem was forthright. Unknowingly echoing Frederick Douglass, he argued that only the amalgamation of black and white could save the South, and the rest of America, from the evil of racism by rendering race redundant.[10]

In light of Caldwell's treatment of the themes of class, gender, religion, and race, it should hardly be surprising to know that he did not consider himself to be "a spokesman for the South." Yet neither did he consider himself to be a defamer of his native region. "I had no intention at all," he said late in life, "to try to make the South look worse than it was." Reality there was bad enough, and he believed that his fictional and nonfictional representations of that reality were valid.[11]

Most of Caldwell's writing belies his oft-expressed assertion from the 1950s on that there was no social purpose to his work, that he was only a storyteller. He was, of course, a storyteller and, at his best, one with few equals. At the same time, most of his strongest fiction was clearly intended to serve the cause of social reform. No doubt his late denial of his early intention reflected his awareness of the critical disfavor in which reformist fiction was held after its halcyon days of the 1930s. Notwithstanding his denigration of critics throughout most of his career, he deeply wanted to be considered a serious artist, and he knew that critics and scholars ultimately determine a writer's standing. In the conservative atmosphere after the Second World War, writing of social protest, according to the formalist standards that dominated criticism, was topical, ephemeral, and not purely literary. Caldwell's concern to rehabilitate his reputation among critics caused him on occasion to disparage the greatest element of his work.[12]

Instead of worrying about what critics thought—despite his repeated claims that he did not care—Caldwell should have dug out the old scrapbooks of clippings that he had kept from the 1930s. He would have been gratified by what he read from the pens of many of his fellow southerners. For every hostile review of one of his books that accused him of being a communist, or a corrupter of morals, or a traitor to the South, he would have found a laudatory review that commended his artistic skill, his social conscience, and his willingness to take seriously people who for too long had been the objects of condescension, ridicule, or mere pity. He would have discovered that he had many more defenders among his homefolk than he realized. In the destitute South of the 1930s, there were people who were able to articulate their knowledge that folk like the Lesters, grotesque as they might seem to literary critics, were all too real.

Despite his frequent claims in the postwar period that he was only a storyteller, from time to time during those years Caldwell acknowledged what he consistently had maintained in the 1930s when his critical reputation was at its zenith. Occasionally, he admitted that a great part of his goal was to reveal injustice in the hope that improvement would occur in the lives of southerners—blacks and poor whites—who had never had a chance to experience the promise of America's Declaration of Independence, who had never had a chance to enjoy economic liberty or to pursue personal happiness. When he was candid rather than cagey, he proudly admitted that much of his work had a purpose that was overtly reformist.[13]

Although Caldwell had no control over the rightward drift of sociopolitical thinking after 1945 that created a climate inimical to his kind of writing, he nonetheless bore considerable responsibility for his fall from critical grace. During the paperback revolution that followed the Second World War, he did his best to insure that his reputation would lie in a slough. He allowed some of his newly written stories to be published in pulp magazines. He allowed his great works of the 1930s to be packaged in ways that obscured their meaning. He allowed the distributor of his paperbacks to use him as a huckster. What is more important, some of his postwar writing is execrable. Yet the critic who judges the body of a writer's work by its worst examples is a bad critic, and such judgment has sometimes been inflicted on Caldwell. His reputation has suffered, as Scott MacDonald says, from "a back-asswards system of values." Moreover, as Sylvia Jenkins Cook has noted, critics bestowed their greatest praise on the very books that were the most popular. Unintentionally, critics reinforced Caldwell's lifelong respect for the perceptiveness of the general reader.[14]

That respect led Caldwell to value the opinions of such readers far above the dicta of critics. As he saw himself, he was the people's writer. The hundreds of letters he received from people who had read his work suggest that there was ample reason for his perception of himself. Although some of those correspondents called him everything but a gentleman, many others expressed their gratitude for his concern for the deprived, and some asked questions about his work that indicated that ordinary people, South, North, and abroad, read it closely and took it seriously. Was the protagonist in "Daughter" black or white? Was Lonnie Newsome in "Kneel to the Rising Sun" black or white? What was Fiddler in "The Growing Season"—a dog, a mule, an imbecilic child? When Caldwell responded to such queries, and he often did, his answer invariably was that the reader should decide for himself, a reply that indicated not only his resolve to let the work speak for itself but also his regard for the intelligence of the reader.[15]

The people's writer was proud of the enormous sales of his books, which occurred after their issue in paperback. Popularity was not something to apologize for, but was instead something to be grateful for. That millions of people bought his books took some of the sting out of critical rejection and reinforced the aggressive anti-intellectualism that he displayed throughout most of his career. That many of those millions bought his books for the wrong reason—for their alluring covers rather than for their somber, and comic, content—did not perturb him. He hoped that his message came through. Yet he realized that, despite the vast sales, his books would not reach all of his intended readers. "Real people," he told two interviewers late in his career, "might not be affluent enough to buy a book—even a fifty cent one." But, he continued, such people "make life, and that's what's worth writing about."[16]

What makes Caldwell unique is his writing about the forebears of people who even in the relatively affluent postwar era could not afford to buy a fifty-cent book. No southern writer before him had presented the poor, white and black, in the manner he did—as victims of a culture of poverty that had developed as a result of oppression that spanned generations. Earlier southern writers would not have understood such a concept.[17]

It is, in fact, Caldwell's ignorance of the history of southern literature that goes far toward explaining the strength of his great work of the 1930s. Although he was aware that plantation romance existed—part of his purpose was to show its limits—he had read the work of only one author who was commonly considered to have written in that genre. He greatly admired Joel Chandler Harris's Uncle Remus tales, which are complex stories that subvert, rather than teach, the lessons of the moonlight-and-magnolias school. What is more to the point, he read nothing by southwestern humorists until 1954, when, on being introduced to George Washington Harris's Sut Lovingood yarns, he expressed his keen appreciation of them. The writer to whom he was sometimes compared by sympathetic critics—Mark Twain—he claimed not to have read. He was likewise unaware of the work of other nineteenth-century southern writers that exhibited themes similar to his: the radical treatment of race by George W. Cable and the frank presentation of sex by Amélie Rives and Kate Chopin. Caldwell's ignorance enabled him to approach his material, the lives of people whose stories had never been fully told, unencumbered by the past.[18]

Caldwell's lack of interest in the history of southern literature—and in the history of almost anything else, including that of his family—was accompanied by a burning concern for the present. In the 1920s, when his ideas were forming, his interests lay in sociological studies, for their attempt to address pressing problems, and in realistic fiction, for its depiction of ordinary people in contemporary settings. Those intellectually formative years set the pattern for virtually all of his writing. Among his 175 works of fiction, only one, a later and lesser novel entitled *Summertime Island,* is set in the past. His ignorance of the South's literary history enabled him to paint a portrait of poor whites that filled a void in regional writing.[19]

Caldwell, who was only refining for fiction what he had seen in life, did not know that his treatment of poor whites was unique until he read Shields McIlwaine's 1939 study of the depiction of poor-whites in southern literature. He thought so highly of *The Southern Poor-White from Lubberland to Tobacco Road* that he reviewed it for publication, something that he seldom did after 1930. Caldwell rightly considered McIlwaine's book to be path-breaking. McIlwaine, who was also a southerner and the son of a Presbyterian minister, rightly considered Caldwell's portrayal of poor whites to be pioneer. It was not until the appearance of Caldwell's fiction, McIlwaine observed, that sex, "a long-neglected side of poor-white life," was fully developed; that a character such as Jeeter Lester, who was the first "completely adequate portrait of a man from his class in American literature," was fashioned; and that the dimension of tragedy was introduced—before *Tobacco Road,* "there was merely the pathetic and the near tragic."[20]

What Caldwell's haphazard formal education failed to supply was compensated manyfold by experience, which, he believed, was the best teacher; by his father's influence, which was profound; by his closeness to the South's poor—white and black—which gave him his subject; by his stint at the *Atlanta Journal,* which enabled him to develop a plain style of writing and which introduced him to a wide array of contemporary literature; and by his genius.

Few were the critics who described Caldwell as a writer of genius. Many of those who esteemed his work of the 1930s—Malcolm Cowley was preeminent among them—nonetheless spoke of the narrowness of his vision. By the mid-1940s, more and more critics were saying that he had exhausted his material. By the end of his career, his work was seldom deemed worthy of notice. Caldwell ignored the charge, increasingly common by the mid-1940s, that he was writing too much. Even so, by that time, writing was usually just a job, not an obsession as it had been earlier. Like a banker who went to his bank or a storekeeper who went to his store, Caldwell went to his study and wrote for eight or nine hours a day, six days a week, sometimes for ten months a year. By the time his final book was issued in the year of his death, he had published twelve volumes of nonfiction, twenty-five novels, and nearly a hundred fifty short stories. Writing was what he did; what else could he do? He could not understand critics who admonished him to stop doing the only thing he knew. Nor could he comprehend his publisher's advice to write a big book—longer than the two-hundred-odd-page novels he was turning out after 1945—and a happy book. Never before had he written a big book, or a happy one.[21]

If critics and scholars often judged Caldwell by his worst work, and if publishers asked him to write books that he could not write, three Nobel laureates expressed great admiration for the best of his work. Late in the 1950s, in an assessment that modified an earlier opinion that had characterized Caldwell's later work as "trash," William Faulkner, to whom Caldwell was often unfavorably compared after the 1930s, said: "I think that the first books, *God's Little Acre* and the short stories, that's enough for any man." Latin America's magic realist likewise praised his work. Gabriel García Márquez, whose avowed debt to journalism and to the language of "country folk," whose radical politics, and whose anti-intellectualism all mirror Caldwell's experience, said in 1982, "I learned a lot from . . . Erskine Caldwell." A year later, Saul Bellow wrote to Caldwell's wife Virginia: "I thought your husband should have won the Nobel Prize."[22]

Those tributes deeply gratified Caldwell. Ever doubtful of the quality of his work, he was doubly pleased by the accolades of writers who had won the prize that always had been denied him. But he appreciated even more the honor bestowed by a hotel porter in Reno, Nevada, early in 1957. Pausing in his duties, the porter asked Caldwell, "May I just shake your hand? . . . I've enjoyed your books so much." "I would rather have a comment like that," Caldwell told his wife, "than the praise of all the great critics." That ordinary people found his work satisfying was enough.[23]

Yet today, despite a reawakening of interest in Caldwell's work among American scholars, few of his countrymen read it, nor have they for many years. What caused his great, though brief, popularity among Americans after 1945 is no longer appealing. Caldwellian sex, once shocking, is now banal. It is regrettable that many Americans are ignorant of his best work. It is deplorable that many southerners have never heard of him. To anyone sympathetic to Caldwell's work, the irony is galling: the descendants of "the people"—poor whites and blacks—of whom and for whom he wrote do not know him. Many of those people, who enjoy a better education, greater prosperity, and the opportunity to engage in the pursuit of happiness to a far greater degree than their parents or grandparents are not aware that Caldwell strived with all his might to contribute to their betterment.

That ignorance is not Caldwell's fault. The books are there to be read: *American Earth, Tobacco Road, God's Little Acre, We Are the Living, Kneel to the Rising Sun,* and *Southways,* along with *Some American People, You Have Seen Their Faces, In Search of Bisco,* and *Deep South.* In fiction and in nonfiction, Caldwell told his story. Notwithstanding its affinities with the work of Charles Dickens, D. H. Lawrence, and Sherwood Anderson, which the young Caldwell knew, and with the work of America's southwestern humorists, which the young Caldwell did not know, his story is sui generis. It is modern but not modernist because, for all of the despair in his work, there is an underlying hope. As the son of a social-gospel clergyman, he never lost his faith in the possibility of social progress.

That faith moved Caldwell to tear down the idols enshrined in the temple that housed the myths of a benign South. In the gospel according to Caldwell, the South was a region where a sense of place meant little more than local boosterism, where the reality of family disintegrated, where the concept of community dissolved, where the image of racial concord was merely illusion, and where the church bestowed its blessing on much that was wrong. Caldwell's desire to spread his gospel caused him to ignore much that was good in the South and to amplify much that was bad. Even so, his myth of the South bore greater resemblance to the lives of millions of southerners than did the myth generated by many other southern writers of the 1920s and 1930s.

The critics and readers who castigated Caldwell for the narrowness of his vision were dead wrong. For as long as some people are ill fed, ill clad, and ill housed; for as long as some people are mired in ignorance; for as long as some people suffer because of their race, their religion, or their sex—for so long do all people fail to achieve full humanity. Caldwell's people were southerners. They, of all people, should honor a man who tried mightily to make the South a better place.

NOTES

SELECT BIBLIOGRAPHY

INDEX

NOTES

PREFACE

1. MacDonald, *Critical Essays on Erskine Caldwell*; Devlin, *Erskine Caldwell*; Cook, *Erskine Caldwell and the Fiction of Poverty*; Klevar, *Erskine Caldwell*; Miller, *Erskine Caldwell*.

INTRODUCTION: The Character of Erskine Caldwell

1. Erskine Caldwell, *With All My Might*, 16–30, 91, 97; "About the Author," in Erskine Caldwell, *Tobacco Road* (1932; repr. New York, n.d.), [172]; Erskine Caldwell, *Call It Experience*, 43.

2. Rahv, "Paleface and Redskin," in Rahv, *Essays on Literature and Politics*, 3–7.

3. Caldwell's first wife, Helen, and his last wife, Virginia, assisted him greatly with his work. Caldwell always did the actual writing.

4. Erskine Caldwell to Helen Caldwell, 19 May 1933, [June 1933], [May 1937], and 23 May 1937; Julius Weiss to Erskine Caldwell, 20 Feb. 1942; Erskine Caldwell to St. Joseph Sanatorium and Hospital, 28 June 1943; I. S. Caldwell to Erskine Caldwell, 23 Mar. 1944; Erskine Caldwell to Richard P. Maner, 11 Sept. 1950, 5 Apr. and 9 Aug. 1951, Erskine Caldwell Collection, Dartmouth College Library. Erskine Caldwell to Alfred Morang, 26 Feb. 1935, 11 June 1942, and 23 Mar. 1951, Alfred Morang Papers, bMS Am 1638, Houghton Library, Harvard University; Erskine Caldwell to Mr. and Mrs. I. S. Caldwell, 25 Apr. 1939 and 6 July 1944, Erskine Caldwell Collection, Hargrett Rare Book and Manuscript Library, University of Georgia Libraries. Hereafter, when citing letters written by Erskine Caldwell and letters written to him, I shall refer to him as EC. Also, I shall cite hereafter the Erskine Caldwell Collection at the Dartmouth College Library as ECC-DC and the Erskine Caldwell Collection at the University of Georgia Libraries as ECC-UGA. Klevar, *Erskine Caldwell*, 235; McClintock, "Erskine Caldwell," in Arnold, *Conversations*, 103–8, esp. 104. Interviews with Mary M. Maner, 25 May and 18 Dec. 1990; interview with Virginia Caldwell Hibbs, 2 July 1992; interview with Erskine Caldwell Jr., 4 July 1992. For further evidence of Caldwell's generosity, see EC to Mr. and Mrs. I. S. Caldwell, 22 Dec. 1940, 9 Nov. 1941, 2 and 22 Oct. 1942, and 31 Mar. and 14 Dec. 1943, ECC-UGA.

5. Frank Daniel, "Erskine Caldwell Keeps Plugging the Basic Need for

Human Dignity," *Atlanta Journal,* 26 Feb. 1959, in *Scrapbooks of Erskine Caldwell,* reel 5; hereafter cited as *EC Scrapbooks.* William A. Sutton to EC, 26 May 1970; Edward R. Fagan to William A. Sutton, 27 July 1970; Ray McIver to William A. Sutton, 15 Sept. 1970; Harry Behn to William A. Sutton, 21 Oct. 1970, ECC-DC.

6. Erskine Caldwell, "Starving Babies Suckled by Dogs in Georgia Wastes," *New York Post,* 21 Feb. 1935, *EC Scrapbooks,* reel 1. The headline of Caldwell's story was supplied by the *Post.*

7. Interview with Henrietta Boyce, Annette Johnson, Lucille M. Parrish, and Helen Williams, 21 Mar. 1991. The incident described was related by Mrs. Boyce.

CHAPTER ONE: The Maverick Preacher's Wayward Son

1. Sources that cite 1902 as the year of Caldwell's birth are as follows: Caldwell's registration card at the University of Virginia, 15 Sept. 1923, Office of the Registrar, University of Virginia; Joe Leigh Camp to EC, 1 Feb. 1965; EC to William A. Sutton, 14 Sept. 1970, ECC-DC. The year 1903 is cited in the following sources: Caldwell's registration card at the University of Virginia, 6 Jan. 1925, Office of the Registrar, University of Virginia; EC to Clerk of Court, Coweta County, Ga., 11 Mar. 1942; Caroline Caldwell to EC, 18 Mar. 1965; William A. Sutton to Thomas H. Frier, 28 Sept. 1972, ECC-DC. See also Klevar, *Erskine Caldwell,* 418–19, n. 9. I am grateful to Robert D. LeHeup, supervisor of transcripts at the University of Virginia, for supplying copies of Caldwell's registration cards.

2. Caldwell, *With All My Might,* 3; Klevar, *Erskine Caldwell,* 3. In 1990, plans were initiated to move the house in which Caldwell was born from White Oak to the town of Moreland, four miles distant. Following relocation and restoration, "the Little Manse" became the Erskine Caldwell Museum, which officially opened on 4 July 1992.

3. Interview with Mary M. Maner, 25 May 1990; Klevar, *Erskine Caldwell,* 4–5. My account of Carrie's ancestry is based primarily on information compiled by her nephew, Alfred W. Maner. I am grateful to Mr. Maner for making those records available.

4. Interview with Mary M. Maner, 25 May 1990; Samuel R. Spencer Jr. to EC, 25 June 1964, ECC-DC.

5. Interview with Mary M. Maner, 25 May 1990; Whit Burnett to EC, 19 Oct. 1951, Archives of *Story Magazine,* Princeton University; Klevar, *Erskine Caldwell,* 7; W. A. Kennedy, *Sesquicentennial History,* 15, 27.

6. Howard Caldwell to I. S. Caldwell, 12 Apr. 1944, ECC-UGA; marginalia by Carrie Caldwell on letter from Robert Cantwell to EC, 23 Aug. 1950, ECC-DC; Mr. and Mrs. George H. Caldwell to Wayne Mixon, 1 Mar. 1991, letter in my possession.

7. *Charlotte News,* 10 Jan. 1961, *EC Scrapbooks,* reel 5; undated statement, Office of the President, Erskine College, Robert Cantwell Papers, Special Collec-

tions, Knight Library, University of Oregon; *Centennial History,* 265; W. A. Kennedy, *Sesquicentennial History,* 104; Erskine Caldwell, *Deep South,* 179–82; interview with Mary M. Maner, 18 Dec. 1990.

8. J. M. Nickles to Robert Cantwell, 11 Sept. 1950, Cantwell Papers; Sutton, "A Lover's Quarrel," IV-7; Official Transcript of the Record of I. S. Caldwell, Office of the Registrar, Erskine College, copy in Cantwell Papers.

9. R. C. Grier to Robert Cantwell, 30 Aug. 1950, Cantwell Papers.

10. Sutton, "A Lover's Quarrel," IV-8; Service Records of Ira S. Caldwell, Military Reference Branch, National Archives and Records Administration. Although Ira's records do not specify the reason for his transfer, he was undoubtedly aware that he would suffer reduction in rank and pay. Michael G. Knapp to Wayne Mixon, 19 July and 23 Aug. 1991, letters in my possession. I am grateful to Mr. Knapp for providing copies of Ira's service records.

11. Gen. Edward F. Witsell to Mrs. Ira S. Caldwell, 9 Dec. 1947, ECC-UGA; undated statement, Office of the President, Erskine College, Cantwell Papers; marginalia by Carrie Caldwell on letter from Robert Cantwell to EC, 23 Aug. 1950, ECC-DC.

12. Interview with Henrietta Boyce, Annette Johnson, Lucille M. Parrish, and Helen Williams; interview with Leroy Lewis, 21 Mar. 1991; interview with Ralph Stephens, 28 Jan. 1991; interview with Harry P. Wren, 21 Mar. 1991; interviews with Mary M. Maner, 25 May and 14 July 1990. Sutton, "A Lover's Quarrel," I-4, IV-8; June Caldwell to *New Yorker Magazine,* 8 Nov. 1951, ECC-DC; interview with Virginia Caldwell Hibbs, 2 July 1992; Farley, "Erskine Caldwell," 202–17.

13. Interview with Mary M. Maner, 14 July 1990; Caldwell, *With All My Might,* 13–14.

14. Interview with Mary M. Maner, 18 Dec. 1990.

15. W. A. Kennedy, *Sesquicentennial History,* 104; June Caldwell to *New Yorker Magazine,* 8 Nov. 1951; Howard Caldwell to EC, 8 Jan. 1947, ECC-DC; Caldwell, *With All My Might.* 9–10.

16. W. A. Kennedy, *Sesquicentennial History,* 104; Caldwell, *With All My Might,* 19–27.

17. Mrs. I. S. Caldwell, "Home Missions," Woman's Presbyterial Missionary Union *Monthly Bulletin* 6 (June 1912): 10–11; Mrs. I. S. Caldwell, "Home Missions," Woman's Presbyterial Missionary Union *Monthly Bulletin* 7 (May 1913): 8–9; Mrs. Ira Caldwell, "Home Missions," Woman's Presbyterial Missionary Union *Monthly Bulletin* 7 (Oct. 1913): 8–9; Mrs. I. S. Caldwell, "Home Missions," *A.R.P. Journal of Missions* 2 (Feb. 1915): 9–11. The title of the magazine was changed from *Monthly Bulletin* to *A.R.P. Journal of Missions* in December 1913. On the ascendancy of extreme racism in the turn-of-the-century South, see Williamson, *The Crucible of Race.*

18. Mrs. I. S. Caldwell, "Home Missions," Woman's Presbyterial Missionary Union *Monthly Bulletin* 6 (Aug. 1912): 6–7.

19. Mrs. Ira Caldwell, "Home Missions," Woman's Presbyterial Missionary Union *Monthly Bulletin* 7 (Oct. 1913): 8–9; Mrs. Ira Caldwell, "Home Missions,"

Woman's Presbyterial Missionary Union *Monthly Bulletin* 7 (Sept. 1913): 4–5; Mrs. I. S. Caldwell, "Home Missions," *A.R.P. Journal of Missions* 2 (Aug. 1915): 6–8. Copies of Carrie's seven columns cited in notes 17–19, along with copies of forty other columns, are in the ECC-UGA.

20. W. A. Kennedy, *Sesquicentennial History,* 104; R. C. Grier to Robert Cantwell, 30 Aug. 1950, Cantwell Papers.

21. Ray A. King, *A History of the Associate Reformed Presbyterian Church,* 101; W. A. Kennedy, *Sesquicentennial History,* 2; "Associate Reformed Presbyterian Church," in Hill, *Encyclopedia of Religion in the South,* 76.

22. Mrs. I. S. Caldwell, "Home Missions," Woman's Presbyterial Missionary Union *Monthly Bulletin* 3 (Jan. 1910): 7, ECC-UGA; Miller, "Tracing Tobacco Road," 9, 27.

23. J. G. McCain et al., "To the Memphis and Louisville Presbytery in Regular Session Assembled," 5 Nov. 1917, copy in ECC-UGA; M. G. Boyce to William A. Sutton, 15 Nov. 1970, ECC-DC.

24. Mrs. Wilo Anderson to Thelma Harmon, undated, ECC-DC; Sutton, "A Lover's Quarrel," unpaginated; John D. Smith to Wayne Mixon, 27 Nov. 1990, letter in my possession.

25. Carrie Caldwell to EC, ? July 1953; Narrative by Carrie Caldwell on letter from Robert Cantwell to EC, 23 Aug. 1950, ECC-DC; Minutes of the Session, Salem Church, 11 Aug. 1916 and 5 July 1919. I am grateful to John D. Smith for supplying copies of records from Salem Church.

26. Caldwell, *With All My Might,* 37; Miller, "Tracing Tobacco Road," 45.

27. Lavinia M. Smith to Dan B. Miller, 25 Jan. 1991, copy in my possession courtesy of John D. Smith; Sutton, "A Lover's Quarrel," unpaginated; Miller, "Tracing Tobacco Road," 38; M. G. Boyce to William A. Sutton, 15 Nov. 1970, ECC-DC.

28. Caldwell, *With All My Might,* 35; Miller, "Tracing Tobacco Road," 43; Lavinia M. Smith to Dan B. Miller, 20 Nov. 1990, copy in my possession courtesy of John D. Smith.

29. Caldwell, *With All My Might,* 29–33.

30. Minutes of the Session, Salem Church, 5 July 1919; W. A. Kennedy, *Sesquicentennial History,* 398, 598; R. C. Grier to Robert Cantwell, 30 Aug. 1950, Cantwell Papers. Caldwell erroneously cited 1918 as the year of the move; *Call It Experience,* 13, and *With All My Might,* 41.

31. Sutton, "A Lover's Quarrel," IV-16; interview with Harry P. Wren; interview with Leroy Lewis. Ira was quoted by Mary M. Maner during the course of the Lewis interview.

32. Interview with Leroy Lewis; interview with Harry P. Wren; interview with Henrietta Boyce, Annette Johnson, Lucille M. Parrish, and Helen Williams; interview with Ralph Stephens.

33. Interview with Harry P. Wren; interview with Ralph Stephens.

34. Sutton, "A Lover's Quarrel," IV-21; interview with Mary M. Maner, 25 May 1990; interview with Ralph Stephens; Miller, "Tracing Tobacco Road," 73; Caldwell, *Call It Experience,* 24–25.

35. *Louisville (Ga.) News and Farmer,* 24 Aug. 1944, obituary of Ira S. Caldwell reproduced in W. A. Kennedy to Robert Cantwell, 5 Sept. 1950, Cantwell Papers; I. S. Caldwell, "A School That Teaches a Community," 764–65.

36. I. S. Caldwell, "The Bunglers," 202–10, 247–51, 293–99, 332–36, 377–83; Degler, *In Search of Human Nature,* 37–48, 139–51; Sutton, "A Lover's Quarrel," IV-35.

37. I. S. Caldwell, "The Bunglers," 203, 249–50.

38. Ibid., 249–51, 297–99.

39. Ibid., 249, 296, 377. Rodger L. Hurley has observed that poverty is sometimes a cause of mental retardation. Hurley, *Poverty and Mental Retardation,* 65.

40. I. S. Caldwell, "The Bunglers," 334, 336.

41. Ibid., 383.

42. Interview with Leroy Lewis; interview with Ralph Stephens; interview with Harry P. Wren; *Louisville (Ga.) News and Farmer,* 24 Aug. 1944, Cantwell Papers; Sutton, "A Lover's Quarrel," IV-2, IV-27; Cy Hood to William A. Sutton, 6 Dec. 1970, ECC-DC.

43. Interview with Harry P. Wren.

44. Interview with Mary M. Maner, 14 July 1990; Sutton, "A Lover's Quarrel," unpaginated; interview with Harry P. Wren; interview with Ralph Stephens; EC to *Chatterbox,* 4 July 1966, ECC-DC; Caldwell, *With All My Might,* 44.

45. Interview with Harry P. Wren; Caldwell, *In Search of Bisco,* 11–15; Caldwell, *Call It Experience,* 15; interview with Ralph Stephens.

46. Sutton, "A Lover's Quarrel," unpaginated; interview with Harry P. Wren; interview with Leroy Lewis.

47. Caldwell, *Call It Experience,* 25; Caldwell, *With All My Might,* 112; Caldwell, *In Search of Bisco,* 12.

48. Sutton, "A Lover's Quarrel," unpaginated.

49. Caldwell, *With All My Might,* 51; Caldwell, *Call It Experience,* 27; Miller, "Tracing Tobacco Road," 71.

50. Official Transcript of the Record of Erskine Caldwell, Office of the Registrar, Erskine College; William A. Sutton to EC, 27 Sept. 1971, ECC-DC; Erskine Caldwell, "Mr. Caldwell Protests," *New Republic* 79 (27 June 1934): 184–85, reprinted in MacDonald, *Critical Essays,* 32–33.

51. Jesse S. Agnew to William A. Sutton, 25 Sept. 1970, ECC-DC; Sutton, "A Lover's Quarrel," various pagination [16, 173].

52. Sutton, "A Lover's Quarrel," 22–23; Al Hansen to William A. Sutton, 11 Feb. 1972; Affidavit for Arrest, City of Bogalusa versus Erskine Caldewell [*sic*], 3 Feb. 1922, ECC-DC; Caldwell, *Call It Experience,* 31–32; Caldwell, *With All My Might,* 58.

53. Miller, "Tracing Tobacco Road," 65; Sutton, "A Lover's Quarrel," IV-3; Cy Hood to William A. Sutton, 8 Dec. 1970, ECC-DC; *Atlanta Journal,* 19 Nov. 1921. Even though Caldwell was in his second year of attendance at Erskine College in November 1921, he was still a freshman in academic standing.

54. EC to Mr. and Mrs. Ira S. Caldwell, 20 Mar. 1921, ECC-UGA; Sutton, "A

Lover's Quarrel," IV-27, IV-29; John D. Smith to Wayne Mixon, 27 Nov. 1990, letter in my possession.

55. Caldwell, *With All My Might,* 7.

CHAPTER TWO: The Making of a Writer

1. Sutton, "A Lover's Quarrel," various pagination [24, 181]; Caldwell, *With All My Might,* 63–64; interview with Mary M. Maner, 14 July 1990; *Jefferson County Reporter,* 6 Sept. 1923, copy in ECC-UGA.

2. Record of Erskine Caldwell, Office of the Registrar, University of Virginia; Caldwell, *With All My Might,* 64; Miller, "Tracing Tobacco Road," 90–92.

3. Record of Erskine Caldwell, Office of the Registrar, University of Virginia. I am grateful to Robert D. LeHeup of the University of Virginia's Registrar's Office for supplying me with copies of Caldwell's transcript and descriptions of the courses that he took.

4. Caldwell, *With All My Might,* 65; George E. Nitzshe to EC, 1 Apr. 1941, ECC-DC; Klevar, *Erskine Caldwell,* 54; Sutton, "A Lover's Quarrel," unpaginated; EC to Mr. and Mrs. Ira S. Caldwell, 5 Sept. 1924, ECC-UGA.

5. EC to Mr. and Mrs. Ira S. Caldwell, 5 Sept. 1924, ECC-UGA.

6. Caldwell, *With All My Might,* 71–73; Sutton, "A Lover's Quarrel," various pagination [50, 207]; EC to Mr. and Mrs. Ira S. Caldwell, 6 Nov. 1924, ECC-UGA.

7. Registration Card of Erskine Caldwell, 6 Jan. 1925, Office of the Registrar, University of Virginia; Record of Erskine Caldwell, Office of the Registrar, University of Virginia; Klevar, "Interview with Helen Caldwell Cushman," in Arnold, *Erskine Caldwell Reconsidered,* 87; Certificate of Marriage of Erskine Caldwell and Helen Lannigan, 3 Mar. 1925, copy in ECC-DC; Klevar, "Caldwell's Women," Arnold, *Erskine Caldwell Reconsidered,* 19, quoting Helen Caldwell Cushman.

8. Record of Erskine Caldwell, Office of the Registrar, University of Virginia; Sutton, "A Lover's Quarrel," V-6, V-7; Caldwell, *Call It Experience,* 36; Caldwell, *With All My Might,* 83; interview with Ralph Stephens; *Jefferson County Reporter,* 6 May 1926, copy in ECC-UGA.

9. Caldwell, *Call It Experience,* 40–41; Flora, "Fiction in the 1920s," Rubin et al., *The History of Southern Literature,* 280–81.

10. Caldwell, *Call It Experience,* 37–39; Caldwell, *With All My Might,* 85–87; E. Caldwell, review of *The Selmans,* by V. R. Emanuel, *Charlotte Observer,* 6 Dec. 1925; E. Caldwell, review of *Snow Rubies,* by "Ganpat" [M. L. A. Gompertz], *Charlotte Observer,* 6 Dec. 1925; E. Caldwell, review of *Thirteen,* by F. Britten Austin, *Charlotte Observer,* 3 Jan. 1926.

11. Erskine Caldwell, review of *A Modernist and His Creed,* by Edward Mortimer Chapman, *Charlotte Observer,* 28 Feb. 1926; Erskine Caldwell, review of *The Land of Mist,* by A. Conan Doyle, *Charlotte Observer,* 25 July 1926; E. Caldwell, review of *The Red Web,* by Blair Coan, *Charlotte Observer,* 13 Dec. 1925; Erskine Caldwell, review of *America and Germany,* by Sidney Brooks,

Charlotte Observer, 10 Jan. 1926; Odum and Willard, *Systems of Public Welfare,* 7; E. Caldwell, review of *Systems of Public Welfare, Charlotte Observer,* 20 Dec. 1925. I am grateful to Erik Bledsoe for supplying a copy of Caldwell's review of *The Land of Mist.*

12. Puckett, *Folk Beliefs of the Southern Negro,* vii; Erskine Caldwell, review of *Folk Beliefs of the Southern Negro, Charlotte Observer,* 15 Aug. 1926.

13. Dowd, *The Negro in American Life,* 581; Erskine Caldwell, review of *The Negro in American Life, Charlotte Observer,* 21 Nov. 1926.

14. Klevar, *Erskine Caldwell,* 70; Record of Erskine Caldwell, Office of the Registrar, University of Virginia; *Catalogue of Courses,* University of Virginia, 1926–27, 163.

15. This paragraph is based upon Caldwell's evaluations of the following articles: Benjamin Stolberg, "American Labor Stands Pat," *Independent* 117 (30 Oct. 1926): 501–2, 512; Ann Washington Craton, "Those Terrible Americans," *New Masses* 1 (Oct. 1926): 18–19, 28–29; J. B. Eggen, "The Fallacy of Eugenics," *Social Forces* 5 (Sept. 1926): 104–9; H. S. Jennings, "Inheritance of Acquired Characters," *Forum* 76 (Nov. 1926): 702–11; Wilson D. Wallis, "Race and Culture," *Scientific Monthly* 23 (Oct. 1926): 313–21; Daniel Hall, "The Relation Between Cultivated Area and Population," *Scientific Monthly* 23 (Oct. 1926): 356–65; Edward Alsworth Ross, "With the Population Mystics," *Social Forces* 5 (Sept. 1926): 32–36; Carl Van Doren, "Why I Am an Unbeliever," *Forum* 76 (Dec. 1926): 864–69; Sara Haardt, "Our Social Revolution," *Virginia Quarterly Review* 2 (Oct. 1926): 517–29; Clarence True Wilson, "Methodist Rights in Politics," *Forum* 76 (Nov. 1926): 668–81; Robert Preston Brooks, "Georgia Goes Marching On," *Forum* 76 (Nov. 1926): 748–55. Caldwell's evaluations are in the Atcheson Hench-Erskine Caldwell Collection (#9150), Manuscripts Division, Special Collections Department, University of Virginia Library.

16. Hench-Caldwell Collection, University of Virginia; Atcheson Hench Oral History (RG-26), University Archives, University of Virginia; emphasis is in original.

17. Hench Oral History, University of Virginia.

18. Registration card of Erskine Caldwell, Office of the Registrar, University of Virginia; interview with Mary M. Maner, 14 July 1990; interview with Harry P. Wren; interview with Ralph Stephens.

19. Klevar, *Erskine Caldwell,* 426 n. 19; E. Haldeman-Julius, "War!" *Haldeman-Julius Monthly* 1 (Dec. 1924): 2; Erskine Caldwell, "The Georgia Cracker," 39–42.

20. EC to Atcheson Laughlin Hench, 26 May 1970, Hench-Caldwell Collection (#9150-a), University of Virginia; Klevar, *Erskine Caldwell,* 76; Record of Erskine Caldwell, Office of the Registrar, University of Virginia.

21. Woodward, *Origins of the New South,* 416; Hall et al., *Like a Family,* 56, 59, 61–63, 77; Tindall, *Emergence of the New South,* 318.

22. Hall et al., *Like a Family,* 187–95, 213–355; Tindall, *Emergence of the New South,* 318–53.

23. Tindall, *Emergence of the New South*, 60–61; Woodward, *Origins of the New South*, 188.

24. Tindall, *Emergence of the New South*, 409, 411; Vance, *Human Geography of the South*, 188, 191; Fite, *Cotton Fields No More*, 4–5.

25. Tindall, *Emergence of the New South*, 416–21; Conrad, *Forgotten Farmers*, 83–104; Grubbs, *Cry from the Cotton*; Robert F. Martin, *Howard Kester*, 88–108.

26. Williamson, *Crucible of Race*, 117, 301–2; Ayers, *Vengeance and Justice*, 241–43; Ayers, *Promise of the New South*, 153–59; Tindall, *Emergence of the New South*, 148, 151, 174–75.

27. Tindall, *Emergence of the New South*, 187–96.

28. Ibid., 99–100; Cash, *Mind of the South*, 137–45.

29. EC to Editor, *The Nation*, 16 June 1927, Oswald Garrison Villard Papers, bMS Am 1323, by permission of the Houghton Library, Harvard University.

30. "Caldwell's Reading Reports, 1926–27," Hench-Caldwell Collection, University of Virginia; Klevar, "Interview with Helen Caldwell Cushman," in Arnold, *Erskine Caldwell Reconsidered*, 92; EC to Alfred Morang, 15 Dec. 1932, Morang Papers, by permission of the Houghton Library, Harvard University.

31. Owen, "Erskine Caldwell's Unpublished Poems," 53–57.

32. Marjorie Lee Sewell to EC, [July 1958], ECC-DC; Miller, "Tracing Tobacco Road," 150; Helen Caldwell to Mrs. I. S. Caldwell, 6 Aug. 1927, ECC-UGA; Klevar, "Erskine Caldwell," 102 (draft of *Erskine Caldwell*, courtesy of Professor Klevar).

33. Helen Caldwell to Mrs. I. S. Caldwell, 27 Nov. 1928, ECC-UGA; Klevar, *Erskine Caldwell*, 85–86; Helen Caldwell to Mrs. I. S. Caldwell, 6 Aug. 1927, ECC-UGA; Caldwell, *With All My Might*, 103; EC to I. S. Caldwell, 13 Mar. 1929, ECC-UGA; Sutton, "A Lover's Quarrel," V-46.

34. Hoffman, Allen, and Ulrich, *The Little Magazine*; Erskine Caldwell, "Joe Craddock's Old Woman," *blues* 7 (Fall 1929): 33–34.

35. Erskine Caldwell, "Midsummer Passion," in Alfred Kreymborg, Lewis Mumford, and Paul Rosenfeld, eds., *The New American Caravan* (New York: Macaulay, 1929), 96–99, reprinted in Erskine Caldwell, *Complete Stories*, 540–43. This story also appeared as "July" in *transition* no. 16–17 (June 1929): 170–73. On the dual publication, see Caldwell, *Call It Experience*, 70–71, and *With All My Might*, 96–97; and MacDonald, "Evaluative Check-List," in MacDonald, *Critical Essays*, 344. Erskine Caldwell, "The Strawberry Season," *Pagany* 1 (Winter 1930): 34–36, reprinted in Caldwell, *Complete Stories*, 34–37; Erskine Caldwell, "Tracing Life with a Finger," in Kreymborg, Mumford, and Rosenfeld, *New American Caravan*, 100–6; Erskine Caldwell, "Inspiration for Greatness," *Pagany* 1 (Winter 1930): 53–60. "Tracing Life with a Finger" and "Inspiration for Greatness" were reprinted as parts 1 and 2 of Erskine Caldwell, *The Sacrilege of Alan Kent* (Portland, Maine, 1936). Quotation is from *Sacrilege*, 29.

36. Caldwell, "Joe Craddock's Old Woman," in Caldwell, *Complete Stories*, 363–64.

37. EC to Vrest Orton, 24 Sept. 1930, ECC-DC; Caldwell, *With All My Might*,

106; Erskine Caldwell, *The Bastard*. The name of Caldwell's fictional town is likely derived from the name of the seat of Jefferson County, Georgia—Louisville. See also Owen, "The Apprenticeship of Erskine Caldwell," 197–204, and Cook, *Erskine Caldwell and the Fiction of Poverty*, 22.

38. Erskine Caldwell, "In Defense of Myself," copy in Erskine Caldwell Papers, Department of Special Collections, University of Tulsa, Oklahoma.

39. EC to Milton A. Abernethy, 7 Mar. 1932, Archive of *Contempo Magazine*, Harry Ransom Humanities Research Center, University of Texas at Austin.

CHAPTER THREE: The Godforsaken South

1. Erskine Caldwell, "Plans for Study," application to John Simon Guggenheim Foundation, [July 1931], ECC-DC.

2. Sutton, "A Lover's Quarrel," V-46; EC to Richard Johns, 12 May, 10 June, and 22 Aug. 1930, Archives of *Pagany* magazine, University of Delaware Library; Miller, "Tracing Tobacco Road," 155. Caldwell was indeed "working like hell." In addition to writing stories, he completed a novel, *Poor Fool* (New York, 1930), with an urban northern setting. He also wrote another novel with a similar setting, "The Bogus Ones," that was not published. Sutton, "A Lover's Quarrel," V-46; typescript of "The Bogus Ones" is in Sutton Papers. It is likely that yet another work was written during this period. "If Only to Remember the Flat-Lands" is an unfinished novel with a southern setting. Like *The Bastard*, it features violence and suggests an incestuous relationship; copy in ECC-UGA.

3. EC to Richard Johns, 7 Jan. and 12 July 1930, *Pagany* Archives.

4. Kuehl and Bryer, *Dear Scott/Dear Max*, 13, 162; Maxwell Perkins to EC, 13 and 26 Feb. and 5 Aug. 1930, Archives of Charles Scribner's Sons, Author Files I, Box 29, Princeton University; Erskine Caldwell, "A Very Late Spring" and "The Mating of Marjorie," *Scribner's* 87 (June 1930): 636–42; Caldwell, *Call It Experience*, 85; Klevar, *Erskine Caldwell*, 91.

5. EC to Maxwell Perkins, 23 May 1930; Maxwell Perkins to EC, 2 June 1930, Scribner Archives.

6. John Hall Wheelock to EC, 12 Nov. 1930; EC to John Hall Wheelock, 15 Dec. 1930; Wheelock to EC, 20 Dec. 1930; EC to Wheelock, 30 Dec. 1930; Wheelock to EC, 2 Jan. and 21 Feb. 1931, Scribner Archives. Scheduled for publication in February 1931, *American Earth* came out in April of that year.

7. Erskine Caldwell, "Savannah River Payday," in Caldwell, *American Earth*, 85–97, reprinted in Erskine Caldwell, *The Caldwell Caravan*, 395–400, esp. 395.

8. Ibid., esp. 398; John Hall Wheelock to EC, 12 Nov. 1930, Scribner Archives.

9. Erskine Caldwell, "Saturday Afternoon," in Caldwell, *American Earth*, 10–22, reprinted in Caldwell, *Complete Stories*, 28–33. "Saturday Afternoon" first appeared in *Nativity*, a little magazine published in Columbus, Ohio, no. 1 (Winter [i.e., Dec.] 1930): 12–16.

10. Caldwell, "Saturday Afternoon," in Caldwell, *Complete Stories*, 28–33.

11. Ibid.

12. Ibid.; John Hall Wheelock to EC, 12 Nov. 1930, Scribner Archives.

13. Erskine Caldwell, "Molly Cotton-Tail," in Caldwell, *American Earth*, 37–46, reprinted in Caldwell, *Complete Stories*, 329–33; Erskine Caldwell, "A Swell-Looking Girl," in Caldwell, *American Earth*, 67–75, reprinted in Caldwell, *Caldwell Caravan*, 391–94. "A Swell-Looking Girl" was first published in *Pagany* 1 (Spring 1930): 43–46.

14. "Erskine Caldwell Shows Marked Power," *Louisville Courier-Journal*, 5 July 1931; "The Literary Lantern," *Charlotte Observer*, 28 June 1931, *EC Scrapbooks*, reel 1. See also reviews of *American Earth* in *Montgomery Advertiser*, 10 May 1931; *Atlanta Journal*, 30 May 1931; *Richmond News Leader*, 1 July 1931; *New Orleans Times-Picayune*, 2 Aug. 1931; and *Raleigh News and Observer*, 2 Aug. 1931, *EC Scrapbooks*, reel 1.

15. A. B. Bernd, review of *American Earth*, by Erskine Caldwell, *Macon Telegraph*, 9 Aug. 1931; *Montgomery Advertiser*, 10 May 1931; *New Orleans Times-Picayune*, 2 Aug. 1931, *EC Scrapbooks*, reel 1.

16. John Hall Wheelock to EC, 5 May 1931, Scribner Archives.

17. EC to Richard Johns, 12 Apr. 1931, *Pagany* Archives. Caldwell's assertion that he worked on "Tobacco Road" for ten months has been challenged by his biographers. Miller, "Tracing Tobacco Road," 208, and Klevar, *Erskine Caldwell*, 103, argue that the actual writing of the manuscript occupied only three months. Yet Klevar acknowledges that the publication of the first installment of Ira Caldwell's "Bunglers" may have planted the idea of the novel in his son's mind. That publication appeared ten months before the completion of "Tobacco Road."

18. Maxwell Perkins to EC, 10 June 1931, Scribner Archives.

19. EC to Maxwell Perkins, 11 June 1931, Scribner Archives; EC to Richard Johns, 15 June 1931, *Pagany* Archives.

20. Maxwell Perkins to EC, 12 and 13 June 1931, Scribner Archives; John Hall Wheelock to William A. Sutton, 6 Aug. 1970, ECC-DC.

21. Maxwell Perkins to John Simon Guggenheim Foundation, undated, Scribner Archives. The secretary of the Guggenheim Foundation acknowledged receipt of Perkins's recommendation of Caldwell on 2 Nov. 1931; Scribner Archives.

22. Maxwell Perkins to EC, 8 Feb. 1932, Scribner Archives. On the matter of revisions, see Maxwell Perkins to EC, 26 June 1931, and John Hall Wheelock to EC, 12 and 18 Nov. 1931, Scribner Archives. On the matter of sales, see Maxwell Perkins to EC, 25 Feb. 1932, Scribner Archives; John Hall Wheelock to William A. Sutton, 6 Aug. 1970, ECC-DC.

23. Erskine Caldwell, *Tobacco Road*, 34, 85, 126.

24. Ibid., 49–50, 86, 138; emphasis is in original.

25. John Hall Wheelock to William A. Sutton, 6 Aug. 1970, ECC-DC; Maxwell Perkins to Guggenheim Foundation, undated, Scribner Archives; Caldwell, *Tobacco Road*, 58–72, 100–104.

26. Caldwell, *Tobacco Road*, 59–62.

27. Ibid., 63, 20.

28. Ibid., 60, 14, 26.

29. Ibid., 28.

30. Ibid., 147, 151.

31. Ibid., 152–55.

32. Ibid., 102, 131, 124, 139.

33. Ibid., 157.

34. Ibid., 157, 45. See also EC to Benjamin W. Farley, 5 July 1978, Farley, "Erskine Caldwell," 217 n. 53.

35. Klevar, *Erskine Caldwell,* 157. This paragraph, except for the statement regarding sales of *Tobacco Road,* is based upon reviews of the novel in the following newspapers: *Augusta Chronicle,* 14. Feb. 1932; *Baltimore Evening Sun,* 26 Feb. 1932; *Charlotte News,* 28 Feb. 1932; *Louisville Courier-Journal,* 28 Feb. 1932; *Richmond News Leader,* 29 Feb. 1932; *Chattanooga News,* 19 Mar. 1932; *Gastonia (N.C.) Gazette,* 28 Apr. 1932, EC Scrapbooks, reel 1. See also the review in *Saturday Review of Literature,* 5 Mar. 1932, by Jonathan Daniels, a North Carolina journalist; *EC Scrapbooks,* reel 1.

36. *Raleigh News and Observer,* clipping [1932], *EC Scrapbooks,* reel 1; EC to Milton A. Abernethy, 30 Oct. and 8 Nov. 1932 and 26 Apr. 1933, *Contempo* Archive.

37. EC to Milton A. Abernethy, 26 Apr. 1933 and 8 Nov. 1932, *Contempo* Archive.

38. EC to Milton A. Abernethy, 17 Sept. 1933, *Contempo* Archive.

39. EC to [William Stanley] Hoole, 22 Feb. 1936, Special Collections, Colby College Library, Waterville, Maine.

40. John Gould Fletcher to Lewis Mumford, 30 Oct. 1929; John Gould Fletcher to Mark van Doren, 21 Apr. 1934; John Gould Fletcher to Van Wyck Brooks, 26 Nov. 1935, John Gould Fletcher Papers, Special Collections Division, University of Arkansas Libraries, Fayetteville; John Gould Fletcher, letter to *The Nation,* 27 Dec. 1933, excerpted in *New Masses* 10 (30 Jan. 1934): 20; EC to Maxim Lieber, undated, reprinted in *New Masses* 10 (30 Jan. 1934): 21.

41. Wade, "Sweet Are the Uses of Degeneracy," in Davidson, *Selected Essays,* 176–92, esp. 192. Wade's essay was first published in *Southern Review* 1 (Winter 1936): 449–66.

42. Davidson, "The Trend of Literature," 204.

43. Caldwell, "Plans for Study," ECC-DC; EC to Atcheson Laughlin Hench, 26 May 1970, Hench-Caldwell Collection, University of Virginia. Since his move to Maine in 1927, Caldwell had been "a Southerner . . . by residence" for only three months of each year.

44. Klevar, *Erskine Caldwell,* 111; Maxwell Perkins to EC, 8 Feb. 1932; EC to Maxwell Perkins, 7 Mar., 21 Apr., and 27 May 1932; Maxwell Perkins to EC, 31 May and 18 June 1932, Scribner Archives; EC to Milton A. Abernethy, 19 Oct. 1932, *Contempo* Archive; EC to William Carlos Williams, 16 Nov. 1932, Erskine Caldwell Correspondence, Yale Collection of American Literature, Beinecke Rare Book and Manuscript Library, Yale University.

45. Erskine Caldwell, *God's Little Acre,* 69, 146–47; EC to Margaret Bourke-White, [1936], Erskine Caldwell Papers, Syracuse University Library, Special

Collections Department. Caldwell's passionate nature is strikingly revealed in his letters to Helen Caldwell of the early 1930s and in his letters to Margaret Bourke-White of the late 1930s. See ECC-DC and the Erskine Caldwell Papers, Syracuse University.

46. Caldwell, *God's Little Acre*, 42, 57. The Maine novel, "Autumn Hill," a story of domestic strife, was not published until 1952, and its title had been changed; Erskine Caldwell, *A Lamp for Nightfall* (New York, 1952).

47. Caldwell, *God's Little Acre*, 115–20, 133.

48. Ibid., 159.

49. Caldwell, *God's Little Acre*.

50. Ibid., 158.

51. Ibid.; Klevar, *Erskine Caldwell*, 92, 117.

52. William Soskin, "D. H. Lawrence and Erskine Caldwell—An Unusual Association," *New York Evening Post*, 7 Feb. 1933.

53. A. B. Bernd, "Georgia Rabelais," *Macon Telegraph*, 12 Mar. 1933.

54. Barry Bingham, "Big Virtues, Big Faults," *Louisville Courier-Journal*, 19 Feb. 1933.

55. Jonathan Daniels, "Strong Story of Forgotten Lives," *Raleigh News and Observer*, 5 Mar. 1933.

56. Ibid. The passage from *God's Little Acre* is reproduced here as it appears in Daniels's review, despite several minor inaccuracies in his transcription.

57. Ibid.

58. *Macon Telegraph*, 12 Mar. 1933; *Louisville Courier-Journal*, 19 Feb. 1933; *Raleigh News and Observer*, 5 Mar. 1933.

59. This paragraph is based upon my examination of the February–April issues of the following newspapers: *Richmond Times-Dispatch*, *New Orleans Times-Picayune*, *Augusta (Ga.) Chronicle*, *Atlanta Constitution*, *Atlanta Georgian*, and *Atlanta Journal*. Contrary to the case for virtually all of Caldwell's other books, there are no copies of reviews of *God's Little Acre* in the *EC Scrapbooks*.

60. Maxim Lieber to EC, 15 June 1933; EC to Helen Caldwell, 25 May 1933, ECC-DC; Klevar, *Erskine Caldwell*, 129.

61. EC to Helen Caldwell, 2 and 3 June 1933, ECC-DC; EC to Milton A. Abernethy, 3 Aug. 1933, *Contempo* Archive.

62. EC to Helen Caldwell, 9 and 18 June 1933, ECC-DC; Caldwell, *Call It Experience*, 130–31; EC to I. L. Salomon, 29 Aug. 1933, I. L. Salomon Papers, Library of Congress.

63. Erskine Caldwell, *We Are the Living*; Owen, "Folk Motifs," 85. The six stories cited are reprinted in Caldwell, *Complete Stories*, 317–28, 214–23, 86–95, 115–18, 340–46, and 169–79.

64. EC to Milton A. Abernethy, 28 Oct. 1932 and 25 Aug. 1933, *Contempo* Archive; Erskine Caldwell, "August Afternoon," *Esquire* 1 (Autumn 1933): 22, 89, 110.

65. Caldwell, "August Afternoon," reprinted in Caldwell, *Caldwell Caravan*, 287–94.

66. There are no southern reviews of *We Are the Living* in the *EC Scrapbooks*.

In my examination of the issues of certain southern newspapers from late September to early November 1933, I failed to find reviews there either. See note 59 for the newspapers examined.

67. Maxim Lieber to EC, 28 Mar. and 5 Apr. 1949; Minna Lieber to EC, 20 Dec. 1949, ECC-DC; EC to Alfred Morang, 23 Nov. 1933, Morang Papers.

68. Jack Kirkland, *Tobacco Road: A Three Act Play* (1934; repr. New York, 1952); *Savannah News,* 14 Nov. 1938, *EC Scrapbooks,* reel 2. See also *Shreveport Times,* 12 Dec. 1937, *EC Scrapbooks,* reel 2; Klevar, *Erskine Caldwell,* 145.

69. Marguerite Stefan in *Augusta Chronicle,* undated clipping in *EC Scrapbooks,* reel 1. Among commentators attributing authorship of the play to Caldwell were those in the following newspapers: *Thomasville (Ga.) Press,* 29 Oct. 1937; *Atlanta Georgian,* 18 Nov. 1938; *Augusta Chronicle,* 18 Nov. 1938; *Cordele (Ga.) Dispatch,* 22 Nov. 1938; *Charlotte News,* 24 Nov. 1938; *Albany (Ga.) Herald,* 26 Nov. 1938; *Greenville (S.C.) Piedmont,* 13 Jan. 1939, *EC Scrapbooks,* reel 2; *Montgomery Advertiser,* 3 June 1941, *EC Scrapbooks,* reel 3.

70. The *Macon Telegraph* editorial was reprinted in the *Kingsland Southeastern Georgian,* 12 Dec. 1935; *Atlanta Georgian,* 24 Jan. 1936; *New York Times,* 10 May 1936; "Kelly Ban on 'Tobacco Road' Praised by Georgia Governor," unidentified, undated clipping, *EC Scrapbooks,* reel 1; John S. Van Gilder to *New York Times,* 23 Nov. 1937, in *Asheville Citizen,* 11 Dec. 1937, and *Charlotte Observer,* 12 Dec. 1937, *EC Scrapbooks,* reel 2.

71. W. J. Cash, "Impossibility of Censorship Again Revealed," *Charlotte News,* 2 Feb. 1936, *EC Scrapbooks,* reel 1; "'Road' Too Tough for Birmingham," unidentified, undated clipping; *Savannah News,* 14 Nov. 1938; *Savannah Press,* 15 Nov. 1938; *Atlanta Journal,* 16 and 23 Nov. 1938; "'Tobacco Road' Will Play in New Orleans," *Greensboro (N.C.) News,* 23 Nov. 1937; *Greenville (S.C.) Piedmont,* 13 Jan. 1939; *Memphis Commercial Appeal,* 16 Jan. 1939, *EC Scrapbooks,* reel 2.

72. "Wrens Chief Asks [Sheriff] Whittle to Ban Play 'Tobacco Road,'" unidentified, undated clipping; *Augusta Herald,* 7 and 20 Nov. 1938; *Savannah Press,* 15 Nov. 1938; *Augusta Chronicle,* 17, 18, and 19 Nov. 1938; *Atlanta Constitution,* 20 and 21 Nov. 1938; *Atlanta Journal,* 20 and 23 Nov. 1938; *Parkersburg (W.Va.) News,* 19 Apr. 1940; *Charlotte News,* 30 Apr. 1939, *EC Scrapbooks,* reel 2.

73. *Atlanta Georgian,* [22 Nov. 1938]; Nashville *Banner,* 3 Dec. 1938; *Montgomery Advertiser,* 29 Nov. 1938, *EC Scrapbooks,* reel 2.

74. *Augusta Herald,* 18 Nov. 1938, *EC Scrapbooks,* reel 2.

75. *Atlanta Journal,* 17 Nov. 1938, *EC Scrapbooks,* reel 2.

76. Marion, "Star Dust Above Tobacco Road," in MacDonald, *Critical Essays,* 174–79.

77. Erskine Caldwell, "Of 'Tobacco Road,'" *New York Times,* 10 May 1936; Julia McCarthy, "'Tobacco Road' True to Life, Says Author," unidentified, undated clipping, *EC Scrapbooks,* reel 1.

78. Caldwell, "Of 'Tobacco Road,'" *EC Scrapbooks,* reel 1.

79. *Montgomery Advertiser,* 3 June 1941, reprinted in *Richmond Times-*

Dispatch, 5 June 1941, *Birmingham Age-Herald,* 17 June 1941, and *Talladega (Ala.) Daily Home,* 17 June 1941, *EC Scrapbooks,* reel 3; *Montgomery Advertiser,* 29 Nov. 1938, *EC Scrapbooks,* reel 2. See also *Charlotte News,* 2 Feb. 1936, *EC Scrapbooks,* reel 1; *Augusta Herald,* 7 and 18 Nov. 1938; *Atlanta Journal,* 17 and 22 Nov. 1938 and 1 Dec. 1940; *Charlotte News,* 24 Nov. 1938; *Memphis Press-Scimitar,* 15 Mar. 1939, *EC Scrapbooks,* reel 2.

80. *New York Herald Tribune,* 4 Dec. 1938, *EC Scrapbooks,* reel 2.

81. *Augusta Chronicle,* 11 Aug. 1940, *EC Scrapbooks,* reel 2; Tindall, *Emergence of the New South,* 423.

82. *Savannah News,* 8 Aug. 1941; *New York Times,* 10 Aug. 1941, *EC Scrapbooks,* reel 3.

83. Howard, "Caldwell on Stage and Screen," in Arnold, *Erskine Caldwell Reconsidered,* 59–72, esp. 62–66.

84. EC to Milton A. Abernethy, 26 Apr. 1933, *Contempo* Archive; EC to Alfred Morang, 29 Oct. 1933 and 17 and 24 Oct. 1934, Morang Papers; Klevar, *Erskine Caldwell,* 142–53, passim. Klevar says that Harcourt Brace offered an advance on *Journeyman* of $200. His source is Caldwell's letter to Morang of 29 October 1933, wherein the sum noted is $2,000. Caldwell often made typographical errors in his correspondence, but he was meticulous with money matters. Moreover, Viking Press subsequently offered a $1,000 advance on the novel, and back in 1930, as Klevar notes, *Scribner's* had paid Caldwell $350 for two short stories. Klevar, *Erskine Caldwell,* 91, 143, 147, 434 n. 8. See also EC to Helen Caldwell, [fall 1933], ECC-DC.

85. EC to Helen Caldwell, 12 July 1933, ECC-DC; EC to Alfred Morang, 29 Oct. 1933, Morang Papers.

86. Erskine Caldwell, *Journeyman.*

87. Farley, "Erskine Caldwell," 217 n. 51, 217 n. 53; *New York World Telegram,* 12 Feb. 1938, *EC Scrapbooks,* reel 2.

88. *Atlanta Journal,* clipping [March 1935]; [*Augusta Herald*], clipping [1935], *EC Scrapbooks,* reel 1; *Durham Herald,* 4 Feb. 1938; *Charlotte Observer,* 28 May 1938; *Winston-Salem Sentinel,* clipping [1938]; *New York Post,* 17 Feb. 1938, *EC Scrapbooks,* reel 2. The disparity of the dates cited above results from the circumstances of publication of *Journeyman.* A limited edition appeared in 1935, copies of which Caldwell must have sent to his friends Frank Daniel and Earl Bell, who wrote reviews in the *Atlanta Journal* and the *Augusta Herald,* respectively. The trade edition of *Journeyman* did not appear until early in 1938.

89. Erskine Caldwell, "Blue Boy," in Erskine Caldwell, *Kneel to the Rising Sun,* reprinted in Caldwell, *Complete Stories,* 286–90.

90. Erskine Caldwell, "Candy-Man Beechum," reprinted in Caldwell, *Caldwell Caravan,* 408–11.

91. Maxim Lieber to EC, 11 Dec. 1933, ECC-DC; emphasis is in original. Erskine Caldwell, "Kneel to the Rising Sun," reprinted in Caldwell, *Caldwell Caravan,* 417–36, esp. 418, 427.

92. Caldwell, "Kneel to the Rising Sun," 435–36.

93. Ibid., 433; Erskine Caldwell, *Some American People,* 241–42, 244–45.

94. Erskine Caldwell, "Daughter," reprinted in Caldwell, *Complete Stories*, 235–40; Erskine Caldwell, "Masses of Men," reprinted in Caldwell, *Complete Stories*, 448–58; Erskine Caldwell, "Slow Death," reprinted in Caldwell, *Complete Stories*, 580–87.

95. Caldwell, "Slow Death," 582.

96. Erskine Caldwell, "The Growing Season," reprinted in Caldwell, *Complete Stories*, 258–62.

97. Ibid., 259–60, 262. Randall Jarrell is quoted in MacDonald, "Evaluative Check-List," in MacDonald, *Critical Essays*, 348.

98. Erskine Caldwell, "Maud Island," reprinted in Caldwell, *Complete Stories*, 38–49; Erskine Caldwell, "Honeymoon," reprinted in Caldwell, *Caldwell Caravan*, 307–12; Erskine Caldwell, "A Day's Wooing," reprinted in Caldwell, *Caldwell Caravan*, 313–19; Erskine Caldwell, "The Shooting," reprinted in Caldwell, *Complete Stories*, 571–75.

99. *Chicago News*, undated clipping; *New York World-Telegram*, undated clipping, *EC Scrapbooks*, reel 1. T. J. Campbell of Knoxville, Tennessee, in *Scribner's Magazine* 97 (May 1935): 320. Hamilton Basso, review of *Kneel to the Rising Sun* and *Tenant Farmer* by Erskine Caldwell, *New Masses*, undated clipping; *Salisbury (N.C.) Post*, 23 June 1935; *Nashville Tennessean*, 9 June 1935, *EC Scrapbooks*, reel 1.

100. *Raleigh News and Observer*, 7 July 1935; *Salisbury (N.C.) Post*, 23 June 1935; "Kneel to Rising Sun for Author Caldwell," *Charlotte News*, undated clipping; "American Stories," *Jacksonville Times-Union*, undated clipping; "Literary Lantern," *Charlotte Observer*, undated clipping, *EC Scrapbooks*, reel 1. See also *Macon Telegraph*, 7 June 1935; *Chattanooga News*, 15 June 1935; *Richmond Times-Dispatch*, 16 June 1935; *Atlanta Journal*, undated clipping, *EC Scrapbooks*, reel 1.

101. For Caldwell's reasons for shifting the focus of his writing from fiction to nonfiction, see Erskine Caldwell, "Attack Upon Sharecropper Stories Makes Caldwell Put Sting in Reply," unidentified clipping [Mar. 1935], *EC Scrapbooks*, reel 1.

102. Erskine Caldwell, *Southways*. See the stories "Snacker," "The Sunfield," "Uncle Henry's Love Nest," and "Hamrick's Polar Bear," reprinted in Caldwell, *Complete Stories*, 59–69, 415–24, 306–9, and 588–95.

103. Erskine Caldwell, "Carnival," reprinted in Caldwell, *Complete Stories*, 147–49; Erskine Caldwell, "Runaway," reprinted in Caldwell, *Complete Stories*, 469–73.

104. Erskine Caldwell, "A Small Day," reprinted in Caldwell, *Complete Stories*, 488–95.

105. Erskine Caldwell, "Man and Woman," reprinted in Caldwell, *Complete Stories*, 18–22.

106. Erskine Caldwell, "Wild Flowers," reprinted in Caldwell, *Complete Stories*, 299–305.

107. Erskine Caldwell, "A Knife to Cut the Corn Bread With," reprinted in Caldwell, *Complete Stories*, 602–9.

108. Erskine Caldwell, "The Negro in the Well," reprinted in Caldwell, *Caldwell Caravan*, 301–6.

109. Ibid.

110. Erskine Caldwell, "Nine Dollars' Worth of Mumble," reprinted in Caldwell, *Caldwell Caravan*, 401–7; Erskine Caldwell, "The Fly in the Coffin," reprinted in Caldwell, *Complete Stories*, 576–79.

111. Erskine Caldwell, "Return to Lavinia," reprinted in Caldwell, *Complete Stories*, 96–101.

112. Jonathan Daniels, "From Comedy to Pity," *Saturday Review of Literature*, 18 June 1938; *Memphis Commercial Appeal*, 19 June 1938; *Nashville Tennesseean*, 19 June 1938; *New Orleans Picayune*, 19 June 1938; *Nashville Banner*, 22 June 1938, EC Scrapbooks, reel 2.

113. *Durham Herald*, 24 July 1938; *Atlanta Constitution*, 10 July 1938; *Macon Telegraph*, 17 June 1938; *Atlanta Journal*, 19 June 1938, EC Scrapbooks, reel 2.

114. Erskine Caldwell, "The People v. Abe Lathan, Colored," *Esquire* 12 (Aug. 1939): 26–27, 145, reprinted in Caldwell, *Complete Stories*, 474–81; Erskine Caldwell, "The End of Christy Tucker," *Nation* 150 (1 June 1940): 673–75, reprinted in Caldwell, *Caldwell Caravan*, 344–48.

115. Caldwell, "End of Christy Tucker," 344–48.

116. Untitled, unidentified clipping [late 1935 or early 1936]; Erskine Caldwell, "A Note," EC Scrapbooks, reel 1; Sutton, "A Lover's Quarrel," 161.

117. Rable, "The South and the Politics of Anti-Lynching Legislation," 201–21; Erskine Caldwell, *Trouble in July*.

118. Caldwell, *Trouble in July*.

119. Ibid., 5, 12, 66, 124, 11.

120. Ibid., 49–50.

121. Ibid., 158–59.

122. Ibid., 89, 9, 135.

123. Ibid., 51, 125.

124. Ibid., 79–81.

125. Ibid., 41–47; Erskine Caldwell, preface to 1977 edition of *Trouble in July*.

126. "Erskine Caldwell Is the Personification of an Earthworm," *Gainesville (Ga.) News*, 29 Mar. 1940, ECC-DC. "Another 'Tobacco Road'," *Raleigh News and Observer*, 3 Mar. 1940; *Chattanooga Times*, 25 Feb. 1940; *Durham Herald*, 17 Mar. 1940; *Charlotte Observer*, 18 Feb. 1940; *Birmingham News*, 17 Mar. 1940; *Atlanta Journal*, 25 Feb. 1940, Erskine Caldwell Collection, University of Virginia.

127. Wright, "Lynching Bee," 351–52; Wright, *Uncle Tom's Children*, 3–15.

128. Lee, "Erskine Caldwell," 372–74, 389.

CHAPTER FOUR: Radical Activism

1. Caldwell, *With All My Might*, 89–173, *passim*; Klevar, *Erskine Caldwell*, 83–230, *passim*; Miller, "Tracing Tobacco Road," 447–48.

2. Norman Macleod, "A Hardboiled Idealist," unidentified, undated clipping, *EC Scrapbooks*, reel 1, reprinted, with magazine identified and date supplied in MacDonald, *Critical Essays*, 6–7; EC to Alfred Morang, 26 Sept. 1932 and 5 Oct. 1933, Morang Papers; Cook, "Erskine Caldwell and the Literary Left Wing," in MacDonald, *Critical Essays*, 362; Miller "Tracing Tobacco Road," 362; John D. Hicks, George E. Mowry, and Robert E. Burke, *The American Nation: A History of the United States from 1865 to the Present*, 4th ed. (Boston: Houghton Mifflin, 1963), 560.

3. Macleod, "A Hardboiled Idealist," *EC Scrapbooks*, reel 1.

4. Hahn, *Roots of Southern Populism*, 282–83; Tindall, *Emergence of the New South*, 423–24.

5. EC to Alfred Morang, 3 June 1931 and 10 Aug. 1934, Morang Papers.

6. Erskine Caldwell, "Ripe for Revolution," *New Masses* 8 (Dec. 1932): 26–27, reprinted in MacDonald, *Critical Essays*, 20–23; EC to Helen Caldwell, 26 May and 1 and 2 June 1933, ECC-DC; EC to Alfred Morang, 16 July 1934, Morang Papers.

7. EC to Helen Caldwell, 23 June 1933, ECC-DC; EC to Mr. and Mrs. I. S. Caldwell, 3 May 1934, ECC-UGA; EC to Frank Daniel, 3 May and 23 June 1934, Frank Daniel Papers, Special Collections, R. W. Woodruff Library, Emory University; EC to Alfred Morang, 10 June 1934, Morang Papers; Erskine Caldwell, "A Story That Got Lost," *New Masses* 10 (16 Jan. 1934): 13; Erskine Caldwell, "'Parties Unknown' in Georgia," *New Masses* 10 (23 Jan. 1934): 16, 18.

8. EC to Alfred Morang, 5 Feb. 1934, Morang Papers; Caldwell, "A Story That Got Lost," 13; Caldwell, "'Parties Unknown' in Georgia," 16.

9. Caldwell, "A Story That Got Lost," 13; "Expect Early Arrest in Jefferson Killing," *Atlanta Constitution*, 14 Jan. 1934; "Jefferson County Race Trouble, Charged by Caldwell, Is Denied," *Atlanta Constitution*, 25 Jan. 1934; "Caldwell Charge Troubles Sheriff," *Atlanta Constitution*, 27 Jan 1934; "Jury Probe of Negro Deaths Urged by Jefferson Sheriff," *Atlanta Constitution*, 28 Jan. 1934; "Group Asks Probe of Negro Killings," *Atlanta Constitution*, 31 Jan. 1934.

10. *Atlanta Constitution*, 25 and 28 Jan. 1934.

11. Ibid., 27 and 28 Jan. 1934.

12. Ibid., 31 Jan. 1934. For a perceptive sketch of Raper, see Singal, *The War Within*, 328–38.

13. *Atlanta Constitution*, 31 Jan. 1934; Caldwell, "A Story That Got Lost," 13.

14. *Atlanta Constitution*, 31 Jan. 1934.

15. Caldwell, "'Parties Unknown' in Georgia," 16.

16. Ibid., 18.

17. Ibid., 16; EC to Alfred Morang, 15 Feb. 1934, Morang Papers; Minutes of Grand Jury, Jefferson County, Ga., 16 May 1934, Jefferson County Courthouse, Louisville, Ga.

18. Erskine Caldwell, "Georgia Is Swept by Poverty, Says Erskine Caldwell," *New York Post*, 18 Feb. 1935; Erskine Caldwell, "U.S. Aid Forces Out Georgia Share Croppers," *New York Post*, 19 Feb. 1935; Erskine Caldwell, "Georgia Land Barons Oust Dying Girl and Her Father," *New York Post*, 20 Feb. 1935; Erskine

1186 Notes

Caldwell, "Starving Babies Suckled by Dogs in Georgia Wastes," *New York Post,*
21 Feb. 1935, *EC Scrapbooks,* reel 1. Coleman, *History of Georgia,* 313–14;
interview with Henrietta Boyce, Annette Johnson, Lucille M. Parrish, and Helen
Williams. The titles of Caldwell's articles were supplied by the *Post.*

19. "Farmers," *Time,* 25 (4 Mar. 1935): 13–14. "Along Tobacco Road," *Time*
[25 Mar. 1935]; Thomas J. Hamilton in *Time,* [25 Mar. 1935]; *Augusta Chronicle,* [4 Mar. 1935]; *Augusta Chronicle,* 10–14 Mar. 1935, *EC Scrapbooks,* reel 1.

20. *Augusta Chronicle,* 10–14 Mar. 1935, *EC Scrapbooks,* reel 1.

21. *Augusta Chronicle,* 14 and 17 Mar. 1935, *EC Scrapbooks,* reel 1.

22. J. T. Avret in *Augusta Chronicle,* 17 Mar. 1935; Abraham Cook in *Time*
[25 Mar. 1935]; James Harrison in *Time,* [25 Mar. 1935]; *Charlotte News,* 13
Mar. 1935, reprinted in *Augusta Chronicle,* 17 Mar. 1935, *EC Scrapbooks,* reel 1.

23. *Augusta Chronicle,* [6 Mar. 1935], *EC Scrapbooks,* reel 1. John R. Lewis
in *Augusta Chronicle,* 10 Mar. 1935, reprinted in MacDonald, *Critical Essays,*
113–15; James Barlow Jr. in *New York Post,* 6 Mar. 1935, reprinted in MacDonald, *Critical Essays,* 111. Frank Rossiter in *Time,* [25 Mar. 1935]; Warren H.
Pierce in *Time,* [25 Mar. 1935]; Mark Valentine in *Time,* [25 Mar. 1935], *EC
Scrapbooks,* reel 1.

24. Erskine Caldwell, "Attack Upon Sharecropper Stories Makes Caldwell Put
Sting in Reply," unidentified, undated clipping, *EC Scrapbooks,* reel 1. This ar-
ticle doubtlessly appeared in March 1935 and was probably published in the *New
York Post.*

25. EC to Helen Caldwell, 29 Mar. 1935, ECC-DC.

26. Erskine Caldwell, "Landlords Chiseling South's Poor on FERA," *New
York Post,* 18 Apr. 1935, *EC Scrapbooks,* reel 1.

27. Ibid.

28. Erskine Caldwell, "Poor Who Ask Pay Beaten in South," *New York Post,*
19 Apr. 1935, *EC Scrapbooks,* reel 1.

29. Erskine Caldwell, "Georgia Tenants, Ousted by Landlords, Eat Dirt as
Change from Bread and 'Lasses," *New York Post,* 20 Apr. 1935, *EC Scrapbooks,*
reel 1.

30. Erskine Caldwell, "Caldwell Finds AAA Is Ruining Thousands," *New
York Post,* 17 Apr. 1935; Caldwell, "Georgia Tenants," *New York Post,* 20 Apr.
1935, *EC Scrapbooks,* reel 1. As in the case of Caldwell's first *Post* series, the
titles of the reports in the second series were supplied by the *Post.*

31. Smith is quoted in the *New York Post,* 19 Apr. 1935, *EC Scrapbooks,* reel
1. In normal times, cash renters were the aristocrats among tenant farmers. In
times of economic depression, however, sharecropping might provide a greater
measure of security. On the varieties of farm tenancy, see Conrad, *Forgotten
Farmers,* 6–8. Much of the material relating to the controversy sparked by Caldwell's articles in the *Post* is reprinted in MacDonald, *Critical Essays,* 97–152.

32. Augusta *Chronicle,* [24 Mar. 1935]; *New Republic,* 27 Mar. 1935, *EC
Scrapbooks,* reel 1; Erskine Caldwell, *Tenant Farmer,* 16, 14; Hamilton Basso,
"Sunny South," *New Masses,* undated clipping, *EC Scrapbooks,* reel 1.

33. On Couch, see Singal, *The War Within,* 265–301.

34. W. T. Couch to EC, 15 June 1932; EC to W. T. Couch, 18 June 1932; Couch to EC, 21 and 23 June and 8 July 1932; EC to Couch, 10 July 1932; Couch to EC, 14 July 1932, Records of the University of North Carolina Press, Southern Historical Collection, Library of the University of North Carolina at Chapel Hill.

35. W. T. Couch, "Caldwell's Tenants," unidentified, undated clipping, *EC Scrapbooks*, reel 1; Couch, "American Peasants," *Virginia Quarterly Review* 10 (Oct. 1934): 636–40; Hoffsommer, "The AAA and the Cropper," 494–502; Johnson, Embree, and Alexander, *Collapse of Cotton Tenancy*, 46–63; Vance, *Human Geography of the South*, 482–98.

36. Couch, "Caldwell's Tenants," *EC Scrapbooks*, reel 1.

37. Grubbs, *Cry from the Cotton*, 49–51; *New York Post*, 22 Apr. 1935, reprinted in MacDonald, *Critical Essays*, 152. See also Conrad, *Forgotten Farmers*, 178–85.

38. Caldwell, *Some American People*, 205–66; Klevar, "Erskine Caldwell," draft of Klevar, *Erskine Caldwell*, 209–10, 586 n. 36. *Macon Telegraph*, 21 Oct. 1935; *Lexington (Ky.) Herald*, 8 Dec. 1935; *Atlanta Journal*, undated clipping, *EC Scrapbooks*, reel 1.

39. *Atlanta Constitution*, undated clipping, *EC Scrapbooks*, reel 1; EC to Frank Daniel, 5 Jan. 1936, Daniel Papers.

40. Caldwell, *Some American People*, 4, 8.

41. Goldberg, *Margaret Bourke-White*, 161–62; Bourke-White, *Portrait of Myself*, 119.

42. Goldberg, *Margaret Bourke-White*, 83–160; Margaret Bourke-White to EC, 9 Mar. 1936, Caldwell Papers, Syracuse University.

43. Bourke-White, *Portrait of Myself*, 115; Ruth Carnall to Margaret Bourke-White, telegram, 16 July 1936; Margaret Bourke-White to EC, 18 July 1936; [Notes of Ruth Carnall], 17–25 July 1936, Caldwell Papers, Syracuse University. See also Goldberg, *Margaret Bourke-White*, 163–65.

44. Bourke-White, *Portrait of Myself*, 125; Goldberg, *Margaret Bourke-White*, 163, 167; Caldwell, *With All My Might*, 150–51.

45. Klevar, *Erskine Caldwell*, 191; Bourke-White, *Portrait of Myself*, 126.

46. Bourke-White, *Portrait of Myself*, 126–27; emphasis is in original.

47. Ibid., 133. See also Stott, *Documentary Expression and Thirties America*, 59–60.

48. Bourke-White, *Portrait of Myself*, 137.

49. Erskine Caldwell and Margaret Bourke-White, *You Have Seen Their Faces*, unpaginated front matter; Stott, *Documentary Expression*, 218. Bourke-White also said that the captions were the result of a collaborative effort; Bourke-White, *Portrait of Myself*, 137. Fifty years later, Caldwell suggested that he alone wrote the captions; Caldwell, *With All My Might*, 157.

50. Caldwell and Bourke-White, *You Have Seen Their Faces*, unpaginated [following 114].

51. Ibid., unpaginated [following 82 and 145].

52. Ibid., unpaginated [preceding 25 and following 31, 56, 82, and 169]; Klevar, "Erskine Caldwell," draft of Klevar, *Erskine Caldwell*, 237.

53. Caldwell and Bourke-White, *You Have Seen Their Faces*, 25–31, 49–56, 73–82, 107–14, 139–45, 163–69.

54. Ibid.; Hoffsommer, "AAA and the Cropper," 496. See also Johnson, Embree, and Alexander, *Collapse of Cotton Tenancy*, 58–59.

55. Caldwell and Bourke-White, *You Have Seen Their Faces*, 167–68, unpaginated [following 56]; Conrad, *Forgotten Farmers*, 3.

56. Caldwell and Bourke-White, *You Have Seen Their Faces*, 168–69.

57. Stott, *Documentary Expression*, 213, 224, 266; Miller, "Tracing Tobacco Road," 372.

58. Tindall, *Emergence of the New South*, 425–26, 431–32, 707–10; Coleman, *History of Georgia*, 348; Frank Freidel and Alan Brinkley, *America in the Twentieth Century*, 5th ed. (New York: Knopf, 1982), 10.

59. *Charlotte Observer*, 14 Nov. 1937; *Augusta Herald*, 21 Nov. 1937; *Winston-Salem Sentinel*, undated clipping; *Atlanta Journal*, undated clipping; *Macon Telegraph*, 9 Dec. 1937; *Nashville Banner*, 28 Nov. 1937 [emphasis is in original], *EC Scrapbooks*, reel 2.

60. *Atlanta Georgian*, 21 Nov. 1937; *Atlanta Constitution*, 8 Feb. 1938, *EC Scrapbooks*, reel 2. See also (Dalton) *North Georgia Citizen*, 2 Dec. 1937, *EC Scrapbooks*, reel 2.

61. "Unionizing Farm Labor," unidentified, undated clipping, *EC Scrapbooks*, reel 2. Internal evidence suggests that the editorial appeared in November 1937 in a newspaper published in Henry County, Alabama. See also *Memphis Commercial Appeal*, 28 Nov. 1937, *EC Scrapbooks*, reel 2.

62. Couch, "Landlord and Tenant," in MacDonald, *Critical Essays*, 56–59.

63. Davidson, "Erskine Caldwell's Picture Book," in MacDonald, *Critical Essays*, 59–67, esp. 59, 61. Caldwell and Bourke-White, *You Have Seen Their Faces*, unpaginated [preceding 25 and following 145]; Erskine Caldwell, "Why I Wanted to Do This Story," *Popular Photography*, undated clipping, *EC Scrapbooks*, reel 2.

64. Davidson, "Caldwell's Picture Book," 64; emphasis is in original. Caldwell and Bourke-White, *You Have Seen Their Faces*, 168; Conrad, *Forgotten Farmers*, [1]–2; Raper, *Preface to Peasantry*, 70; EC to Liv Smith, 29 Dec. 1937, Caldwell Papers, Syracuse University. See also National Emergency Council, *Report on Economic Conditions of the South*, 45.

65. Caldwell and Bourke-White, *You Have Seen Their Faces*, 25; Davidson, "Caldwell's Picture Book," 61.

66. Davidson, "Caldwell's Picture Book," 62, 67.

67. Ibid., 66.

CHAPTER FIVE: Changing South, Unchanging Writer

1. The trip began in October and ended in December; Caldwell, *Call It Experience*, 192. The two other collaborations were *North of the Danube* (New York: Viking, 1939) and *Russia at War* (London: Hutchinson, 1942).

2. Erskine Caldwell and Margaret Bourke-White, *Say, Is This the U.S.A.*, 138, 146, 154–56.

3. Thad Snow to EC, 12 Feb. 1941; George Wolf to EC, 14 Feb. 1941, ECC-DC; Erskine Caldwell, "Flight from the Land," 20–22, 92.

4. Ethridge, Caldwell, and Graves, "Are We a United People?" 3–30, esp. 4–5, ECC-DC.

5. Caldwell, *Call It Experience,* 22–23; Ethridge, Caldwell, and Graves, "Are We a United People?," 5–11, ECC-DC.

6. *Birmingham News,* 21 Feb. 1941, *EC Scrapbooks,* reel 2; Ethridge, Caldwell, and Graves, "Are We a United People?" 11–15, ECC-DC.

7. Ethridge, Caldwell, and Graves, "Are We a United People?" 16–19, ECC-DC.

8. Ibid., 21; *Birmingham News,* 21 Feb. 1941, *EC Scrapbooks,* reel 2.

9. Charles A. Pearce to Lucy Bailey, 17 Mar. 1947, ECC-DC; EC to Hamilton Basso, 19 Aug. 1940, Caldwell Correspondence, Yale University; Klevar, *Erskine Caldwell,* 219; Miller, "Tracing Tobacco Road," 445–48.

10. Goldberg, *Margaret Bourke-White,* 176, 224–25; EC to Kenneth and Genevieve [Taggard], 22 Nov. 1939, Genevieve Taggard Papers, Rare Books and Manuscripts Division, New York Public Library, Astor, Lenox and Tilden Foundations; *Ashland (Ky.) Independent,* 19 Apr. 1940, *EC Scrapbooks,* reel 2; EC to Mr. and Mrs. I. S. Caldwell, 16 Dec. 1939, ECC-UGA.

11. Caldwell, *Call It Experience,* 185; Earl L. Bell to EC, 15 Nov. and 6 Dec. 1939; EC to Earl Bell, 17 Dec. 1939, Caldwell Papers, Syracuse University.

12. [Erskine Caldwell], Prospectus for American Folkways: A Series, undated, ECC-DC. See also *St. Paul Dispatch,* 23 May 1941, *EC Scrapbooks,* reel 3.

13. *New York Herald Tribune Book Review,* 20 Aug. 1950, *EC Scrapbooks,* reel 4; *Ashland (Ky.) Independent,* 19 Apr. 1940; *Hot Springs (Ark.) New Era,* 23 Oct. 1940, *EC Scrapbooks,* reel 2; *Jacksonville Times-Union,* 13 July 1941, *EC Scrapbooks,* reel 3.

14. *Jacksonville Times-Union,* 13 July 1941; *Miami Herald,* 25 Apr. 1943, *EC Scrapbooks,* reel 3; EC to Stetson Kennedy, 25 Aug. 1940, ECC-UGA.

15. EC to Stetson Kennedy, 5 Sept. 1940 and 7 and 8 Jan. 1941, ECC-UGA.

16. Stetson Kennedy to EC, 3 Mar. 1941, ECC-DC; EC to Stetson Kennedy, 12 June [1941], ECC-UGA. [Stetson Kennedy], "Prospectus" [for American Folkways], 5 June 1941. I am grateful to Mr. Kennedy for supplying a copy of this document.

17. EC to Stetson Kennedy, 28 Nov. 1941, ECC-UGA; Martin, *Howard Kester,* 72–73; Stetson Kennedy, *Palmetto Country,* 201–11.

18. EC to Stetson Kennedy, 18 Dec. 1941, ECC-UGA; Kennedy, *Palmetto Country,* 183–91, esp. 184, 191.

19. EC to Stetson Kennedy, 18 Dec. 1941 and 25 Jan. and 22 May 1942, ECC-UGA.

20. Kennedy, *Palmetto Country,* 193–200, esp. 193–96.

21. EC to Stetson Kennedy, 5 Mar. 1942, ECC-UGA; Kennedy, *Palmetto Country,* 43–107.

22. EC to Stetson Kennedy, 22 May 1942, ECC-UGA; John Selby, "Books and Things," *Mankato (Minn.) Free Press,* 21 Dec. 1942, *EC Scrapbooks,* reel 3.

23. Arnold, "Interview with Erskine Caldwell," in Arnold, *Conversations,* 286; EC to Hamilton Basso, 19 Aug. 1940, Caldwell Correspondence, Yale University.

24. EC to Rhoda Lynn, 28 Mar. 1941, ECC-DC; EC to Stetson Kennedy, 12 June [1941], ECC-UGA.

25. Stetson Kennedy to EC, 13 Oct. 1946; Charles Duell to EC, 16 Mar. 1942, quoting George Milburn; MacEdward Leach to EC, 19 Mar. 1945, ECC-DC.

26. Klevar, "Erskine Caldwell," draft of Klevar, *Erskine Caldwell,* 312, 375, 382, 413, 435.

27. Bonetti, "A Good Listener Speaks," in Arnold, *Conversations,* 244–51, esp. 250; Caldwell and Bourke-White, *Russia at War;* Erskine Caldwell, *Moscow Under Fire: A Wartime Diary, 1941* (London: Hutchinson, 1942); Erskine Caldwell, *All-Out on the Road to Smolensk* (New York: Duell, Sloan and Pearce, 1942); Erskine Caldwell, *All Night Long: A Novel of Guerrilla Warfare in Russia* (New York: Book League of America, 1942).

28. Goldberg, *Margaret Bourke-White,* 239; Caldwell, *Call It Experience,* 204, 217.

29. Goldberg, *Margaret Bourke-White,* 199, 219, 222–23, 252–53.

30. Ibid., 252–53; Miller, "Tracing Tobacco Road," 511; Klevar, *Erskine Caldwell,* 247–53.

31. Caldwell, *Call It Experience,* 217; Erskine Caldwell, *Georgia Boy.*

32. Caldwell, *Georgia Boy,* 193–205, 57–66, 69–83, 117–33.

33. Ibid., 227–39; EC to Charles A. Pearce, 8 Dec. [1942], ECC-DC.

34. EC to Charles A. Pearce, 8 Dec. [1942], ECC-DC; Caldwell, *Georgia Boy,* jacket blurb for 1950 reprint.

35. Caldwell, *Georgia Boy,* jacket blurb for 1950 reprint; *Houston Post,* 25 Apr. 1943; *Dallas News,* 2 May 1943; *Montgomery Advertiser,* 23 May 1943; *Chattanooga Times,* 13 June 1943, *EC Scrapbooks,* reel 3.

36. *Houston Post,* 25 Apr. 1943; *Montgomery Advertiser,* 23 May 1943, *EC Scrapbooks,* reel 3; *Columbus (Ga.) Enquirer-Sun,* 9 May 1943, Erskine Caldwell Collection, University of Virginia.

37. Erskine Caldwell, *Tragic Ground,* 74, 127.

38. Ibid., 7, 15, 26, 42, 56, 58, 79, 114, 124, 128.

39. Ibid., 66, 95.

40. Ibid., 94, 95, 121, 126.

41. Ibid., 96, 128.

42. For the impact of the Second World War on the South's economy, see Tindall, *Emergence of the New South,* 694–701.

43. Ibid., 703.

44. *Charlotte News,* 20 Oct. 1944; *Louisville Courier-Journal,* 12 Nov. 1944; *Saturday Review of Literature,* 14 Oct. 1944, *EC Scrapbooks,* reel 4. See also *Montgomery Advertiser,* 5 Nov. 1944; *Winston-Salem Sentinel,* 12 Nov. 1944; and *Raleigh News and Observer,* 10 Dec. 1944, *EC Scrapbooks,* reel 4.

45. EC to Alfred Morang, 5 and 23 Oct. 1944, Morang Papers.

46. Caldwell, *Call It Experience,* 222; EC to James Gray, 11 Sept. 1948, Papers of James Gray and Family, Minnesota Historical Society.

47. Erskine Caldwell, *A House in the Uplands.*

48. Ibid., 27, 11–12.

49. Erskine Caldwell, *The Sure Hand of God.*

50. Ibid.

51. Ibid., 163.

52. Erskine Caldwell, *This Very Earth*, 63.

53. Erskine Caldwell, *Place Called Estherville.*

54. Ibid.

55. Ibid., 231–32.

56. Ibid., 234–44.

57. Erskine Caldwell, *Episode in Palmetto.*

58. Philip Lightfoot Scruggs, "A Southern Miscellany: Crusaders and Artists," *Virginia Quarterly Review* 21 (Summer 1946): 449 (quotation); *Savannah Morning News,* 14 Apr. 1946; *Memphis Commercial Appeal,* 28 Apr. 1946; *Charleston News and Courier,* 5 May 1946; *Dallas News,* 5 May 1946 and 25 Sept. 1949; *Athens (Ga.) Banner Herald,* 27 Oct. 1947; *Charlotte Observer,* 16 Nov. 1947; *Louisville Courier-Journal,* 23 Nov. 1947; *Lynchburg (Va.) Advance,* 26 Aug. 1948; *Atlanta Constitution,* 29 Aug. 1948 and 4 Sept. 1949; *Greensboro Daily News,* 29 Aug. 1948; *Atlanta Journal,* 11 Sept. 1949; *Birmingham News,* 17 Sept. 1949; *Augusta Herald,* 29 Sept. 1949; *Winston-Salem Journal,* 24 Oct. 1949, *EC Scrapbooks,* reel 4. For favorable reviews, see *Atlanta Journal,* 12 Oct. 1947 and 18 Aug. 1948; *Houston Post,* 19 Oct. 1947; *Anderson (S.C.) Daily Mail,* 27 Oct. 1947; *Phylon* (First Quarter 1949), *EC Scrapbooks,* reel 4.

59. *Atlanta Journal,* 11 Sept. 1949; *Dallas News,* 25 Sept. 1949; *Augusta Herald,* 29 Sept. 1949, *EC Scrapbooks,* reel 4.

60. Caldwell, *Call It Experience,* 5.

61. Erskine Caldwell, *Gulf Coast Stories;* Erskine Caldwell, "The Story of Mahlon," Erskine Caldwell, *When You Think of Me,* 30–38, esp. 33, 38. Devlin, *Erskine Caldwell,* 115, conjectures that the "melancholy impressionistic style" of "The Story of Mahlon" is evidence that Caldwell wrote the story "very early" in his career. Whenever the story might have been written, what is certain is that Caldwell allowed it to be published late in his career.

62. Erskine Caldwell, *Jenny by Nature;* Erskine Caldwell, *Close to Home;* Erskine Caldwell, *The Last Night of Summer;* Erskine Caldwell, *Miss Mamma Aimee;* Erskine Caldwell, *Summertime Island;* Erskine Caldwell, *The Earnshaw Neighborhood;* Erskine Caldwell, *Annette.*

63. Erskine Caldwell, *Claudelle Inglish;* Erskine Caldwell, *The Weather Shelter;* Caldwell, *Jenny by Nature;* Caldwell, *Close to Home;* Caldwell, *Summertime Island.*

64. Caldwell, *Claudelle Inglish.*

65. Miller, "Tracing Tobacco Road," 545, 549–50; Bonn, *Heavy Traffic and High Culture,* 10. Collectively, Caldwell's publishers received more than $6 million from the sale of his books during this period. His share from the sale of each twenty-five-cent book was usually one and a half cents.

66. Shaplen, "The Quarter Books," 4, quoting Caldwell. Donald Demarest to

Jerry Burke, 5 Nov. 1948; Donald Demarest to EC, 19 Aug. and 30 Dec. 1949; "Self-Interview by Erskine Caldwell," [summer 1950], ECC-DC.

67. Caldwell, *Call It Experience*, 225–27; Caldwell, *With All My Might*, 211–13. "Famous Author at Katz," unidentified, undated clipping; *Kansas City Star*, 24 June 1948; Kansas Writers' Conference: University of Kansas, 21 June to 2 July 1948 (brochure); Margaret Young, "Enterprise Book Corner," *Beaumont (Tex.) Enterprise*, 4 July 1948; Margaret Young, "Writers Conference Gets Acescent Report," *Dallas Morning News*, 18 July 1948, *EC Scrapbooks*, reel 4.

68. Weybright, "Georgia Boy," 120.

69. A. D. Kirby to EC, 6 Dec. 1947; Mrs. Russell Taylor to EC, [1947]; Anna Smith to EC, [postmarked 25 May 1951]; "A Sophomore" to EC, [postmarked 25 May 1951]; Estelle Holleran to EC, 25 May 1951; Barbara Linan to EC, 24 May 1951, ECC-DC.

70. In addition to the correspondence cited in note 69, see Mabel D. Tillman to Editor, *The Journal*, Atlanta *Journal*, 25 June 1948; Eugene Anderson, "Around the Circle," *Macon Telegraph*, 30 July 1949, *EC Scrapbooks*, reel 4; anonymous writer to New American Library, 13 Apr. 1949; Theresa Winchester to EC, 25 May 1951; William Wilson to EC, [1951?], ECC-DC.

71. Larry W. King to EC, 28 Feb. 1954; B. W. Middlebrook to EC, 18 June 1959; Mary J. Jones to EC, 8 Feb. 1952; "An American" to EC, 9 Mar. 1952, ECC-DC; *Albany (Ga.) Herald*, 16 June 1948, *EC Scrapbooks*, reel 4.

72. *Jacksonville Times-Union*, 31 Oct. 1959, *EC Scrapbooks*, reel 5; Theodore Waller to Charles Duell, 8, 15, and 22 June 1953, ECC-DC; *Atlanta Journal*, 21 Sept. 1957, *EC Scrapbooks*, reel 5; Victor Weybright to EC, 3 Oct. 1957, ECC-DC; *Augusta Chronicle*, 27 July 1957, quoting G. Pierce King, *EC Scrapbooks*, reel 5; Howard, "Caldwell on Stage and Screen," 67–70; Caldwell, *With All My Might*, 255–56.

73. James Stokely to EC, 23 Feb. 1938; Charles A. Bly Jr. to EC and Margaret Bourke-White, 11 Apr. 1938; Tom P. Moye to EC, 23 Oct. 1938; Lorena Lester to EC, 15 Oct. 1940, ECC-DC.

74. Walter B. Powell to EC, 6 Feb. 1952; Bert H. Hatch to EC, 1 Nov. 1950; Gloucester Caliman Coxe to EC, 27 Nov. [1950?], ECC-DC. See also William W. Seward Jr. to EC, 25 Sept. 1948; Donald Demarest to Jerry Burke, 5 Nov. 1948; Cena B. Howard to EC, 15 Feb. 1950; Raymond G. Perkinson to EC, 29 Nov. 1952; Mrs. Fred Powell to EC, 14 Mar. 1958, ECC-DC; Albert E. Idell to Editor, *Saturday Review of Literature*, 29 June 1946, *EC Scrapbooks*, reel 4.

75. James F. Mitchell to EC, 29 Nov. 1947, ECC-DC; John O. West to Wayne Mixon, 27 Jan. and 9 Feb. 1991, letters in my possession.

76. "Hillbilly Peyton Place," *Time* 70 (30 Sept. 1957): 102, *EC Scrapbooks*, reel 5.

77. James Oliver Brown to EC, 30 Apr. 1952, ECC-DC; Klevar, *Erskine Caldwell*, 298–99; Snyder, "Spying on Southerners," 275–77. See also *Firing Line* 4 (15 May 1955): [49]–51. *Firing Line* was the organ of the American Legion's National Americanism Commission.

78. James Oliver Brown to EC, 5 May 1952; EC to June Caldwell, [June 1952], ECC-DC; Klevar, *Erskine Caldwell*, 307.

79. Klevar, "Erskine Caldwell," draft of Klevar, *Erskine Caldwell*, 350–52, 362, 369–70, 383, 402, 414, 424, 426, 428, 439, 451.

80. After 1959, Caldwell published no new short stories except for *The Deer at Our House* (New York: Collier, 1966), an illustrated children's story issued in book form. MacDonald, "Evaluative Check-List," in MacDonald, *Critical Essays*, 357–59.

81. Harvey L. Klevar, interview with Erskine Caldwell, 30 Nov. 1978, quoted in Klevar, *Erskine Caldwell*, 151–52; Klevar, *Erskine Caldwell*, 375–76.

82. Ibid., 364, 374.

83. Erskine Caldwell, *Around About America*, 41, 44–45.

84. Caldwell quoted in *Los Angeles Mirror*, 17 Jan. 1961, *EC Scrapbooks*, reel 5; Caldwell, *Around About America*, 63–64, 221.

85. Caldwell, *Around About America*, 54–59.

86. In *With All My Might*, written when he was nearly eighty, Caldwell asserted that he knew Bisco in White Oak, Georgia. When his family left White Oak, Caldwell was only three years old. Doubtlessly Caldwell knew Bisco, but the acquaintance probably was made while the Caldwells were living in Prosperity, South Carolina. By the time the family left Prosperity, Erskine was nearly nine. Caldwell, *With All My Might*, 4–6.

87. Caldwell, *In Search of Bisco*, 49–58, 71–82, 86–87, 109, 112.

88. Ibid., 170–71.

89. Ibid., 123–28, 156–64.

90. Ibid., 213–14.

91. *Austin American-Statesman*, 11 Apr. 1965; *Pensacola News Journal*, 9 May 1965; *Charleston News and Courier*, 18 Apr. 1965, ECC-DC. See also *Charlotte Observer*, 4 Apr. 1965; *New Orleans Picayune*, [?] May 1965; *Louisville Courier-Journal*, [?] July 1965, ECC-DC.

92. *Nashville Banner*, 30 Apr. 1965; *Dallas News*, 4 Apr. 1965; *Norfolk Pilot*, 11 Apr. 1965; *High Point (N.C.) Enterprise*, 4 Apr. 1965; *Rocky Mount (N.C.) Telegram*, 18 Apr. 1965; *Winston-Salem Journal-Sentinel*, 18 Apr. 1965; *Atlanta Daily World*, 20 May 1965; *Atlanta Journal*, 11 Apr. 1965, ECC-DC. See also *Birmingham News*, 4 Apr. 1965; *Nashville Tennesseean*, 18 Apr. 1965; *Houston Chronicle*, 30 May 1965; *Chattanooga Times*, undated clipping, ECC-DC.

93. Frank Daniel to Virginia and Erskine Caldwell, 22 Mar. 1965, ECC-DC.

94. Klevar, *Erskine Caldwell*, 381–82.

95. Caldwell, *Deep South*. *Deep South* is divided into two parts. The first section, which comprises 187 of the volume's 257 pages, was first published in England in 1966 as a book entitled *In the Shadow of the Steeple*. The second section, "At the Other End of Town," was original to *Deep South*.

96. Ibid., 53, 147, 149.

97. Ibid., 127.

98. Ibid., 250, 247; Klevar, "Erskine Caldwell," draft of Klevar, *Erskine Cald-*

well, 521; EC to Martin Luther King Jr., 11 Nov. 1964, quoted in Klevar, *Erskine Caldwell,* 377.

99. *San Antonio Express,* 10 Mar. 1968; *Atlanta Constitution and Journal,* 25 Feb. 1968, ECC-DC; Edwin M. Yoder Jr., "Are Pianos Holier than Pipe Organs?" *Chicago Tribune Book World,* 19 Mar. 1968, ECC-UGA.

100. Interview with Virginia Caldwell Hibbs, 2 July 1992.

101. A. A. Taylor to Mr. and Mrs. Erskine Caldwell, 13 Jan. 1947; Invitation from Fisk University [to Mr. and Mrs. Erskine Caldwell] to attend openings of collections at Fisk's Carl Van Vechten Gallery of Fine Arts on 4 November 1949; Virginia Caldwell to James Oliver Brown, 5 Aug. 1958; Phillip J. Walker to EC, 7 Dec. 1959 and 21 Apr. 1960, ECC-DC; interview with Ralph Stephens; John D. Smith, "Recollections of the Events Surrounding Erskine Caldwell's Visit to Erskine College in December 1959," 3 Nov. 1970. As president of Erskine College's Euphemian Literary Society, Smith, a native of Atoka, Tennessee, and a member of Salem Church many years after Ira Caldwell had served as pastor, was the target of protests from Erskine College alumni and other people who opposed Caldwell's visit. I am grateful to Mr. Smith for supplying a copy of his "Recollections." See also John Cook Wyllie to EC, 8 Sept. 1962; W. G. Malcolm to Edgar F. Shannon Jr., undated, enclosed with Janet L. Sketchley to EC, 21 Apr. 1965, ECC-DC.

102. Ralph McGill, "Tobacco Road Is Now Paved," *Atlanta Constitution,* 19 Nov. 1966; Ralph McGill, "The Culture of Poverty," *Atlanta Constitution,* 7 Dec. 1966; EC to Ralph McGill, 9 and 22 Dec. 1966, Ralph McGill Papers, Special Collections, R. W. Woodruff Library, Emory University; EC to Chris Eckl, 24 July 1965; EC to Governor [Lester] Maddox, 24 Oct. 1967; EC to John Pennekamp, 28 Mar. 1969, ECC-DC. For further evidence of recognition of Caldwell by southern academicians, see Gerald M. Garmon to EC, 8 Jan. and 13 May 1964; Samuel R. Spencer Jr. to EC, 14 Sept. 1964 and 19 Mar. and 8 and 16 Apr. 1965; Charles N. Carnes to Mr. and Mrs. Erskine Caldwell, 25 Feb. 1966, ECC-DC; Emory University *Campus Report* 17 (1 Feb. 1965): 1, Daniel Papers.

103. EC to John Pennekamp, 28 Mar. 1969, ECC-DC.

104. *New York Times,* 18 Dec. 1978; Virginia Caldwell to Mills Lane IV, 4 Nov. 1976; Virginia Caldwell to Cornelia and Waller Barrett, 4 Dec. 1976 and 3 Dec. 1978, Erskine Caldwell Collection, University of Virginia; Mills Lane IV to EC, 25 Mar. and 3 June 1975, ECC-DC; Thomas with Eidsvik, producers, *In Search of Caldwell's Georgia;* Moser, producer, *Erskine Caldwell;* interview with Mary M. Maner, 25 May 1990.

105. Caldwell, *Earnshaw Neighborhood;* Erskine Caldwell, *Afternoons in Mid-America,* 13–69; EC to Frank Daniel, 10 Feb. and 27 Mar. 1977, ECC-UGA.

106. Arnold, "Interview with Virginia Caldwell," in Arnold, *Erskine Caldwell Reconsidered,* 104, 106; Klevar, *Erskine Caldwell,* 409–10.

107. Klevar, *Erskine Caldwell,* 414; Arnold, "Interview with Virginia Caldwell," in Arnold, *Erskine Caldwell Reconsidered,* 106–8.

108. *With All My Might* was issued by Peachtree Publishers of Atlanta in March 1987. Telephone conversation with Kathleen Herndon of Peachtree Publishers, 12 Feb. 1993.

CHAPTER SIX: Caldwell's Achievement

1. Cowley, "The Two Erskine Caldwells," in MacDonald, *Critical Essays,* 198–200; Maxwell Perkins to EC, 2 June 1930, Scribner Archives.

2. Bourke-White, *Portrait of Myself,* 196; McClintock, "Erskine Caldwell," in Arnold, *Conversations,* 107; Tharpe, "Interview with Erskine Caldwell," in Arnold, *Conversations,* 138–47, esp. 144. Tharpe conducted his interview with Caldwell in August 1971.

3. EC to Milton A. Abernethy, 17 Sept. 1933, *Contempo* Archive.

4. Klevar, *Erskine Caldwell,* 260–61; Kelley, *Weeds;* Scarborough, *In the Land of Cotton;* Kroll, *The Cabin in the Cotton.* See also Bradbury, *Renaissance in the South,* 75–79.

5. Rubin, *The Writer in the South,* 82–116; Caldwell, *With All My Might,* 7, 9, 22, 29, 39.

6. Thomas Jefferson is quoted in Rubin, *The Literary South,* 57.

7. Brinkmeyer, "Is That You in the Mirror, Jeeter?" in MacDonald, *Critical Essays,* 370–74.

8. Burke, "Caldwell: Maker of Grotesques," in MacDonald, *Critical Essays,* 167–73; Wade, "Sweet Are the Uses of Degeneracy," 176–92; Frohock, "Erskine Caldwell," in MacDonald, *Critical Essays,* 201–13; Bradbury, *Renaissance in the South,* 100–101; Gray, "Southwestern Humor, Erskine Caldwell, and the Comedy of Frustration," in MacDonald, *Critical Essays,* 298–314; Cook, *From Tobacco Road to Route 66,* 64–84; Flynt, *Dixie's Forgotten People,* 75; Jacobs, "*Tobacco Road,*" 206–26; Mellard, "The Fiction of Social Commitment," 351–55, esp. 354–55; Kirby, *Media-Made Dixie,* 51–63, passim; Kirby, *Rural Worlds Lost,* 186; Peeler, *Hope Among Us Yet,* 171–72; Cook, *Erskine Caldwell and the Fiction of Poverty,* 116–21; Broadwell and Hoag, "'A Writer First,'" in Arnold, *Conversations,* 160–78, esp. 168.

9. Rubin et al., *History of Southern Literature,* 283, 355, 436–37; Eric J. Sundquist, *Faulkner: The House Divided* (Baltimore: Johns Hopkins Univ. Press, 1983), 63–130, passim.

10. Waldo E. Martin Jr., *The Mind of Frederick Douglass* (Chapel Hill: Univ. of North Carolina Press, 1984), 220–24.

11. Broadwell and Hoag, "'A Writer First'", 167.

12. [Carvel Collins], "Erskine Caldwell at Work," 21–27; Lewis and Wertman, "The Art of Fiction," in Arnold, *Conversations,* 109–19, esp. 119; Tharpe, "Interview with Erskine Caldwell," 138; Helen C. Smith, "Erskine Caldwell," in Arnold, *Conversations,* 156–59, esp. 157; Arnold, introduction to *Conversations,* xii; EC to James Korges, 20 June 1969, James Korges Papers, Rice University; EC to Guy Owen, 18 Mar., 9 May, 11 July, and 9 Aug. 1978, Guy Owen Papers, Southern Historical Collection, Library of the University of North Carolina at

Chapel Hill. Caldwell appreciated James Korges's perceptive summary of his work; Korges, *Erskine Caldwell*.

13. Guccione, "Sex, Sin and Society Through the Eyes of Erskine Caldwell," in Arnold, *Conversations,* 52–57, esp. 53; Renek, "'Sex Was Their Way of Life,'" in Arnold, *Conversations,* 66–80, esp. 77; Bonetti, "A Good Listener Speaks," 244–45; Staats, "Erskine Caldwell at Eighty-One," in Arnold, *Conversations,* 257–64, esp. 258; Arnold, "Interview with Erskine Caldwell," in Arnold, *Conversations,* 274–75; EC to Jon Allan, 13 Jan. 1974, Erskine Caldwell Collection, University of Virginia.

14. MacDonald, "Enough Good Reasons," 7; Cook, *Erskine Caldwell and the Fiction of Poverty,* 269. For examples of acutely myopic evaluations of Caldwell, see Harrison Smith, "Comic Citizens of the South," in MacDonald, *Critical Essays,* 89–90; Carl Bode, "Erskine Caldwell," in MacDonald, *Critical Essays,* 246–48; and Devlin, *Erskine Caldwell,* preface, 139.

15. See, for example, Jack Reese to EC, 6 Mar. 1945; Mrs. A. D. Shorter to EC, 16 Oct. 1946; H. V. Hopkins to EC, 5 Oct. 1950; Nell R. Payne to EC, 3 Apr. 1951; Frank White Sr. to EC, 29 June 1951; Ethel Roark to EC, 18 Aug. 1951; EC to Ethel Roark, 6 Sept. 1951; Emmett Dismuke to EC, 11 Jan. and 26 May 1954; Kathryn J. Robertson to Erskine and Virginia Caldwell, 19 Dec. 1958; Karen Ristau to EC, 7 Nov. 1964; EC to Karen Ristau, 23 Nov. 1964; Mary Martin to EC, 9 Feb. 1965; Ralph A. Gougis to EC, 13 Aug. 1966, ECC-DC.

16. Lelchuk and White, "An Interview with Erskine Caldwell," in Arnold, *Conversations,* 83–102, esp. 94.

17. On the matter of a culture of poverty, see Lewis, *La Vida,* xlii–lii, esp. li; and Jones, *The Dispossessed,* 1–10, 73–89.

18. *Atlanta Journal,* 16 Dec. 1959, *EC Scrapbooks,* reel 5; Erskine Caldwell, foreword to *On the Plantation,* [vii]–xi. On Harris as a subverter of plantation romance, see Wayne Mixon, "The Ultimate Irrelevance of Race: Joel Chandler Harris and Uncle Remus in Their Time," *Journal of Southern History* 56 (Aug. 1990): 457–80. EC to Brom Weber, 18 Aug. 1954, Brom Weber Papers, University of California at Davis; Brom Weber to EC, 26 Sept. 1954, ECC-DC; Broadwell and Hoag, "'A Writer First,'" 174; Broadwell and Hoag, "The Art of Fiction LXII," in Arnold, *Conversations,* 179–204, esp. 197; Jay Martin, "Erskine Caldwell's Singular Devotions," 40–56, esp. 40–41; Arlin Turner, *George W. Cable: A Biography* (1956; repr. Baton Rouge: Louisiana State Univ. Press, 1966), 243–62; Wayne Mixon, "New Woman, Old Family: Passion, Gender, and Place in the Virginia Fiction of Amélie Rives," in Elizabeth Jacoway et al., eds., *The Adaptable South: Essays in Honor of George Brown Tindall* (Baton Rouge: Louisiana State Univ. Press, 1991), 124–47, esp. 124–35; Anne Rowe, "Kate Chopin," in Rubin et al., *History of Southern Literature,* 228–32.

19. Caldwell's lack of interest in family history mirrored yet another of his father's traits. Conversely, his mother's interest in her family's background bordered on conceit.

20. Erskine Caldwell, "The White Man's Poverty," *New York Herald-Tribune,* 29 Oct. 1939, *EC Scrapbooks,* reel 2; McIlwaine, *The Southern Poor-White,* 224,

230, 231. Biographical information about McIlwaine is presented in the dust jacket of his book.

21. Stanley Salmen to EC, 30 Nov. 1953, ECC-DC. For perceptive commentaries on Caldwell's reputation among critics, see MacDonald, introduction to *Critical Essays*, xi–xxxvii, and Cook, *Erskine Caldwell and the Fiction of Poverty*, 255–84.

22. Faulkner is quoted in Cook, *Erskine Caldwell and the Fiction of Poverty*, 272; Marlise Simons, "A Talk With Gabriel García Márquez," *New York Times Book Review*, 5 Dec. 1982, 7, 60–61; Bellow is quoted in Miller, "Tracing Tobacco Road," 615.

23. Trueheart, "Erskine Caldwell," in Arnold, *Conversations*, 297–305, esp. 304.

SELECT BIBLIOGRAPHY

Primary Sources

MANUSCRIPT COLLECTIONS

Caldwell, Erskine. Collection. Dartmouth College Library, New Hanover, N.H.
———. Collection. Hargrett Rare Book and Manuscript Library, University of Georgia Libraries, Athens.
———. Collection. Manuscripts Division, Special Collections Department, University of Virginia Library, Charlottesville.
———. Correspondence. Yale Collection of American Literature, Beinecke Rare Book and Manuscript Library, Yale University, New Haven, Conn.
———. Papers. McFarlin Library, University of Tulsa, Okla.
———. Papers. Syracuse University Library, Special Collections Department, Syracuse, N.Y.
———. Records. Office of the Registrar, Erskine College, Due West, S.C.
———. Records. Office of the Registrar, University of Virginia, Charlottesville.
Caldwell, Ira S. Records. Military Reference Branch, National Archives and Records Administration, Washington, D.C.
Cantwell, Robert. Papers. Special Collections, Knight Library, University of Oregon, Eugene.
Charles Scribner and Sons. Archives. Princeton University, Princeton, N.J.
Contempo Magazine. Archives. Harry Ransom Humanities Research Center, University of Texas at Austin.
Daniel, Frank. Papers. Special Collections, R. W. Woodruff Library, Emory University, Atlanta, Ga.
Fletcher, John Gould. Papers. Special Collections Division, University of Arkansas Libraries, Fayetteville.
Grand Jury, Jefferson County, Ga. Minutes. Louisville, Ga.
Gray, James and Family. Papers. Minnesota Historical Society, St. Paul.
Hench, Atcheson. Oral History. University Archives, University of Virginia Library, Charlottesville.
Hench, Atcheson, and Erskine Caldwell. Collection. Manuscripts Division, Special Collections Department, University of Virginia Library, Charlottesville.
Korges, James. Papers. Woodson Research Center, Library of Rice University, Houston, Tex.

McGill, Ralph. Papers. Special Collections, R. W. Woodruff Library, Emory University, Atlanta, Ga.

Morang, Alfred. Papers. Houghton Library, Harvard University, Cambridge, Mass.

Owen, Guy. Papers. Southern Historical Collection, Library of the University of North Carolina at Chapel Hill.

Pagany Magazine. Archives. University of Delaware Library, Newark.

Salomon, I. Lawrence. Papers. Manuscript Division, Library of Congress, Washington, D.C.

Session, Salem Associate Reformed Presbyterian Church. Minutes. Atoka, Tenn.

Special Collections, Colby College Library, Waterville, Maine.

Story Magazine. Archives. Princeton University, Princeton, N.J.

Sutton, William A. Papers. Special Collections, Library of the University of Illinois at Urbana-Champaign.

Taggard, Genevieve. Papers. Rare Books and Manuscripts Division, New York Public Library, Astor, Lenox and Tilden Foundations.

University of North Carolina Press. Records. Southern Historical Collection, Library of the University of North Carolina at Chapel Hill.

Villard, Oswald Garrison. Papers. Houghton Library, Harvard University, Cambridge, Mass.

Weber, Brom. Papers. Special Collections, Library of the University of California, Davis.

INTERVIEWS

Unpublished

Boyce, Henrietta; Johnson, Annette; Parrish, Lucille M.; and Williams, Helen. Interview by author. Wrens, Ga., 21 Mar. 1991.

Caldwell, Erskine Jr. Interview by author. Moreland, Ga., 4 July 1992.

Hibbs, Virginia Caldwell. Interview by author. Moreland, Ga., 2 July 1992. Telephone interview by author. 23 Aug. 1992.

Lewis, Leroy. Interview by author. Louisville, Ga., 21 Mar. 1991.

Maner, Mary M. Interviews by author. Louisville, Ga., 25 May, 14 July, and 18 Dec. 1990.

Stephens, Ralph. Interview by author. Athens, Ga., 28 Jan. 1991.

Wren, Harry P. Interview by author. Wrens, Ga., 21 Mar. 1991.

Published

Caldwell, Erskine. Arnold, Edwin T. "Interview with Erskine Caldwell." In Arnold, Edwin T., ed., *Conversations with Erskine Caldwell*. Jackson: Univ. Press of Mississippi, 1988.

——. Bonetti, Kay. "A Good Listener Speaks." *Saturday Review* 9 (July-Aug. 1983): 8–11; reprinted in Arnold, *Conversations*.

——. Broadwell, Elizabeth Pell, and Ronald Wesley Hoag. "The Art of Fiction LXII: Erskine Caldwell." *Paris Review* No. 86 (Winter 1982): 126–57; reprinted in Arnold, *Conversations*.

——. Broadwell, Elizabeth Pell, and Ronald Wesley Hoag. "'A Writer First': An Interview with Erskine Caldwell." *Georgia Review* 36 (Spring 1982): 83–101; reprinted in Arnold, *Conversations*.

——. Collins, Carvel. "Erskine Caldwell at Work: A Conversation with Carvel Collins." *Atlantic Monthly* 202 (July 1958): 21–27.

——. Guccione. "Sex, Sin, and Society Through the Eyes of Erskine Caldwell." *London American* (23/29 Mar. 1961): 7; reprinted in Arnold, *Conversations*.

——. Lelchuk, Alan, and Robin White. "An Interview with Erskine Caldwell." *Per/Se*, Spring 1967, 11–20; reprinted in Arnold, *Conversations*.

——. Lewis, Donald, and Richard Wertman. "The Art of Fiction: An Interview with Erskine Caldwell." *University of Virginia Magazine* 132 (Nov. 1968): 4–9, 24, 26; reprinted in Arnold, *Conversations*.

——. McClintock, Jack. "Erskine Caldwell: Down South Storyteller." *Florida Accent*, 2 June 1968, 8–9; reprinted in Arnold, *Conversations*.

——. Renek, Morris. "'Sex Was Their Way of Life': A Frank Interview with Erskine Caldwell." *Cavalier*, Mar. 1964, 12–16, 40–42; reprinted in Arnold, *Conversations*.

——. Smith, Helen C. "Erskine Caldwell: A Georgia Boy Returns Home." *Atlanta Constitution*, 7 Oct. 1975; reprinted in Arnold, *Conversations*.

——. Staats, Marilyn Dorn. "Erskine Caldwell at Eighty-One: An Interview." *Arizona Quarterly* 41 (Autumn 1985): 247–57; reprinted in Arnold, *Conversations*.

——. Tharpe, Jac. "Interview with Erskine Caldwell." *Southern Quarterly* 20 (Fall 1981): 64–74; reprinted in Arnold, *Conversations*.

——. Trueheart, Charles. "Erskine Caldwell: The Final Chapter." *Washington Post*, 1 Mar. 1987; reprinted in Arnold, *Conversations*.

Caldwell, Virginia. Arnold, Edwin T. "Interview with Virginia Caldwell." In Arnold, Edwin T., ed., *Erskine Caldwell Reconsidered*, Jackson: Univ. Press of Mississippi, 1990.

Cushman, Helen Caldwell. Klevar, Harvey L. "Interview with Helen Caldwell Cushman." In Arnold, *Erskine Caldwell Reconsidered*.

GOVERNMENT DOCUMENTS

National Emergency Council. *Report on Economic Conditions of the South.* Washington, D.C.: U.S. Government Printing Office, 1938.

NEWSPAPERS

Atlanta Constitution, Jan. 1934, Nov.–Dec. 1966.
Atlanta Journal, Nov. 1921.
Charlotte Observer, Dec. 1925–Dec. 1926.

Louisville Courier-Journal, Feb. 1933.
Macon Telegraph, Mar. 1933.
New York Evening Post, Feb. 1933.
Raleigh News and Observer, Mar. 1933.
Scrapbooks of Erskine Caldwell. Microfilm ed. Ann Arbor: Xerox University
  Microfilms, 1974.

MAGAZINES

Haldeman-Julius Monthly, Dec. 1924.
New Masses, Jan.–Feb. 1934.

BOOKS BY ERSKINE CALDWELL

Afternoons in Mid-America: Observations and Impressions. New York: Dodd,
  Mead, 1976.
American Earth. New York: Charles Scribner's Sons, 1931.
Annette. New York: New American Library, 1973.
Around About America. New York: Farrar, Straus, 1964.
The Bastard. 1929. Repr. New York: Novel Selections, n.d.
The Caldwell Caravan: Novels and Stories by Erskine Caldwell. Cleveland: World
  Publishing, 1946.
Call It Experience: The Years of Learning How to Write. New York: Duell, Sloan
  and Pearce, 1951.
Claudelle Inglish. Boston: Little, Brown, 1958.
Close to Home. New York: Farrar, Straus, and Cudahy, 1962.
The Complete Stories. Boston: Little, Brown, 1953.
Deep South: Memory and Observation. New York: Weybright and Talley, 1968.
The Earnshaw Neighborhood. New York: World Publishing, 1971.
Episode in Palmetto. New York: Duell, Sloan and Pearce, 1950.
Georgia Boy. 1943. Repr. New York: Grosset and Dunlap, 1950.
God's Little Acre. 1933. Repr. New York: New American Library, n.d.
Gulf Coast Stories. Boston: Little, Brown, 1956.
A House in the Uplands. New York: Duell, Sloan and Pearce, 1946.
In Search of Bisco. New York: Farrar, Straus and Giroux, 1965.
Jenny by Nature. New York: Farrar, Straus and Cudahy, 1961.
Journeyman. 1935. Repr. New York: Duell, Sloan and Pearce, 1950.
Kneel to the Rising Sun and Other Stories. New York: Viking, 1935.
The Last Night of Summer. New York: Farrar, Straus, 1963.
Miss Mamma Aimee. New York: New American Library, 1967.
Place Called Estherville. New York: Duell, Sloan and Pearce, 1949.
Some American People. New York: Robert M. McBride, 1935.
Southways. New York: Viking, 1938.
Summertime Island. New York: World Publishing, 1968.
The Sure Hand of God. 1947. Repr. New York: Grosset and Dunlap, n.d.

Tenant Farmer. New York: Phalanx Press, 1935.
This Very Earth. New York: Duell, Sloan and Pearce, 1948.
Tobacco Road. 1932. Repr. New York: New American Library, n.d.
Tragic Ground. 1944. Repr. New York: New American Library, n.d.
Trouble in July. 1940. Repr. Savannah: Beehive Press, 1977.
We Are the Living. New York: Viking, 1933.
The Weather Shelter. New York: World Publishing, 1969.
When You Think of Me. Boston: Little, Brown, 1959.
With All My Might: An Autobiography. Atlanta: Peachtree Publishers, 1987.

    With Margaret Bourke-White

Say, Is This the U.S.A. New York: Duell, Sloan and Pearce, 1941.
You Have Seen Their Faces. New York: Viking, 1937.

ARTICLES BY ERSKINE CALDWELL

"Flight from the Land." *McCall's* 68 (May 1941): 20–22, 92.
Foreword to *On the Plantation: A Story of a Georgia Boy's Adventures during the War,* by Joel Chandler Harris. Athens: Univ. of Georgia Press, 1980.
"The Georgia Cracker." *Haldeman-Julius Monthly* 4 (Nov. 1926): 39–42.
" 'Parties Unknown' in Georgia." *New Masses* 10 (23 Jan. 1934): 16, 18.
"A Story That Got Lost." *New Masses* 10 (16 Jan. 1934): 13.

RADIO AND VIDEO MATERIALS

Ethridge, Mark, Erskine Caldwell, and John Temple Graves II. "Are We a United People?" *Town Meeting: Bulletin of America's Town Meeting of the Air* 6 (24 Feb. 1941): 3–30. Printed version of radio broadcast of 20 Feb. 1941.
Moser, Chris, producer. *Erskine Caldwell: Georgia Revisited.* Videotape. Atlanta: Georgia Endowment for the Humanities, 1986.
Thomas, David O., with Charles Eidsvik, producers. *In Search of Caldwell's Georgia.* Videotape. Athens: University of Georgia, 1980.

Secondary Sources

BOOKS

Arnold, Edwin T., ed. *Conversations with Erskine Caldwell.* Jackson: Univ. Press of Mississippi, 1988.
————, ed. *Erskine Caldwell Reconsidered.* Jackson: Univ. Press of Mississippi, 1990.
Ayers, Edward L. *The Promise of the New South: Life after Reconstruction.* New York: Oxford University Press, 1992.

——. *Vengeance and Justice: Crime and Punishment in the Nineteenth-Century American South.* New York: Oxford University Press, 1984.

Bonn, Thomas L. *Heavy Traffic and High Culture: New American Library as Literary Gatekeeper in the Paperback Revolution.* Carbondale: Southern Illinois Univ. Press, 1989.

Bourke-White, Margaret. *Portrait of Myself.* New York: Simon and Schuster, 1963.

Bradbury, John M. *Renaissance in the South: A Critical History of the Literature, 1920–1960.* Chapel Hill: Univ. of North Carolina Press, 1963.

Cash, W. J. *The Mind of the South.* 1941. Repr. New York: Vintage, n.d.

The Centennial History of the Associate Reformed Presbyterian Church, 1803–1903. Charleston, S.C.: Walker, Evans, and Cogswell, 1905.

Coleman, Kenneth, ed. *A History of Georgia.* Athens: Univ. of Georgia Press, 1977.

Conrad, David Eugene. *The Forgotten Farmers: The Story of Sharecroppers in the New Deal.* Urbana: Univ. of Illinois Press, 1965.

Cook, Sylvia Jenkins. *Erskine Caldwell and the Fiction of Poverty: The Flesh and the Spirit.* Baton Rouge: Louisiana State Univ. Press, 1991.

——. *From Tobacco Road to Route 66: The Southern Poor White in Fiction.* Chapel Hill: Univ. of North Carolina Press, 1976.

Couch, W. T., ed. *Culture in the South.* Chapel Hill: Univ. of North Carolina Press, 1935.

Cowley, Malcolm. *—And I Worked at the Writer's Trade: Chapters of Literary History.* New York: Viking, 1978.

Degler, Carl N. *In Search of Human Nature: The Decline and Revival of Darwinism in American Social Thought.* New York: Oxford Univ. Press, 1991.

Devlin, James E. *Erskine Caldwell.* Boston: Twayne, 1984.

Dowd, Jerome. *The Negro in American Life.* New York: Century, 1926.

Fite, Gilbert C. *Cotton Fields No More: Southern Agriculture, 1865–1980.* Lexington: Univ. Press of Kentucky, 1984.

Flynt, J. Wayne. *Dixie's Forgotten People: The South's Poor Whites.* Bloomington: Indiana Univ. Press, 1979.

Goldberg, Vicki. *Margaret Bourke-White: A Biography.* Reading, Mass.: Addison-Wesley, 1986.

Grubbs, Donald H. *Cry from the Cotton: The Southern Tenant Farmers' Union and the New Deal.* Chapel Hill: Univ. of North Carolina Press, 1971.

Hahn, Steven. *The Roots of Southern Populism: Yeoman Farmers and the Transformation of the Georgia Upcountry, 1850–1890.* New York: Oxford Univ. Press, 1983.

Hall, Jacquelyn Dowd et al. *Like a Family: The Making of a Southern Cotton Mill World.* Chapel Hill: Univ. of North Carolina Press, 1987.

Hobson, Fred C. Jr. *Serpent in Eden: H. L. Mencken and the South.* Chapel Hill: Univ. of North Carolina Press, 1974.

Hoffman, Frederick J., Charles Allen, and Carolyn F. Ulrich. *The Little Magazine:*

A History and a Bibliography. Princeton, N.J.: Princeton University Press, 1946.

Hurley, Rodger L. *Poverty and Mental Retardation: A Causal Relationship*. New York: Vintage, 1969.

Johnson, Charles S., Edwin R. Embree, and W. W. Alexander. *The Collapse of Cotton Tenancy: Summary of Field Studies and Statistical Surveys, 1933–35*. Chapel Hill: Univ. of North Carolina Press, 1935.

Jones, Jacqueline. *The Dispossessed: America's Underclasses from the Civil War to the Present*. New York: Basic Books, 1992.

Kelley, Edith Summers. *Weeds*. New York: Harcourt, Brace, 1923.

Kennedy, Stetson. *Palmetto Country*. Ed. Erskine Caldwell. New York: Duell, Sloan and Pearce, 1942.

Kennedy, W. A., ed. *Sesquicentennial History of the Associate Reformed Presbyterian Church*. Clinton, S.C.: Jacobs Brothers, 1951.

King, Ray A. *A History of the Associate Reformed Presbyterian Church*. Charlotte, N.C.: Board of Christian Education of the Associate Reformed Presbyterian Church, 1966.

King, Richard H. *A Southern Renaissance: The Cultural Awakening of the American South, 1930–1955*. New York: Oxford University Press, 1980.

Kirby, Jack Temple. *Media-Made Dixie: The South in the American Imagination*. Rev. ed. Athens: Univ. of Georgia Press, 1986.

——. *Rural Worlds Lost: The American South, 1920–1960*. Baton Rouge: Louisiana State Univ. Press, 1987.

Kirkland, Jack. *Tobacco Road: A Three Act Play*. 1934. Repr. New York: New American Library, 1952.

Klevar, Harvey L. *Erskine Caldwell: A Biography*. Knoxville: Univ. of Tennessee Press, 1993.

Korges, James. *Erskine Caldwell*. University of Minnesota Pamphlets on American Writers, No. 78. Minneapolis: Univ. of Minnesota Press, 1969.

Kroll, Harry Harrison. *The Cabin in the Cotton*. New York: Ray Long and Richard R. Smith, 1931.

Kuehl, John, and Jackson R. Bryer, eds. *Dear Scott/Dear Max: The Fitzgerald-Perkins Correspondence*. New York: Scribner's, 1971.

Lewis, Oscar. *La Vida: A Puerto Rican Family in the Culture of Poverty — San Juan and New York*. New York: Random House, 1966.

Lindberg, Stanley W. *The Legacy of Erskine Caldwell*. Atlanta: Georgia Humanities Council, 1989.

MacDonald, Scott, ed. *Critical Essays on Erskine Caldwell*. Boston: G. K. Hall, 1981.

Martin, Robert F. *Howard Kester and the Struggle for Social Justice in the South, 1904–77*. Charlottesville: Univ. Press of Virginia, 1991.

McIlwaine, Shields. *The Southern Poor-White from Lubberland to Tobacco Road*. Norman: Univ. of Oklahoma Press, 1939.

Miller, Dan B. *Erskine Caldwell: The Journey from Tobacco Road*. New York: Knopf, 1995.

Odum, Howard W., and D. W. Willard. *Systems of Public Welfare.* Chapel Hill: Univ. of North Carolina Press, 1925.

Peeler, David P. *Hope Among Us Yet: Social Criticism and Social Solace in Depression America.* Athens: Univ. of Georgia Press, 1987.

Puckett, Newbell Niles. *Folk Beliefs of the Southern Negro.* Chapel Hill: Univ. of North Carolina Press, 1926.

Raper, Arthur F. *Preface to Peasantry: A Tale of Two Black Belt Counties.* Chapel Hill: Univ. of North Carolina Press, 1936.

Rubin, Louis D. Jr. *The Literary South.* New York: Wiley, 1979.

———. *The Writer in the South: Studies in a Literary Community.* Athens: Univ. of Georgia Press, 1972.

Rubin, Louis D. Jr., et al., eds. *The History of Southern Literature.* Baton Rouge: Louisiana State Univ. Press, 1985.

Scarborough, Dorothy. *In the Land of Cotton.* 1923. Repr. New York: Macmillan, 1925.

Singal, Daniel Joseph. *The War Within: From Victorian to Modernist Thought in the South, 1919–1945.* Chapel Hill: Univ. of North Carolina Press, 1982.

Stott, William. *Documentary Expression and Thirties America.* New York: Oxford Univ. Press, 1973.

Sutton, William A. *Black Like It Is/Was: Erskine Caldwell's Treatment of Racial Themes.* Metuchen, N.J.: Scarecrow Press, 1974.

Tannenbaum, Frank. *Darker Phases of the South.* New York: Putnam, 1924.

Tindall, George Brown. *The Emergence of the New South, 1913–1945.* 1967. Repr. Baton Rouge: Louisiana State Univ. Press, 1970.

Vance, Rupert B. *Human Factors in Cotton Culture: A Study in the Social Geography of the American South.* Chapel Hill: Univ. of North Carolina Press, 1929.

———. *Human Geography of the South: A Study in Regional Resources and Human Adequacy.* 2d ed. Chapel Hill: Univ. of North Carolina Press, 1935.

Williamson, Joel. *The Crucible of Race: Black-White Relations in the American South since Emancipation.* New York: Oxford Univ. Press, 1984.

Woodward, C. Vann. *Origins of the New South, 1877–1913.* 1951. Repr. Baton Rouge: Louisiana State Univ. Press, 1967.

Wright, Richard. *Uncle Tom's Children.* 1938. Repr. New York: Harper and Row, 1976.

ARTICLES

Arnold, Edwin T. Introduction to *Conversations with Erskine Caldwell.* Jackson: Univ. Press of Mississippi, 1988.

"Associate Reformed Presbyterian Church." In Samuel S. Hill, ed., *Encyclopedia of Religion in the South.* Macon, Ga.: Mercer Univ. Press, 1984, 76.

"Behind the Scenes." *Scribner's* 97 (May 1935): 320.

Bode, Carl. "Erskine Caldwell: A Note for the Negative." *College English* 17 (Oct. 1955): 357–59. Reprinted in MacDonald, *Critical Essays,* 246–48.

Brinkmeyer, Robert H. Jr. "Is That You in the Mirror, Jeeter? The Reader and
    Tobacco Road." *Pembroke* 11 (1979): 47–50. Reprinted in MacDonald, *Criti-
    cal Essays,* 370–74.
Burke, Kenneth. "Caldwell: Maker of Grotesques." *New Republic* 82 (10 Apr.
    1935): 232–35. Reprinted in MacDonald, *Critical Essays,* 167–73.
Caldwell, I. S. "The Bunglers: A Narrative Study in Five Parts." *Eugenics* 3 (June-
    Oct. 1930): 202–10, 247–51, 293–99, 332–36, 377–83.
———. "A School That Teaches a Community." *Survey* 59 (15 Mar. 1928): 764–65.
Cantwell, Robert. "Caldwell's Characters: Why Don't They Leave?" *Georgia Re-
    view* 11 (Fall 1957): 252–64.
Cook, Sylvia Jenkins. "Erskine Caldwell and the Literary Left Wing." In Mac-
    Donald, *Critical Essays,* 361–69.
Couch, W. T. "American Peasants." *Virginia Quarterly Review* 10 (Oct. 1934):
    636–40.
———. "Landlord and Tenant." *Virginia Quarterly Review* 14 (Spring 1938): 309–
    12. Reprinted in MacDonald, *Critical Essays,* 56–59.
Cowley, Malcolm. "Erskine Caldwell's Magic." *Pembroke* 11 (1979): 6–7.
———. "The Two Erskine Caldwells." *New Republic* 111 (6 Nov. 1944): 599–600.
    Reprinted in MacDonald, *Critical Essays,* 198–200.
Davidson, Donald. "Erskine Caldwell's Picture Book." *Southern Review* 4 (1938–
    39): 15–25. Reprinted in MacDonald, *Critical Essays,* 59–67.
———. "The Trend of Literature: A Partisan View." In W. T. Couch, ed., *Culture
    in the South.* Chapel Hill: Univ. of North Carolina Press, 1935, 183–210.
Farley, Benjamin W. "Erskine Caldwell: Preacher's Son and Southern Prophet."
    Journal of Presbyterian History 56 (Fall 1978): 202–17.
"Farmers." *Time* 25 (4 Mar. 1935): 13–14.
Flora, Joseph M. "Fiction in the 1920s: Some New Voices." In Louis D. Rubin et
    al., eds., *The History of Southern Literature.* Baton Rouge: Louisiana State
    Univ. Press, 1985, 279–90.
Frohock, W. M. "Erskine Caldwell: Sentimental Gentleman from Georgia."
    Southwest Review 31 (Autumn 1946): 351–59. Reprinted in MacDonald,
    Critical Essays, 201–13.
Gray, R. J. "Southwestern Humor, Erskine Caldwell, and the Comedy of Frustra-
    tion." *Southern Literary Journal* 8 (Fall 1975): 3–26. Reprinted in MacDon-
    ald, *Critical Essays,* 298–314.
Hobson, Fred. "The Savage South: An Inquiry into the Origins, Endurance, and
    Presumed Demise of an Age." *Virginia Quarterly Review* 61 (Summer 1985):
    [377]–95.
Hoffsommer, Harold. "The AAA and the Cropper." *Social Forces* 13 (May
    1935): 494–502.
Howard, William L. "Caldwell on Stage and Screen." In Edwin T. Arnold, *Erskine
    Caldwell Reconsidered.* Jackson: Univ. Press of Mississippi, 1990, 59–72.
Jacobs, Robert D. "*Tobacco Road:* Lowlife and the Comic Tradition." In Louis
    D. Rubin Jr., ed., *The American South: Portrait of a Culture.* Baton Rouge:
    Louisiana State Univ. Press, 1980, 206–26.

Klevar, Harvey L. "Caldwell's Women." In Edwin T. Arnold, ed., *Erskine Caldwell Reconsidered.* Jackson: Univ. Press of Mississippi, 1990, 15–35.

Lee, Ulysses. "Erskine Caldwell: Profound Comedian." *Opportunity: The Journal of Negro Life* 18 (Dec. 1940): 372–74, 389.

MacDonald, Scott. "Enough Good Reasons for Reading, Studying and Teaching Erskine Caldwell." *Pembroke* 11 (1979): 7–18.

———. "An Evaluative Check-List of Erskine Caldwell's Short Fiction." In MacDonald, *Critical Essays,* 342–60.

———. Introduction to *Critical Essays on Erskine Caldwell.*

———. "Repetition as Technique in the Short Stories of Erskine Caldwell." In MacDonald, *Critical Essays,* 330–41.

Magee, Rosemary M. "Erskine Caldwell." In Samuel S. Hill, ed., *Encyclopedia of Religion in the South.* Macon, Ga.: Mercer Univ. Press, 1984, 122–24.

Marion, J. H. Jr. "Star-Dust Above Tobacco Road." *Christian Century* 55 (16 Feb. 1938): 204–6. Reprinted in MacDonald, *Critical Essays,* 174–79.

Martin, Jay. "Erskine Caldwell's Singular Devotions." In Louis Filler, ed., *A Question of Quality: Popularity and Value in Modern Creative Writing.* Bowling Green, Ohio: Bowling Green Univ. Press, 1976, 40–56.

Mellard, James. "The Fiction of Social Commitment." In Louis D. Rubin et al., eds., *The History of Southern Literature.* Baton Rouge: Louisiana State Univ. Press, 1985, 351–55.

Owen, Guy. "The Apprenticeship of Erskine Caldwell: An Examination of *The Bastard* and *Poor Fool.*" In Jack D. Durant and M. Thomas Hester, eds., *A Fair Day in the Affections: Literary Essays in Honor of Robert B. White Jr.* Raleigh, N.C.: Winston Press, 1980, 197–204.

———. "Erskine Caldwell's Unpublished Poems." *South Atlantic Bulletin* 43 (1978): 53–57.

———. "Folk Motifs in Erskine Caldwell's Cyclorama of the South." *North Carolina Folklore Journal* 27 (1979): 80–87.

Rable, George C. "The South and the Politics of Anti-Lynching Legislation, 1920–1940." *Journal of Southern History* 51 (May 1985): 201–21.

Rahv, Philip. "Paleface and Redskin." In *Essays on Literature and Politics, 1932–1972.* Ed. Arabel J. Porter and Andrew J. Dvosin. Boston: Houghton Mifflin, 1978, [3]–7.

Shaplen, Robert. "The Quarter Books." *Tomorrow* 10 (Dec. 1950): 4–12.

Simons, Marlise. "A Talk with Gabriel García Márquez." *New York Times Book Review,* 5 Dec. 1982, 7, 60–61.

Smith, Harrison. "Comic Citizens of the South." *Saturday Review of Literature* 32 (10 Sept. 1949): 14–15. Reprinted in MacDonald, *Critical Essays,* 89–90.

Snyder, Robert E. "Spying on Southerners: The FBI and Erskine Caldwell." *Georgia Historical Quarterly* 72 (Summer 1988): 248–81.

Thompson, James J. Jr. "Erskine Caldwell and Southern Religion." In MacDonald, *Critical Essays,* 268–78.

Wade, John Donald. "Sweet Are the Uses of Degeneracy." *Southern Review* 1 (Winter 1936): 449–66. Reprinted in Donald Davidson, ed., *Selected Essays and Other Writings of John Donald Wade.* Athens: Univ. of Georgia Press, 1966, 176–92.

Weybright, Victor. "Georgia Boy: A Recollection from the Inner Sanctum." *Pembroke* 11 (1979): 115–20.

Wright, Richard. "Lynching Bee." *New Republic* 102 (18 Mar. 1940): 351–52.

UNPUBLISHED MATERIALS

Klevar, Harvey L. "Erskine Caldwell: A Life." Draft of Klevar, *Erskine Caldwell: A Biography.* Copy courtesy of Prof. Klevar.

Miller, Dan B. "Tracing Tobacco Road: A Life of Erskine Caldwell." Draft of Miller, *Erskine Caldwell: The Journey from Tobacco Road.* Copy courtesy of Dr. Miller.

Smith, John D. Letters to the author, 14 Oct. and 11 and 27 Nov. 1990; 18 Jan. and 4 and 18 Feb. 1991.

———. "Recollections of the Events Surrounding Erskine Caldwell's Visit to Erskine College in December 1959." Copy courtesy of Mr. Smith.

Sutton, William A. "A Lover's Quarrel." Biography of Erskine Caldwell. Sutton Papers.

West, John O. Letters to the author, 27 Jan. and 9 Feb. 1991.

INDEX

ARP Associate Reformed Presbyterian 11 [handwritten annotation]

Abernethy, Milton A., 48
Agricultural Adjustment Act (AAA),
103–4
Agricultural Adjustment Administra-
tion (AAA), 106
American Eugenics Society, 15–16
American Federation of Labor, 27,
107
American Folklore Society, 126
American Folkways, 121–26
Associate Reformed Presbyterian
Church, 6, 11
Atlanta Constitution, 76, 95–96, 107,
114
Atlanta Daily World, 149
Atlanta Georgian, 59, 114
Atlanta Journal, 25, 61, 76, 81, 107,
149
Atoka, Tenn., 10, 12–13
Augusta (Ga.) Chronicle, 14, 48,
99–100
Augusta (Ga.) Herald, 14, 61
Augusta (Va.) Female Seminary, 6
Austin American-Statesman, 149

Baltimore Evening Sun, 47
Barr, Stringfellow, 48
Bartow, Ga., 95–98
Basso, Hamilton, 70, 104
Bell, Earl L., 61
Bellow, Saul, 165
Bernd, Aaron Blum ("A. B."), 41, 54,
55, 107
Best, Marshall, 57
Bingham, Barry, 54, 55
Birmingham News, 81
Bontemps, Arna, 82
Bourke-White, Margaret, 108–9, 121,
126–27

Works: *Say, Is This the U.S.A.,* 118;
You Have Seen Their Faces,
109–17

Caldwell, Caroline Preston Bell ("Carrie"), 5–6, 8, 9–10, 13–14,
28–29
Caldwell, Dabney, 29
Caldwell, Erskine
adolescence of, 13, 18–19
birth of, 5
as book reviewer, 25–27
childhood of, 8–9
and Communist Party, 93–95
as contributor to *New York Post,*
98–99, 101–3
death of, 154
as editor of American Folkways,
121–26
at Erskine College, 20–22
exceptionalism as southern writer,
156–60
and Guggenheim Foundation,
50–51
on Martin Luther King Jr., 151
in Mt. Vernon, Maine, 25, 32–34,
37
neglect by southerners of, 165–66
paperback books of, readers' reactions, 139–43
as participant on NBC radio,
119–21
in Pennsylvania, 24
as poet, 33
popularity of paperback books of,
139
in Portland, Maine, 34, 36
and publishers, 51, 64–65, 121,
126, 139–40, 145, 149–50

Caldwell, Erskine (*cont.*)
  readers' reactions to paperback
    books of, 140–43
  recognition by southerners of,
    152–53
  as reporter for *Atlanta Journal*, 25
  and screenwriting, 56
  and southern cyclorama, 132
  on the southern literary renaissance,
    48–49
  theory of writing of, 38
  at the University of Virginia, 23–24,
    25, 27–29
  Works: *Afternoons in Mid-America*,
    153; *American Earth*, 38;
    Around About America,
    146–47; "August Afternoon,"
    57–58; *The Bastard*, 35–36;
    "Blue Boy," 66; *Call It Experi-
    ence*, 137–38; "Candy-Man
    Beechum," 66–67; "Carnival,"
    72; *Claudelle Inglish*, 138–39;
    "Daughter," 68; "A Day's Woo-
    ing," 69; *Deep South*, 149–51;
    "The End of Christy Tucker,"
    76–77; *Episode in Palmetto*,
    136; "The Face Beneath the
    Sky," 33; "Flight from the
    Land," 119; "The Fly in the
    Coffin," 75; *Georgia Boy*,
    127–28; "The Georgia
    Cracker," 29; *God's Little Acre*,
    51–53; "The Growing Season,"
    69; *Gulf Coast Stories*, 138;
    "Honeymoon," 69; *A House in
    the Uplands*, 132–33; "In De-
    fense of Myself," 36; *In Search
    of Bisco*, 147–48; "Inspiration
    for Greatness," 34–35; "Joe
    Craddock's Old Woman," 35;
    Journeyman, 65; *Kneel to the
    Rising Sun*, 66, 69, 70; "Kneel
    to the Rising Sun," 67–68; "A
    Knife to Cut the Corn Bread
    With," 73; "Man and Woman,"
    73; "Masses of Men," 68;
    "Maud Island," 69; "Meddle-
    some Jack," 57; "The Medicine
    Man," 57, 72; "Midsummer
    Passion," 34; "Molly Cotton-
    Tail," 40–41; "The Negro in
    the Well," 74; "Nine Dollars'
    Worth of Mumble," 74–75;
    "The People's Choice," 57;
    "The People *v.* Abe Lathan,
    Colored," 76–77; "Picking Cot-
    ton," 57; "The Picture," 57;
    Place Called Estherville,
    135–36; "Return to Lavinia,"
    75; "Runaway," 72; "Saturday
    Afternoon," 39–40; "Savannah
    River Payday," 39; *Say, Is This
    the U.S.A.*, 118–19; "The
    Shooting," 69–70; "Slow
    Death," 68; "A Small Day," 72;
    Some American People, 106–7;
    Southways, 71–72, 74, 75;
    "The Story of Mahlon," 138;
    "A Story That Got Lost,"
    95–97; "The Strawberry Sea-
    son," 34; *The Sure Hand of
    God*, 133–34; "A Swell-
    Looking Girl," 41; *Tenant
    Farmer*, 104; *This Very Earth*,
    134–35; *Tobacco Road*,
    42–47; "Tracing Life with a
    Finger," 34–35; *Tragic Ground*,
    129–31; *Trouble in July*, 77–80;
    We Are the Living, 57; *The
    Weather Shelter*, 139; "Wild
    Flowers," 73; *With All My
    Might*, 154; "Yellow Girl," 57;
    You Have Seen Their Faces,
    109–13
Caldwell, Erskine Jr., 27
Caldwell, Helen Lannigan, 25, 56, 65
Caldwell, Ira Sylvester, 5, 6–8, 9, 10,
    13–14, 17–18, 29, 64, 66, 100
  Works: "The Bunglers," 15–17; "A
    School That Teaches a Commu-
    nity," 15
Caldwell, Janet, 56
Caldwell, Jay, 145
Caldwell, June Johnson, 127, 144–45
Caldwell, Virginia Moffett Fletcher,
    145, 152, 165
Carnall, Ruth, 108–9
Carter, Hodding, 122

Carter, Jimmy, 153
Cash, W. J., 32, 60
Charles Scribner's Sons, 38, 51
Charleston (S.C.) News and Courier, 149
Charlotte News, 60, 131
Charlotte Observer, 25, 81
Chattanooga Times, 80
Commission on Interracial Cooperation, 96–97
Communism, 93–95
Contempo Magazine, 48
Cook, Sylvia Jenkins, 162
Couch, William Terry, 104–6, 114–15
Cowley, Malcolm, 155, 164

Daily Worker, 95
Daniel, Frank, 25, 56, 61, 76, 107, 149, 153
Daniels, Jonathan, 54–55, 75, 132
Davidson, Donald, 50, 115–17
Dos Passos, John, 57
Douglass, Frederick, 160
Duell, Sloan and Pearce, 121, 126
Due West Female College, 6
Durham Herald, 76, 80–81

Erskine College, 6, 20–22, 152
Ethridge, Mark, 120

Fair Labor Standards Act, 120
Farm Security Administration (FSA), 113, 119
Farm Tenancy, 30–31
Farrar, Straus and Cudahy, 145
Farrar, Straus and Giroux, 150
Faulkner, William, 1, 71, 82, 165
Federal Emergency Relief Administration (FERA), 99, 101
Fisk University, 152
Fitzgerald, F. Scott, 1, 38
Fletcher, John Gould, 49
Folk Beliefs of the Southern Negro (Newbell Niles Puckett), 26–27
Forty Acres and Steel Mules (Herman Clarence Nixon), 113

Gable, Clark, 56, 94
García Márquez, Gabriel, 165

Georgia Endowment for the Humanities, 152
Gold, Mike, 94
Gordon, Caroline, 48, 140
Graves, John Temple II, 120–21
Green, Paul, 56

Hahn, Steven, 94
The Hard-Boiled Virgin (Frances Newman), 25
Hardwick, Elizabeth, 107
Harper's Magazine, 67
Hemingway, Ernest, 1, 38, 57
Hench, Atcheson Laughlin, 27–29
Hoole, William Stanley, 49
Howard, William L., 64

I'll Take My Stand (Twelve Southerners), 49

Jacksonville, Fla., 118
Jefferson, Thomas, 157
Johns, Richard, 37, 42
Johnson, Nunnally, 64
Josephson, Matthew, 48

Kane, Harnett T., 122
Kennedy, Stetson, 122–26
King, Martin Luther Jr., 151
Kirkland, Jack, 58, 64
Ku Klux Klan, 32

Labor unrest
    in southern agriculture, 31
    in sourthern industry, 30
Lee, Robert E., 152
Lee, Ulysses, 81–82
Let Us Now Praise Famous Men (James Agee and Walker Evans), 113
Lieber, Maxim, 49, 65, 108–9, 144
Little magazines, 34
Louisville Courier-Journal, 41, 54, 131–32
Lynching, 31

McCall's Magazine, 119
MacDonald, Scott, 162

McGill, Ralph, 152
McIlwaine, Shields, 164
McIver, Ray, 149
Macleod, Norman, 93–94
Macon Telegraph, 41, 54, 59, 76, 107
Marion, J. H. Jr., 62
Memphis Commercial Appeal, 75
Mencken, H. L., 25, 29
Milburn, George, 126
Mississippi College Arrowhead,
   143–44
Mitchell, Margaret, 25
Morang, Alfred, 33, 58, 65
Montgomery Advertiser, 63
Montgomery, Robert, 94
Myers, Mary Connor, 106

Nashville Banner, 76
Nashville Tennessean, 70–71, 75–76
The Negro in American Life (Jerome
   Dowd), 27
New American Library (NAL),
   139–40
Newman, Frances, 25
New Masses, 49, 95, 97, 98
New Orleans Picayune, 76
New Republic, 81, 95, 104
New York Post, 91, 100, 101, 106
Nixon, Herman Clarence, 122

Odum, Howard W., 26
Opportunity Magazine, 81

Pagany Magazine, 37–38
Palmetto Country (Stetson Kennedy),
   123–25
Penguin Books, 139
Pensacola News Journal, 149
Perkins, Maxwell, 38, 42, 155
Populism, 94
Porter, Katherine Anne, 140
Poverty, 29–31
Preface to Peasantry (Arthur F.
   Raper), 116
Prosperity, S.C., 9

Race relations, 31
Rahv, Philip, 1–2

Raleigh News and Observer, 54, 75
Raper, Arthur F., 96, 116
Rayburn, Otto Ernest, 122
Riggs, Lynn, 56
Roosevelt, Franklin D., 99

Salem Associate Reformed Presbyte-
   rian Church, 10–12
Saluda, S.C., 118–19
Scribner's Magazine, 38
Selby, John, 125
Smith, Ellison Durant, 103
Smith, J. J., 96
Soskin, William, 53–54
Soso, Miss., 118
*The Southern Poor-White from Lub-
   berland to Tobacco Road* (Shields
   McIlwaine), 164
Southern Tenant Farmers Union, 101,
   107
Stefan, Marguerite, 59
Straus, Roger, 145
Stribling, T. S., 82
Systems of Public Welfare (Howard
   W. Odum), 26

Talmadge, Eugene, 59, 96, 99
Tate, Allen, 48, 140
Thomas, Jean, 122
Time Magazine, 99, 100, 101, 144
Tobacco Road (movie), 64
Tobacco Road (play), 58–59
   reactions by southerners to, 59–63

University of Georgia, 152, 153
University of Kansas Writers' Conference, 140
University of Virginia, 23–25, 27–29,
   152, 153

Viking Press, 64–65, 106–7, 121
Vinson, Carl, 64

Wade, John Donald, 50
Wallace, Henry A., 64
Weybright, Victor, 140
Wheelock, John Hall, 38, 39, 42
White Oak, Ga., 5, 8

Williams, William Carlos, 51
Wilson, Woodrow, 10
Winesburg, Ohio (Sherwood Anderson), 33
Wolfe, Thomas, 38

Wrens, Ga., 13, 19–20
Wright, Richard, 81

Yoder, Edwin M. Jr., 151